D0842714

# LIFE IN THE PIT LANE

## MECHANIC'S STORY OF THE BENETTON GRAND PRIX YEAR

# LIFE IN THE PIT LANE
## MECHANIC'S STORY OF THE BENETTON GRAND PRIX YEAR

## STEVE MATCHETT

*edited by* Alan Henry

*photographs by*
Steven Tee/LAT Photographic

Motorbooks International
Publishers & Wholesalers ®

This edition first published in 1995 by
Motorbooks International Publishers & Wholesalers,
PO Box 2, 729 Prospect Avenue, Osceola, WI 54020 USA

© Steve Matchett 1995

Previously published in Great Britain by Weidenfeld & Nicolson 1995

All rights reserved. With the exception of quoting brief passages
for the purpose of review no part of this publication may be
reproduced without prior written permission from the Publisher.

Motorbooks International is a certified trademark,
registered with the United States Patent Office.

The information in this book is true and complete
to the best of our knowledge. All recommendations are
made without any guarantee on the part of the author or publisher,
who also disclaim any liability incurred in connection with
the use of this data or specific details.

We recognize that some words, models, names and designations,
for example, mentioned herein are the property of the trademark holder.
We use them for identification purposes only. This is not an official publication.

Motorbooks International books are also available at discounts in bulk
quantity for industrial or sales-promotional use. For details write to
Special Sales Manager at the Publisher's address.

Library of Congress Cataloging-in-publication Data Available.

ISBN: 0 7603 0026 7

Printed and bound in Great Britain by
Butler & Tanner Ltd, Frome and London

# CONTENTS

**WRITTEN FOR MY MUM** *and dedicated to the memory of Ayrton and Roland*

'Try not to feel too sad. Remember him, for everything he achieved in life. Ayrton was Formula One. He'll never be forgotten'

Sheila Matchett
*Monday 2 May 1994*

# FOREWORD

When Steve asked me to write this foreword, it was an invitation which I quickly accepted.

In the past, much has been written about the lives of Grand Prix drivers, but suprisingly very little about their mechanics. Steve's account of the 1994 season, as we fought for the Drivers' and Constructors' World Championships, in what turned out to be one of the most turbulent years in Formula One's history, gives a tremendous insight into life within our sport.

The dedication and effort required of the mechanics to ensure that the cars are prepared and maintained, and made ready to race, coupled with their ability to work under pressure, and to seemingly impossible deadlines is simply staggering. To have written such an entertaining and informative book in what little spare time a mechanic has available is a remarkable achievement, and I am only too pleased to be able to give him my full support.

Michael Schumacher

# AUTHOR'S NOTE

The management of Benetton Formula and the Benetton family have been very supportive during the writing of this book, but I feel I must point out that the views and opinions I express are exactly that: my opinions. Because of the controversy surrounding the '94 season, some people might be inclined to think that **LIFE IN THE PIT LANE** is an official release or a commissioned work by Benetton Formula. This is certainly not so. The work is entirely the result of my own independent efforts.

I hope you enjoy it.

# ACKNOWLEDGEMENTS

I would just like to say thank you for the help and encouragement I have received throughout the year:

to Luciano Benetton, Alessandro Benetton, and Flavio Briatore, for lending me their full support; Joan Villadelprat, and Mick Ainsley-Cowlishaw for their encouragement, and allowing me the time to work on the book; Michael Schumacher, for writing the foreword in between Suzuka and Adelaide (at a time when he obviously had an awful lot of other things to think about); Jos Verstappen, for keeping me busy all year; Patrick Spinelli, John Postlethwaite, and Rod Vickery for all their help, time and advice; Kenny Handkammer, for the loan of his printer, and constant interest in how 'our' book was progressing; Bat for patiently explaining and re-explaining the basics of how to drive a Compaq 486 lap-top; Diane Ball, for being such a wonderful sister; Sarah Rouche, for her month-by-month proof-reading (her wonderful appreciation and correct use of the English language, combined with her complete lack of interest of motor-racing has proved invaluable); Alan Henry, for sub-editing the manuscript (our long telephone discussions about the immense problems and irritations caused by different computer languages were most reassuring); Steven Tee, for his superb photographs; Michael Dover, for his enthusiasm and faith in the project; and finally, the Benetton Race Team for being themselves.

Thank you all very much indeed.

Steve Matchett

*Chipping Norton*
*Oxfordshire*
*January 1995*

# JANUARY

Last September I decided to buy the cottage which I had previously been renting, thereby transforming overnight my social status within our small community. Before then I had been just another 'here today, gone tomorrow' temporary tenant, only using the Cotswolds for as long as it suited me. Now I had become a fully-fledged permanent resident, perfectly within my rights to complain about the day-trippers and tourists stealing all the parking spaces.

I spent most of December '93 encamped in the bathroom, tiling the walls and re-panelling the bath with old, pine floor boards I had come across in an antique shop in Faringdon, a village about twenty miles away from my new home at Chipping Norton. Admittedly, this was tedious DIY work, but it had to be done for I knew that if I didn't get on and finish it during the Christmas holidays, it would be another twelve months before I would have the chance to complete it. Once the holidays were over I would be either working, or away from home for almost 90 percent of the year.

The cottage had originally been a small stable block at one end of a large barn. It was apparently one of the first 'barn conversions' in the country, being transformed into cottages well over three hundred years ago. What had originally been built to accommodate two or three horses and their tackle now provided a compact, but comfortable dwelling for a coffee machine, two people and three small unenthusiastic vines, which I had planted at the rear.

The property has many attractive features: exposed beams, Cotswold stone walls, an inglenook fireplace, a row of grave-yard head-stones leaning against the garden wall. Even a body buried in the back yard. These centuries-old remains were discovered (and later reburied) by the builders during the course of restoration work. Everything in fact to make an Estate Agent rub his hands together and remember the good old days of the 'low effort/ high profit' 1980s.

However, amongst the key features which sold the place to me, was the fact that I was already living there and thus didn't have to bother with the time-consuming trouble of physically looking for a house to buy, and endure all the accompanying frustration and irritation of actually moving. That, and the fact that the cottage is only a ten minute drive to work, made it the perfect purchase.

I work for a company which is based just between the tiny Oxfordshire villages of Middle Barton and Gagingwell, two quiet and sleepy hamlets that have remained unchanged for hundreds of years. The majority of their residents are farm animals and the farmers who tend them.

It is sometimes difficult to believe as you drive through this idyllic English countryside that right next door to the grazing sheep and snoozing pigs is the most advanced production facility for sophisticated racing vehicles anywhere in the world.

For this is where the new headquarters for Benetton Formula are based, and it is for Benetton that I work, as a mechanic on the company's Grand Prix racing team.

By a clever piece of architectural design, the whole factory has been built in a hollow. The roof is set at ground level, and from a short distance the whole factory appears almost invisible. The only signs that we are there are the small security office, the Benetton Formula One emblem carved out of stone and set into a traditional dry stone wall, and three flagpoles. One flying the Italian flag, one the Union Jack, and a third the new flag of the EEC.

There had been a lot of changes since the chequered flag had fallen on the Australian Grand Prix at the end of the 1993 season, and I was keen to catch up on the latest developments. After being a major sponsor for the last three years, Camel cigarettes (the brand name of R.J. Reynolds Tobacco), had decided to pull out of Formula One, terminating their relationship with both Benetton and Grand Prix racing. The writing had been on the wall early the previous season and our commercial director Flavio Briatore had wasted no time in replacing Camel with another major sponsor.

A press statement had been released before the '93 Japanese Grand Prix, proclaiming that from the beginning of 1994, Camel Benetton Ford would henceforth be known as Mild Seven Benetton Ford. In a deal said to be worth close to 30 million dollars over the next two years, Flavio had convinced Japan Tobacco that Benetton Formula was the best and most effective vehicle for promoting their Mild Seven brand.

Everyone in the Benetton workforce was very relieved. There had been rumours of redundancies amongst the factory-based staff before the Mild Seven deal was announced. In the present financial climate of world recession, nobody relishes the prospect of having to look for new employment. However, now we were all able to look forward to strong financial support for the next two years.

A new major sponsor also meant a new colour scheme for the car. When Camel signed with Benetton at the beginning of 1991, the livery changed from the bright blue, red and green primary colours of our parent company, the Benetton fashion house, to the rather sudden yellow, of a Camel cigarette packet.

Even after three years, that yellow hadn't become any easier on the eye, and I was certainly looking forward to seeing the car in the new Mild Seven livery.

On my first morning back I was pleasantly surprised by what I saw. The majority of the remaining Benetton B193 cars had already been painted in the new livery and overlaid with Mild Seven logos. The new colours blended a predominant white with differing shades of blue. Beneath these mixed streams of pastel and rich colour, lay a solid, bold green. The overall effect would be to advertise to the world, without the need for words, that the new B194 was a product of Benetton Formula.

Even so, I felt certain that the new car would undergo many subtle changes to its livery, until both Benetton and Mild Seven were happy with the final outcome, but my initial impression was that the graphic designer had done a good job. In particular, the absence of any yellow meant that we shouldn't be infested with those small and very irritating flies which swarmed over both ourselves and the Ferrari mechanics at Silverstone last Summer, attracted to our bright yellow shirts like moths to a candle.

I was also expecting to hear the identity of the new driver to replace Riccardo Patrese who had been released from his two year contract with a year of it still left to run, in a deal made between himself and the directors of the team back at Magny-Cours, during the French Grand Prix weekend. It was a deal with which Riccardo wasn't very happy, but at least he kept his drive until the end of the '93 season at a time when even this looked to be in some doubt, following his poor results during the first few races of the season.

After his first test for us shortly after the end of the '92 season, it was possible to sense that he wasn't at ease. He had been at Williams for five years, where he had felt comfortable and at home, and I suspect he was regretting his decision to leave. He only decided to leave when the stories about Alain Prost's return to Formula One with the Williams team began buzzing around the pit lane.

At the same time, Mansell was on course to win the 1992 Drivers' Championship and would presumably be staying at Williams to defend his title the following year. Having at last won the Championship, he would surely want to prove himself worthy of it by defending his crown during the '93 season pitted against a previous World Champion in equal equipment.

I assume this is how Riccardo assessed the situation and, rather than wait for Frank Williams to explain that there would be no seat for him after Adelaide, he decided to make the move and was amongst the first to sign a driver/team contract for the following year.

However, as things transpired, Mansell declined the offer of a showdown with Prost, handed in his notice and left for America intent on showing the Indycar fraternity some of his Bulldog spirit.

This all meant, of course, that Patrese hadn't really needed to leave Williams in the first place, as Prost would simply have taken Mansell's job. But by this time it was too late. Riccardo had already signed with Flavio, and happy or not, he would be driving a Benetton-Ford at the beginning of the '93 season.

I liked Riccardo and got on with him very well. He is an open and honest man, who comes complete with a touch of Italian irascibility. He could be quick tempered when things were not going well, never with myself, or any of the mechanics, but the engineers, the people that formulate the changes which the mechanics then effect, could easily fall prey to Riccardo's Latin temperament, and occasionally did.

I remember, in particular, an incident in Monaco in 1993, during the final few minutes of practice on the Saturday morning. Riccardo was completing his last few quick laps of the session in preparation for final qualifying that afternoon. He came thundering through the tunnel, doing well over 170mph, when all of a sudden he backed off the throttle and shouted over the radio link, 'I'm coming in. There is a red light (on the dashboard). I repeat, there is a red light. I'm coming in slowly'.

The warning light that Riccardo had seen would automatically illuminate if any of the car's systems developed a problem such as excessively high oil or water temperature or the engine being over-revved.

What Riccardo was most concerned about was that it might have been prompted by the active suspension system losing pressure, and the possibility of the car suddenly pitching itself off the circuit. His anxiety would have been quite understandable at any of the circuits we visit, but here at Monte Carlo, with no gravel traps to scrub the speed off the car before hitting the tyre barriers and only the harbour waiting to greet any luckless driver that managed to break through the armco, his anxious concern for the warning light was more than justifiable.

Riccardo drove the car very slowly back into the pit lane and switched the engine off. Dave Redding, the car's number one mechanic, took control of the steering wheel, while both Bobby Bushell (the number two mechanic, responsible for the rear half of the car) and I (the other number two mechanic, responsible for the front) pulled the car back into the cramped work area of the pit lane.

Riccardo was breathing hard. 'What's wrong?' he demanded of the engineers over the radio. 'Did it lose active pressure?'

'No Riccardo, it's not an active fault. Nothing too serious really. It's just that the fuel pressure dropped for a second,' replied Rory Byrne. 'Cosworth are looking at the data now to see what happened.'

'Nothing too serious? Nothing too serious?' exclaimed Riccardo. 'I'm doing my fastest lap of the session and you want to tell me that the fuel pressure is a little low!'

'It's an automatic function of the car Riccardo. Nothing to worry about,' countered Rory, trying to calm the situation.

'Rory, what do you want to tell me the fuel pressure is low for? What am I supposed to do about it, stop out on the circuit and fix the bloody thing? You know you have a problem with the fuel pressure Rory. I don't need to know!'

The seat belts were undone now, allowing Riccardo more freedom of movement to express himself with body language as well as speech. 'There is nothing I can do to fix the fuel pressure! This bloody light!' He slammed his gloved hand against the steering wheel. 'I want the light disconnected for qualifying Rory. I don't want that happening again!' With that, he pulled the steering wheel off, snatched the medical air-pipe from his helmet, stood up in the car, tugged at his radio wires until the jack plug sprang out and stomped off to get a drink.

'Well,' exclaimed Rory, via his radio, 'that was the best one for a long while! Not as good as Brian Henton, though, I remember him pinning me up against the wall threatening to punch me!' Henton, a straight-talking former British F3 champion, had worked with Byrne during the Toleman team's maiden F1 season in 1981. By a curious twist of fate, Toleman's F1 operation was later sold to Benetton to form the foundations on which today's World Championship winning operation is based.

The question of Patrese's low fuel pressure was traced to a faulty pressure sensor, a problem which Cosworth cured within a few minutes. Riccardo still wanted the warning light disconnected, but the engineers wouldn't give their consent, on the grounds that the driver needed to know if there were any potential problems. Besides which, the active system pressure wasn't connected into that circuit. That was linked to a larger and more noticeable light.

After Riccardo had rested for a while he felt more relaxed, and eventually agreed to drive with the light connected. A couple of minutes before qualifying began, he donned his balaclava, helmet and gloves and climbed into the car. As I strapped him in, I noticed him pull a piece of black tape from one of his gloves, which he must have concealed when no one was looking. He stuck it over the warning light. 'That should stop it!' he whispered in my ear.

Riccardo is a driver who needs to feel completely confident with the car in order to drive quickly and if the car is not exactly right he cannot perform to his full ability. It took our engineers a long while to get the Benetton active system to work correctly. There were a lot of problems with the corner-weights of the car and until they were sorted out the car had a tendency to react erratically when cornering. Schumacher had never driven an active suspension car before, so he had no standards against which compare the handling characteristics. This meant that when we were testing the active car at the beginning of '93 every problem we cured, and every improvement we made, gave Michael more confidence, and a more positive outlook for the future of the car.

Riccardo, on the other hand, had been racing the Williams active car throughout the '92 season and was used to the way their thoroughly tried and tested system operated. There is no doubt that the information Riccardo gave us about the Williams system helped our project advance very quickly, but he found it difficult to adjust to the fact that the Williams system had worked in conjunction with all the traits of a Williams chassis.

The Benetton system, while obviously following similar theories, was unique to us, and was, of course, being used in our chassis. The two systems were never going to react in precisely the same way, and it was these differences that made Riccardo uneasy.

By mid-season both Riccardo and the Benetton management had decided that they would part company at the end of the year. After the Australian Grand Prix, while we were packing the cars and equipment away, Riccardo shook everybody warmly by the hand, thanking us all for the work we had done for him during the season, and said goodbye. I enjoyed working with him very much. We had become firm friends during the course of the year, and I wish him well in whatever he decides to do in the future.

Consequently I was expecting to hear news of who the new driver was going to be, as he would be assigned to the car I work on, race car number 6. There had been no press statement, but the whole world knew that there were only two likely candidates for the seat: Michele Alboreto, and J.J. Lehto.

Lehto had been under serious consideration for quite a while. He had been at the factory for a seat fitting in early December. His young, handsome and clean cut features seemed perfect for the Benetton marketing image and although certainly not the only factor, it would work in his favour if the test times, and driver 'feed-back' were the equal of any other candidates.

Alboreto had been a late contender for the seat. I knew he was to be given a chance at the job before I went on holiday, as he too had been in for a seat fitting. Apart from Flavio and Ross Brawn, Benetton's Technical Director, nobody knew the identity of this second candidate, and it remained a well-kept secret until he walked through the door into the race bay.

All we had known was that sombody was arriving to have a seat made, and that the team's composite specialists should prepare a B193 chassis for a seat fitting. Every time the door opened we all looked round, disappointed that it was only Ross, or one of the drawing office staff, housed in the attics of the building.

When eventually the door did open to reveal Alboreto, it is fair to say that everyone in the race bay was a little surprised, and if any bets had been placed as to who they thought the potential driver would be, then nobody had won any money.

I was pleasantly surprised to see who it was. Michele had driven for Ferrari, and for me that meant he was a bit of a hero. I had been working for a main Ferrari dealership in my home town of Loughborough, when Alboreto was still employed by the Ferrari F1 team in '87.

I thus was able to spend a very special half an hour chatting with him about his days at the Scuderia. I was pleased to discover that he was just a normal chap, with no chip on his shoulder, and we talked like old friends about our very different histories at Ferrari – he was the race team driver and I was the humble mechanic, still learning my trade in the company's road car division.

I was pleased to hear that Michele would have to return to the factory the following day, to finalize his seat fitting. When I returned home that night I went through my book collection, putting aside two volumes to take to the factory the following morning. As soon as Michele showed up I asked him if he would mind signing them for me. He seemed delighted and instantly obliged.

I didn't think he would get the drive at Benetton. It's sad to say, but I think his most competitive days have come and gone. I wished him good luck for the test at Barcelona, and I certainly had no objection to working with him should he be successful in his quest for the seat. The lap times from Barcelona were to add weight to my thoughts about Michele's chances. J.J. had been quicker during the test, and on the strength of that alone there would be little chance of

Flavio offering Michele the race contract.

There was always the possibility he could be interested in signing Michele as the test driver. He would certainly bring a lot of experience to the team, having been in Formula One since 1981. As testing is all about consistency and a feel for any change in the handling of the car, a testing contract might well be right up the Italian's *strada*. In the end, however, Michele held out for a race contract, and a few weeks later he signed with Minardi.

Flavio, meanwhile, hadn't said a word about the identity of the second Benetton driver, even after the times of the Barcelona test had become public knowledge. I don't think he needed to. Most of the international press had written articles, more or less, confirming that J.J. Lehto would soon be elevated by Benetton into the premier division of Formula One motor sport. The lack of any announcement was, I'm sure, a deliberate ploy by Flavio to keep the press on their toes, and ensure continued media coverage of his team.

The teams that had announced their driver line up earlier on had ceased to become pressworthy weeks ago, and until they produced their new cars, for the media to look at and report upon, they would sink into anonymity. Flavio is someone who never makes the same mistake twice, and he was keen to keep the press writing about Benetton for as long as possible. Maybe he had learnt this lesson from the very early signing of Riccardo, the previous year.

I was informed that the driver line-up would be confirmed at the press launch of the new B194, the following Friday, the 14th, at two o'clock precisely. The new car was to be driven through an enormous paper screen, and into the race bay, by our new team member. It was to be a high profile launch, with all the world's sporting press invited. It was to be the launch of all launches. The journalists were to be treated to a lavish lunch of fine food and wine. This would be followed by a tour of the more 'non-sensitive' production areas of the factory. After the tour, there would be wine, the arrival of the new car and driver, press information packs and models of the new Mild Seven liveried Benetton B194.

However, before we could have the launch, we needed to finish the new car, and as the race team mechanics returned from their Christmas holidays, this became priority job number one. Work had begun on the car the previous week, prior to my return to the factory. Everything seemed to be going as well as could be expected, apart from the usual hiccups involved in building the first example of a new car.

Components which had fitted together flawlessly when drawn on the CAD (Computer Aided Design) system, and while trapped in the perfect world of computer generation, simply refused to co-operate after they had been transferred onto paper, manufactured, and been born into the real world. The draughtsman's argument, 'I can't understand it. It seemed to fit all right on the computer,' is one frequently heard by mechanics from every team, up and down the Formula One pit lane.

It does little, though, to ease a situation of immense irritation, when after being at work for over eighteen hours, and remaining as calm as possible during that time, the component in question still has no intention of attaching itself to the chassis.

There are, of course, other problems to overcome on a 'first chassis build'. These include finding that the components you need to fit next are still in Inspection (the department responsible for checking machining tolerances, carbon strength, material hardness and so on). There is the famous 'Ah yes, that part is still being drawn'. Or the classic 'I'm afraid you can't have that yet, as the material for making it is still in the ground. We're just going to start mining it now.'

Annoying as they may be, these problems are normal and to be expected. They are due to the tight deadline imposed upon us out of necessity and are in no way anybody's deliberate fault.

During the final two days leading up to the launch of the new car, our chief mechanic, Mick Cowlishaw, organized a split shift system so that work could continue around the clock. The rota was twelve hours on followed by twelve hours off.

We all preferred this to the twenty-four hours on, followed by another twenty-four hours on which we sometimes have to run at the race circuits. Cosworth were very keen that the B194 should be driven into the race bay under its own power, to prove to the engine manufacturers' critics that work on the new ZR engine was proceeding according to schedule.

Although this request from Cosworth placed great demands on the time we had available to finish the car for the scheduled press launch, the work was duly completed with about an hour to spare. At just after one o'clock in the afternoon, of Friday, January 14th 1994, the first car of the year was pushed out of the Build Shop, and wheeled into the race bay. It was pulled backwards out of the large roller door at the end, to be united with our new driver, the engine fired up and driven back inside for the inspection of the awaiting media representatives.

The large paper screen was manoeuvred into the the door aperture. It was carefully scored with a scalpel to enable the new car to burst through without taking the whole screen with it, thus avoiding the possibility of accidentally blindfolding the driver as he hurtled down the race bay.

The notion of the car crashing into the photographers may well have seemed in line with the current Benetton advertising campaign, and would certainly have literally guaranteed Flavio instant press coverage, but none of the factory staff would relish the prospect of having chassis 01 'written off' so early on in the season.

Just before two o'clock, Flavio came out to where we were waiting with the new car and announced that there would be a slight change of plan regarding drivers. He was about to play his trump card in order to keep one step ahead of the press and confirmed to us that Lehto had been signed and that he would be driving car number six during the coming season.

He would not, however, be driving the new car for the launch. 'Everyone has guessed that Lehto is the new driver,' he explained. 'It would be too predictable to let him drive the car in. We shall instead let that privilege fall to our new Test Team driver. May I introduce to you all, Mr Jos Verstappen. Get him into the car and let's go.' Flavio then turned on his heels, and disappeared back into the race bay to meet the press.

We all said a quick hello to Jos and fitted him into the car while Mick briefly introduced him to the numerous controls and switches. Suddenly it was two o'clock, no more time to explain.

'You'll get the hang of it,' Mick told the rather confused looking Verstappen and gave the signal to fire the engine. After a slight problem raising fuel pressure, the engine burst into life.

The lights were dimmed in the race bay and off she went. The sound of the tearing screen and the bang of the accompanying pyrotechnics was drowned by the roar of the ZR engine, as the car hurtled into the race bay. I was most impressed that Jos didn't stall the car – a very easy thing to do, even when you are fully conversant with a Formula One car.

The clutch is very fierce and unforgiving – remember Prost and the Williams Renault last year? Jos managed a spectacular entrance, to the applause of the entire Benetton staff and journalists, as he brought the car to a standstill at the bottom end of the race bay.

Instantly the car was pounced upon by photographers. 'J.J,' they cried, 'take the helmet off. Lets get a shot of you behind the wheel.' And 'Whose helmet have you got on, J.J.? Won't Flavio let you wear your own? Doesn't it go with the new colour scheme?'

This was followed by audible gasps of astonishment, as both Lehto and Schumacher entered from stage left and sat down, one on each front wheel. 'Who is sitting in the driving seat then?' asked one of the journalists in true Agatha Christie style.

I was enjoying this. I love all the theatricals of Formula One, and Flavio had choreographed this production to perfection. Jos then removed his helmet to end any speculation surrounding the whodunit mystery and another round of applause echoed around the house.

This seemed to bring the photographers to a frenzy, and they clamoured for position at the front of the car. Flash. Flash. Flash. 'Over here boys!' cried one, waving at the drivers to make them look at his lens. Flash. Flash. Flash.

'This way Michael, look at me, over here! Over here!' demanded another, insisting that they look at his camera instead. Flash. Flash. Another decided on a more dramatic approach, and simply screamed at the top of his voice. Everyone looked over at him. You had to, it was a natural reaction.

One chap even produced a toy parrot from his camera bag, and began to wave it violently in the air. 'Watch the birdie, boys!' Flash. Flash. Flash. Flash. These photographers weren't just from the motoring press. They were Fleet Street's finest, more used to catching celebrities leaving clubs and restaurants, or chasing Madonna through the middle of Hyde Park than covering the launch of a new racing car.

Formula One is watched by millions of people the world over. The sport only survives through press exposure. We are all used to the presence of the press, especially the race team, but the photographers, film crews and journalists that we know, are on the whole, much more subdued and placid than these people. The drivers seemed bemused by their antics and they turned to us, laughing.

Neither Schumacher, Lehto nor Verstappen were about to barge past the photographers and stomp off, pretending that they didn't want to be photographed, as their Hollywood counterparts might be inclined to do. On the contrary, they were here to be photographed. They would listen to and answer any questions that were asked of them. There was no need for the media to push, barge and shove each other out of the way.

The Formula One press regulars knew this, of course, and just stood at the back, letting the paparazzi get on with it. There would be plenty of time to get all the shots they needed, when the more eager boys were speeding down the M40 and back to Docklands, to meet deadlines, perhaps shouting 'HOLD THE BACK PAGE!' down their mobile phones.

The launch lasted for around ninety minutes, with all three drivers answering questions about how they anticipated the coming season. When everybody had finished their speeches and note pads were bulging with facts about where Verstappen was born, and if he was looking forward to working with Benetton (was he ever going to answer 'No'?), the Formula One media slowly drifted off, some perhaps to see if there was 'any possibility of just one more glass of that wonderful Chablis?'

By four o'clock that afternoon the new car was back inside the Build shop, up on high stands, and work began to prepare for its initial shakedown run at Silverstone the following Monday morning. Cosworth needed the engine back, to carry out some more test work, and the gearbox needed to be removed in order to fit some updated gear selection components.

By 8.30 p.m. the car was in pieces again, with the chassis in the build shop, the transmission being re-worked in the Sub-Assembly area and the engine winging its way back to the Cosworth headquarters at Northampton. We decided to call it a day, unable to progress any further with the shakedown preparation because until we received the components back from their various departments, the car had more or less ceased to exist!

By Monday morning the B194 had been rebuilt and was waiting in the pit lane garage at Silverstone for the circuit to open at 10.00 a.m. when the shakedown could begin. We needed to check that the electrical systems were operating correctly, and that there were no obvious faults with the transmission, handling, brakes, and cooling of the water and oil systems.

A shakedown, as the name suggests, amounts to a general check that everything is well. It is not a test of speed, that would come later, after the car had been completely stripped back at the factory, and every last nut and bolt had been checked over. Initial impressions were good, the car behaved itself, and everyone was in fine spirits when they returned to the factory that evening.

Two days later, Paul Howard, Paul Seaby and Lee Calcut, the three mechanics who run the race team's spare car, had stripped and rebuilt chassis 01 and were back at Silverstone for a two day test. The test team mechanics were also there, with a B193 car, converted to 'passive' suspension. Computer controlled active systems had been banned by new technical regulations which came into force for the start of the 1994 season.

Schumacher was to drive the B194, while Lehto was to carry out evaluation work on a new damper system fitted to the earlier B193. While this test was going on, Dave, Bobby and I were back at the factory starting to collect parts together to start building chassis 02. We were to go testing in Spain with the second new car, together with the spare car crew, who would again be running chassis 01. We were to carry out a four day test, at the *Circuito Permanente de Catalunya*, the Grand Prix circuit located just outside Barcelona.

We were also going to take one of last year's cars, in order to give Verstappen a drive, and be able to evaluate his ability, without risking a '94 chassis. If we wrote off one of the new chassis during testing, it would be touch and go whether we would be able to replace it before the first race.

The saying that 'No news is good news' is especially true in the world of Grand Prix racing. You can be sure that everything is going well, at a test where you are not present, if you don't hear any news from it. The only time the test team contacts the factory is when something has broken, failed or gone wrong.

It was Friday afternoon, January 21st, and I was building the brake pedal assembly prior to installing it in our new chassis, when our team manager, Gordon Message, came down into the race bay from his office with word from the Silverstone test.

It was bad news. Lehto had crashed. It had been a big impact. Approaching Stowe at around 150mph, he had lost control as the car slid on the late afternoon dew which had started to settle on the track surface.

Lehto had been rushed to Northampton General Hospital, where he was diagnosed as having a broken neck. Gordon didn't know any more details at the time, but promised to keep us informed of any developments.

That night I sat pondering Lehto's accident. What must he be going through? He had just been given the best drive of his life, and exactly one week after the official launch of the driver line up he was lying in a hospital bed recovering from the biggest accident of his career, not yet sure if he would be able to walk again, never mind drive a Formula One car. The next day the news was a little better. Lehto had been transferred to the London Clinic, a specialist hospital, and was receiving attention from John O'Brien, one of the world's leading surgeons. He had been recommended by Professor Syd Watkins, the President of the FIA Medical Commission and an eminent neuro-surgeon who attends all the Grands Prix throughout the world.

J.J. would need to be operated upon, but all being well, he would make a full recovery. A week after his accident he was on his feet again. Although still in hospital, he was already making plans to fly home to Monte Carlo and commence a gentle exercise programme.

He was making a remarkable recovery. I am sure that his determination to drive for us was a contributing factor in this. Despite his rapid progress, I nevertheless felt uncertain whether J.J. would be fit enough to race the car in Brazil, but his determination to do so greatly impressed me and I hoped sincerely he would be able to regain his fitness in time for the first race.

# FEBRUARY

I think we were all pleased to be going off to the Barcelona test. Racing mechanics are, by the very nature of their business, in a state of permanent migration and although it had only been twelve weeks, almost to the day, since the Australian Grand Prix had brought the 1993 season to a close, most of us had become a little restless with home life.

Those married members of the team had endured all the arguments with their wives they could cope with, and – presumably – had seen enough broken Christmas presents being returned by their children to ensure their eagerness to get away.

For myself, the forthcoming test gave me a much needed reason not to complete the bathroom restoration which had, in any case, more or less ground to a standstill since my return to work.

We were to fly out to Barcelona on Sunday the fifth after being driven down to Heathrow by coach which would leave the factory at 6.20 that morning.

It is fair to say that I am not at my personal best first thing in the morning, requiring at least two large cups of strong espresso coffee to shock me back into life. It requires an act of great commitment simply to make it to the bathroom for a shower, and I try to take as much stress as possible out of an early start to the day. Saturday evening therefore was spent finding my passport and team travel clothes, and packing my bright red and green, team issue Benetton suitcase with sufficient kit to last me the five days I would be away.

Throughout the season my suitcase remains permanently packed, with everything a constant traveller needs. I have a separate wash bag and alarm clock which never come out of the suitcase when I am at home, and my team clothing (the race shirts, emblazoned with sponsors' logos, trousers and wet-weather clothing) is stored in my suitcase as soon as it returns from Sketchleys. This enables me to pack for a test or race in about five minutes flat, and is a great help to someone who nurtures a strong aversion to early mornings.

Packing just once a year for a holiday in Greece is bad enough when you start with an empty suitcase, but the idea of having to start looking for shirts, socks and shaving foam, twenty-odd times a year, would drive me insane.

The alarm clock started irritating me at 5.15 a.m., again at 5.20 and yet again at 5.25. Then Judd, my girlfriend, (who hates being called Judith or even worse Judy) took sides with the clock by pushing me out of bed. 'You'll be late,' she pointed out and rolled over to resume her slumber.

This first early rise of the year took some getting used to. It does get easier as the season goes on, although for me, not much. I went downstairs to get a coffee.

We have an automatic espresso machine in the cottage. It remains switched on twenty-four hours a day. It's a great bonus not to have to mess around with filter coffee first thing in the morning. Simply press a button and the machine jumps into action. First grinding the rich, dark roasted Italian Segafredo beans then forcing the water, pre-heated to a perfect 97 degrees, through the freshly ground powder and then gently releasing the beautifully aromatic coffee down into the cup below, which has been run under the hot tap in order to preserve the heat of the coffee.

When viewed through a Bodum glass cup, the coffee looks just like Guinness, as the rich creamy head forms out of the black liquid. This is not due to the addition of any milk, of course, but a natural and essential endproduct of correctly made espresso.

To me, coffee is one of the most appealing perfumes in the world. I find it very difficult to walk past a coffee shop without being drawn inside and breathing in the aroma. I once read that coffee lovers are more obsessed with their addiction than smokers are with tobacco. I have never been a smoker, but I can appreciate how difficult it must be to kick the habit. I certainly wouldn't want to give up coffee.

The first cup was drunk in one go, and the machine instantly fired up a second time. Once the next cup had half gone I began to feel more awake and went back upstairs for a shower.

'You're going to be late! It's five past six!' Judd called from the bedroom. I jumped out of the shower, quickly dried myself and pulled my clothes on. I bade her farewell, grabbed my suitcase, ran downstairs, dashed out to the car and promptly swore.

There had been a vicious frost overnight, and the car was covered with a thick layer of ice. Just what I needed! No time to de-ice it now, I would have to do it on the move. I wound the window down on the Fiesta, and while steering with one hand, I leant out of the car and began spraying de-icer on the screen. The roads were lethal with black ice and I was lucky to keep the car between the ditches as I made my way to the factory.

The clock in the Fiesta pronounced it to be 6.22 a.m. as I entered the factory gates. I had no need to worry about missing the coach, however, as nearly everyone had been caught out by the sudden change in the weather and the unexpected, dramatic drop in temperature.

Not the ideal start to the first test of the year, and it was close to 6.45 a.m. before we got under way for Heathrow. The flight for Barcelona took off at around 9.30 a.m. We were at Terminal One with well over an hour in hand, giving us plenty of time to check in, have breakfast and wander through duty-free to kill some time.

It always surprises me that there are so few leisure facilities at airports. The owners have a captive audience, usually bored and frequently with a surplus of cash to spend. There are lots of restaurants, bars and an increasing number of shops to visit, but there are only so many 'All Day Breakfasts' you can physically eat.

We eventually walked out of Barcelona International arrivals hall and into the bright Catalan sunshine at a little after 12.30 p.m. Although quite chilly, it was a vast improvement on the drab winter we had left behind in England. Loading the suitcases into minibuses which the hire company had reserved for us, we set off through the middle of the city and on to where the circuit is located, a few miles north of the centre.

I like the city of Barcelona, particularly enjoying the work of Miro, Dali and Gaudi, all three of whom have their work displayed in abundance in or around the city. The architecture of Gaudi is easy to spot – his buildings seem to almost drip and melt in front of the eyes as you drive along the streets. Barcelona is the home of Gaudi's most famous work, the *Sagrada Familia,* the spectacular cathedral, with its massive towers, intricate sculptures and carved stone snails over three feet long which appear to slowly climb the huge walls. It is a mammoth project of civil engineering and the last time I visited the site, when I stayed in Spain for a couple of days after the '91 race, it was only about 30 per cent complete, after over a hundred years of continuous work. In order to finish the project many of the existing buildings around the perimeter of the site will need to be demolished as the cathedral slowly grows. However, at the present rate of construction, the builders will not need to expand the site for well over another century. I doubt very much that this project will be completed in my life time, and I have grave suspicions that it will never be finished. Even now the original sections of the cathedral are beginning to crumble with decay.

In complete contrast, the Barcelona circuit is very new, having been built – and only just in time – for the 1991 Grand Prix. The first time we came here was directly after the Portuguese race, with all the teams flying straight to Barcelona from Lisbon, while the cars and all the equipment were driven overland in the transporters.

There was only a week between these last two European races of the season and therefore not enough time to return the teams to their factories scattered around Europe, and get them back again in time for the race. The answer was to get everybody to Spain and do the 'turnaround' – that is to say the stripping, checking, rebuilding and specification changes that we would normally carry out back at home – once we arrived at the Barcelona circuit.

Doing two races back to back is known as a 'double-header'. Some people like them, some people hate them. I fall into the first group, enjoying travel and being away from England's drizzle, but I can sympathize with people who have a family and an urge to be with them.

When we arrived there in '91, the construction of the circuit had fallen behind schedule to the point where it seemed likely we would have the cars rebuilt and ready to run for the first practice session well before the race track would be ready for us. The builders were working around the clock in a desperate race against time to finish the pit lane garages, hospitality suite and press rooms.

It made a pleasant change to leave the circuit in the evening, knowing that there were people other than ourselves still hard at work long after we had gone. We had several drinks for them in the hotel bar, toasting their hard work and dedication well into the night. To our immense surprise – and I suspect theirs too – the work was completed in time. There had been no time to plant any grass seed on the huge earth banks that had been created during the building work, and presumably no time to lay any turf to give the effect of landscaping, but the constructors were not to be beaten and had sprayed the mud banks with green paint. Hundreds of gallons of it. Judging by the somewhat excessive over-spray, which in places was half way across the road, I can only assume that they had used a crop-dusting plane to complete the job. Perhaps if Bernie Ecclestone was to be given the task of overseeing all the Catalan building projects, the people of Barcelona might be celebrating Christmas mass in Gaudi's cathedral before the end of next year.

Now though, three years later, the paint had washed away. Not that it had been replaced with lush grass, but a few of the more hardy weeds had taken hold. We pulled up in front of the security hut at the entrance gate. A window opened and a guard looked out.

'Who are you with?' he asked. From within the two minibuses, sixteen people, all dressed in Benetton blazers, embroidered with the Benetton Formula One logo, looked back at him. 'Minardi!' shouted someone from the back of the bus. 'Thank you,' replied the guard and happily waved us through.

The first job of the afternoon was to prepare a 'flat patch'. This is achieved by placing shims under the set-up wheels, so that when checked with a spirit level the car is sitting perfectly square. The separate shims from each corner are taped together and labelled 'left front', 'left rear' etc., to ensure they don't get mixed up. The floor is then marked around the shims with a paint pen, so that the shims can be replaced in precisely the same position.

Every time any set-up changes need to be carried out on the car, it is positioned on the flat patch. It is imperative that the flat patch is perfectly square as it becomes a datum point of true zero. This is because we are making fine adjustments to the geometry and ride height of the car. It is usual, for example, to alter the ride height (the distance between the floor of the car and the surface of the track) by only half a millimetre.

Any error in the set-up readings will greatly effect the handling of the chassis when running on the circuit. Once the flat patch was finished, we carried out the usual checks on the car to make sure that nothing had happened during its journey from England. A spanner check of all the suspension bolts and a visual check to make sure all the hydraulic connections were still dry is followed by routinely firing up the engine, again just to check that everything is as it should be. A final polish of the bodywork and by five o'clock we thought we were looking good for an early finish.

The engineers then decided that they would like to swap the gearbox differentials from one car to the other. The internals of the two units had been manufactured to different specifications and the idea was to try both in order to evaluate their comparative performance.

The original plan was to run chassis 02 first thing in the morning. This would be its initial shakedown, remembering that, unlike chassis 01, our car hadn't turned a wheel since Dave, Bobby and I had built it back at the factory. Schumacher would then switch into 01 for the remainder of the test, leaving us free to carry out any necessary work on 02.

The problem now seemed to be that the engineers didn't want to run 02 with the differential to its current specification. The easiest way out of this situation was to exchange the whole gearbox with the other car, rather than strip the transmission to extract the differential unit, which would take twice as long.

'Ah well,' Dave said, sounding a little deflated, 'the sooner we get started, the sooner we get done.' We all thought we had been done alright – well and truly.

The bodywork and nose were removed and the car lifted back into the air and put on high stands. The floor was removed, followed by the rear wing. The engine oil was drained out of the oil tank, which is housed in the gearbox casing. The clutch and rear brake lines were disconnected and finally the gearbox itself was removed, before being wheeled over to chassis 01.

Meanwhile the gearbox from 01 was undergoing a similar operation and within a short time was being wheeled over to us. We refitted this back onto our car, along with all the other components. The brake and clutch lines were bled and the engine replenished with fresh oil. The engine was fired back into life and Bobby – who 'drives' the car whenever we are working on it – went through the gears, selecting each one in turn, to check that everything was functioning correctly. The floor was then bolted back into place.

The car was fitted with set-up wheels and lowered down onto the repositioned shims of the flat patch in order to check the geometry of the newly acquired 'rear end' of the car in relation to the original front end. This must be done, as although components interchanged between cars are theoretically identical, drawing and machining tolerances of these various components can be sufficient to affect the set-up.

After a slight adjustment to the ride height, the bodywork and nose were refitted, the paintwork was once again given a final polish and the car-cover was pulled over.

This extra work added I suppose, around two hours to the length of our working day. A little annoying perhaps but not too bad. We are always being given extra work and on the whole accept it as an occupational hazard. There have been many times in the past when the cars have been built and are ready to run, but, before you know it, they are being stripped down again because the engineers have decided to change this or that to the specification. For example, we have arrived at a given circuit for a test or race with a car that has just been rebuilt and set-up for that track, to discover that the engineers want us to change the gear ratios, even before the car has done an installation lap.

I'm certainly not saying that the engineers change their mind without reason. Indeed they always have an explanation to defend the desired changes (sometimes more than one depending on who you ask first). I'm not even questioning the changes that the engineers ask us to make. I don't think for a moment that they create extra work for us out of devilment. All of us are there working towards the same goal. It just seems that occasionally the goalposts keep moving.

We managed to get away from the circuit by around 7.30 p.m. and were showered, changed and ready to go out to dinner by 8.00 p.m. Seven of us had decided to go into the town of Grenolliers, to a small Pizzeria we had discovered last time we were there. Not very traditional Catalan fare I grant you, but a good pizza should never be passed up, wherever in the world one might be.

The pizza was delicious. Piping hot, oozing garlic and topped with local strong black olives. We washed it down with lots of good Chianti, and with the absence of any Grappa, we finished off with a shot or two of Tequila. We were in good spirits and chatted around the table well into the night. We were looking forward to the start of the racing season. Some more so because the first race was in Brazil, and for the unattached members of the team that means girls. Pretty girls and lots of them.

'Bat', one of the race team electricians (whose real name is Alan but had acquired the nickname 'Bat' from the days when he worked with the test team and used to hang around all day until the night-time rebuilds forced him out of the transporter), was already beginning to plan his social time in Sao Paulo, telling us which clubs he was intending to visit, and even for how long, before he would have to move on to the next one.

'The Masque!' he said, 'we must go to the Masque. The things those girls get up to is unbelievable! Straight off the plane. No messing!' I had never been to the Masque, or for that matter to any of the clubs that Bat talked about. Not due to any 'holier than thou' attitude by any means (I just prefer my social time to be a little quieter), but I had a fairly good idea of what the girls in question got up to, and after seeing the tired looking faces of some of my team mates 'the morning after', I found the things the girls got up to quite believable.

'You're out this year Matchett,' he informed me, 'you're not stopping at the hotel bar drinking that bloody prawn juice stuff all night!' Bat was referring to a local Brazilian cocktail called Caipirinha, which curiously does contain some sort of prawn juice. When mixed and consumed, it has the effect of being hit over the head with a cricket bat. Drinking two of them has a similar effect, but with the added sensation of being pushed out of a very tall building.

I haven't told anybody from Benetton that I am writing this diary, fearing that people may be put off acting naturally when in my company, thus removing the very reason for writing it.

I accepted Bat's offer – purely as a matter of research you understand. 'Alright Bat, I'll go. One or two quick drinks! Make sure I'm home by midnight and I'll go with you!' It was a pointless clause. Most nights they don't even go out until after midnight, and asking Bat (or for that matter any of the mechanics) to take care of you is like trusting Sweeney Todd to shave you with his favourite cut-throat. I knew that if I stepped out of the hotel with any of them, dawn would be breaking before I would be allowed back again.

The bottle of tequila that the waiter had left with us was empty. Bobby ordered another. 'We'll just have one each and hand the bottle back. A settler!' Bat informed us, and burst out laughing. I had no idea what a 'settler' was, but looking at the red faces sat around the table, I had a suspicion we didn't really need one.

It was never going to be as simple as having a final drink and handing the bottle back. The waiter brought out lime segments and a huge salt cellar, in order for us to have our last tequila in the traditional manner. Lick some salt from the back of your hand, gulp the spirit down in one go, and then suck the lime. Bobby then demonstrated an extra part to this tradition by snatching the bottle top off the table, throwing it to the floor and stamping on it. 'Its all got to go now!' Bobby said. 'They won't have the bottle back without the top. We have to finish it!'

At work, Bobby is the kindest, quietest and most gentle man you could ever wish to know. He looks as innocent as a choir boy. After a couple of drinks, however, he becomes mischievous, taking on a whole new persona. He changes from 'Good Old Bobby', the man who will do anything to help, to Bob, 'The Devil's Advocate'. As the evening goes on, and develops into a late night, he will encourage people to stay for one last drink. Or despite the fact that it is no longer 'late', but with the sun rising it must now be classed as being 'early', he will urge people to visit just one more club. 'Don't worry!' he'll say, 'we've got plenty of time before we have to catch the flight home, trust me!'

The next day stories were going around that some of the boys had been straddling the bar and attempting to ride it, holding a bizarre rerun of the Grand National. At around four in the morning the hotel manager found three people fast asleep in the corridor of the third floor. He wasn't annoyed, or even upset, just concerned for them. He had removed their shoes and was in the process of fetching blankets and pillows, when the two gearbox mechanics happened to stroll past. With the aid of the hotel register they managed to match room numbers to faces and eventually got them to bed.

After that first day, the rest of the test was fairly uneventful. We were pleased with Michael's performance in the new car and he was very positive about the coming season.

Williams were also at Barcelona, testing last year's type FW15 car with Damon Hill at the wheel. I don't know what they were testing, and everyone knows that testing times can be misleading, but we were nearly a second quicker than the Williams. That too made us all feel very optimistic.

The test finished on Thursday the 10th, and we returned to England that night. This gave us two days off while we waited for the transporters to make their way home overland. This gave the team time to relax a little, and gave me the chance to write about what had happened to us during January.

The next test was at Silverstone. As soon as the cars were back, we were at the factory working on them. They were checked over, the engines removed and returned to Cosworth, and fresh engines installed. There was a slight change to the set-up and we were off.

The weather forecast predicted snow, but there was no way the test would be called off on the strength of it. It wouldn't even be called off if it did snow. We would still go up to the circuit, set the flat patch and stand about waiting for the snow to melt. There is no way that Formula One will defer to mere global climatic conditions. We would go to the circuit and stare at the snow in exactly the same manner as King Canute stared at the rising tide. Silverstone is at the best of times a fairly bleak place to be, but during the winter months, 'bleak' takes on a whole new meaning and the itinerary of a winter test there deserves its own individual description.

The circuit is notoriously flat and apart from the slight climb from the bottom of Club corner up to the relatively new Priory complex, is more or less devoid of any contour. This allows the rain, sleet and snow to have free reign over the circuit and the wind picks up a vicious pace as it howls around the old airfield. It gathers speed as it hurtles through Woodcote, enters the pit lane and slams into the garage doors with more force than all the Italian Ferrari fans at Imola and Monza put together – which I will return to later.

From December to February, Silverstone must rank amongst the top ten most desperate places in the world to be, jockeying for the number one spot alongside the permafrost of the Russian Steppes. The wind is bitterly cold and not merely penetrates the layers of clothing a mechanic wears in an attempt to keep warm, but it simply slices through to the bone with all the ease of a surgeon's scalpel. You can be wearing a T-shirt, race shirt, sleeveless sweater, heavy knit sweater, duckdown body warmer, and wet weather anorak but within five minutes of climbing out of the minibus in the morning and entering the pit lane garages, you are frozen.

Some people try wearing two pairs of trousers to try and encourage the legs to stay a little warmer. I wear snug fitting cycling trousers underneath the rather lightweight, team issue cotton trousers. One chap once told me that he always got good results by wearing a pair of his girlfriend's tights underneath his team kit. I assumed that we were still talking about keeping warm, but I didn't think I knew him well enough to inquire any further.

The feet are also easy prey for the icy cold weather during winter testing in Britain and especially at Silverstone, and these also require special attention if you expect them to support you during what could turn out to be a sixteen or eighteen hour working day. At Benetton, both the race and test teams are given Timberland boat shoes to wear. These are a very good quality, leather, casual shoe.

Once you have worn them in they will remain one of your best friends for many races, indeed sometimes for two or three seasons. They are though, as the name 'boat shoe' suggests, designed for warm weather. In Italy in September or Australia in November they are perfect. They are alas, no defence against a Silverstone test in February.

Two pairs of socks are the absolute minimum you should try to get away with. Anything less will result in instant frostbite. Some people swear by the shoe liners that can be bought from Clarks or Hush Puppies, but in my opinion this is like trying to stop a charging bull elephant with a fly swatter.

I have found that the best thing to use is 'Bubblewrap' – the plastic sheeting filled with air pockets which is used for wrapping such delicate items as Ming vases, or in the case of Formula One, encasing suspension wishbones, electronic control units, brake callipers, front and rear wing elements, in fact just about every component, when it isn't actually fitted to the car. Two pieces of this, folded in half and fitted inside the shoes is like slipping your feet into a warm toaster. Wonderful.

There are three other pieces of personal equipment required to survive a winter test. They include a woolly hat (which must cover the ears) and a pair of woolly gloves. These are never a problem for us to get hold of, as companies like Sparco and Champion give armfuls of them to us at the races, in the hope that we will wear them when doing engine or brake changes in between the untimed and qualifying sessions, when everything on the car is red hot, and give them some free publicity.

As far as the free publicity goes, you only have to look in *Autosport* or watch TV coverage of a Grand Prix to see mechanics wearing gloves emblazoned with this or that company's logo. At a test, though, there are very few cameras to film anything we are up to, let alone what we are wearing, and the gloves are worn to stop the fingers freezing not burning. The final thing you need is a beard. A good thick beard is best, but this is only possible if there is sufficient time to grow one, of course. We often go testing with just one or two days notice, so my advice is think positive, and grow the best one you can.

For the handful of people who come to watch, a winter test must appear similar to trench warfare. There are long periods of inactivity as the mechanics work on the cars, changing, or adjusting this or that. This is followed by short bursts of activity, as the driver is sent out to evaluate the effect of the changes he has just carried out. He will be told to do three or four timed laps, then come back in.

Depending on where we are, this takes about eight minutes. It is during these brief periods, when the car is running, that we have a coffee, eat a quick sandwich, or nip to the loo. Due to the amount of warm clothing we wear the latter has to be carefully timed. You don't want to be too desperate to go, as it can take a good two minutes to remove the necessary garments to accomplish the task. Apart from which the toilet block at Silverstone is out at the back of the paddock and this can also take a couple of minutes to reach. Correct planning is vital.

If the test lasts for more than one day, we normally stay at one of the hotels around Northampton. The day begins when the alarm goes off at around 6.30 a.m. This allows ample time to immediately switch the alarm off, and go back to sleep for another fifteen minutes. I have one of those Braun 'voice activated' clocks, and find it far less stressful to simply shout at it, rather than physically throwing it against the wall.

The leave time is usually seven o'clock, and so with fifteen minutes to go, we have to get up, shower, remember not to shave, find a clean T-shirt, race shirt, sleeveless jumper etc. and blearily climb aboard one of the two minibuses to go to the circuit. Exactly who should be in which minibus is listed in the Movement Schedule, a copy of which is issued to everyone attending the test.

This contains details of our hotel, which chassis are being tested and who will be driving them. It's important to always travel in the same minibus. This way we know who is still asleep when they don't show up at seven, and gives the chance to shock the 'late boys' into life by ringing them from the reception.

There are few more distressing starts to the day than waking up to the sound of the telephone ringing, looking at the clock to see that it's ten past seven, and having to get dressed without a shower, brush your teeth while pulling on your socks and stumble out to the minibus still half asleep. We've all done it and we all know what it's like. Have a start like this and the rest of the day only gets worse.

The drive to the circuit is normally a quiet affair. People have little to talk about at that time of the day, apart from throwing insults at any traffic daring to get in the way. There is a special urgency about Formula One. If a minibus has a top speed of ninety miles an hour, then it must be driven at ninety miles an hour, when and wherever possible.

Breakfast is at 7.30 a.m. but the first job of the day is to see if anybody has broken into the garages and tampered with the cars. There is twenty-four hour security at nearly all of the circuits we visit, but security, however tight, can be breached and there are some Formula One fans who will stop at nothing to get a closer look at the cars they adore. Without meaning any harm they may damage one of the scores of sensors or delicate telemetry units connected to the electronics.

First thing in the morning the garages are frighteningly cold, so as soon as possible the 'space heaters' are fired into life. There is little danger of the engine's cylinder blocks freezing overnight because the water in the cooling system is treated with a corrosion inhibitor and anti-freeze solution, but the engine and gearbox oils, along with the magnesium gearbox casings, must be heated to around 50 before attempting to fire the engine.

This ensures running tolerances are reached and so avoids the engine 'nipping up', or the oil coolers and pipes splitting due to excessive pressure which can be caused by the viscosity of the oils when cold. In the heat of South Africa or Brazil this isn't a problem, of course, but in a British winter it is a very real problem.

After the first checks of the day are complete it is time for breakfast. If the catering crew has been booked, there is normally a full English breakfast available, along with various cereals, fruit, fruit juices, milk, tea – and always the espresso machine!

After breakfast it is time to fire the engine up and go through the gears. This is to warm both the engine and gearbox and check that the gear selection is working correctly. Since the advent of the semi-automatic gearbox, this check has become more important than ever since we are no longer dealing with straightforward mechanical linkages, but now rely on micro-chip technology and computer software in order to change gear.

Although the systems are on the whole very effective and reliable in operation, occasionally the gearbox controller will decide not to talk to the sensors in the selector mechanism, or not allow a gear change when the driver demands one.

The Silverstone pit lane opens at 10.00 a.m. and providing that it isn't either snowing or raining (and at Silverstone it's normally doing a combination of both) the real business of the day begins. The engineer in charge of the test will have briefed the driver on any changes we carried out the night before. Fuel is added, the pre-heated tyres are fitted and the car is sent out.

If a new engine has been fitted, the driver will be told to do a single lap. This is known as an 'installation lap' and is done in order to check for any fuel, water or oil leaks. Any other new components will also be inspected, to check that everything is correct and that the car is ready to be driven at speed. Car and driver are sent out again and the test schedule begins in earnest.

Depending on what we are testing, be it new dampers, set-up changes, new profile floors or diffusers, the car will do three or four laps and then return to the pits. We will have a record of the lap-times of the run, triggered by the speed trap, every time it passes by the start/finish line.

The engineers will try to obtain 'feed back' from the driver, about what the car felt like to drive with the modifications, and see if they have made an improvement or not. Then we will either alter the set-up of the car, adjust wing angles, or change the floor, depending on what we are testing and send the car out again. Times are compared against previous laps, and more adjustments are made. More laps, more adjustments.

At 1.00 p.m. the circuit is closed for lunch. The marshals and circuit staff disappear into the canteen for warmth and food. We, however, aren't so lucky. Due to the massive cost of running a Formula One car, and the price the teams have to pay for the hire of the circuit, no one can afford to stop work for such a trivial thing as lunch. On the contrary, the hour that the circuit is closed is used for any time consuming work, so we are not losing any of the precious track time.

As soon as the pit lane opens again there is an urgency to get the car back out on the track. More changes and ever more laps continue on, all afternoon, until the circuit is finally closed at five thirty. This is when the real work of the day begins.

The majority of engines that Cosworth bring to a test have already seen operation at race meetings, where the majority of their 'serviceable life' has been used. After the car has been running for a day it is fairly standard procedure to have to change the engine, and allow the 'out of life' unit to return to the Cosworth factory for rebuild.

Therefore the first thing we need to find out is whether the engine needs changing. We can be getting on with that, while the engineers begin to compile the 'job list' of other changes to the car, for the test schedule the next day. The brakes, like the engines, have normally been used at a race meeting and it is normal to use up the remainder of their serviceable life at a test.

Every night the carbon components are measured with a micrometer and their dimensions are recorded on the 'brake wear sheet'. When the discs and pads fall below a specified level they are removed from service, and so a complete brake change is also very likely.

Providing that all we have to do to the car – apart from the standard checks to the suspension, bearings of the upright assemblies, condition of the chassis, floor and diffuser carbon work – is to change the engine and brakes, we could

Jos drives the first B194 into the race bay.

Michael, Jos and JJ at the press launch.

The Benetton factory in Oxfordshire.

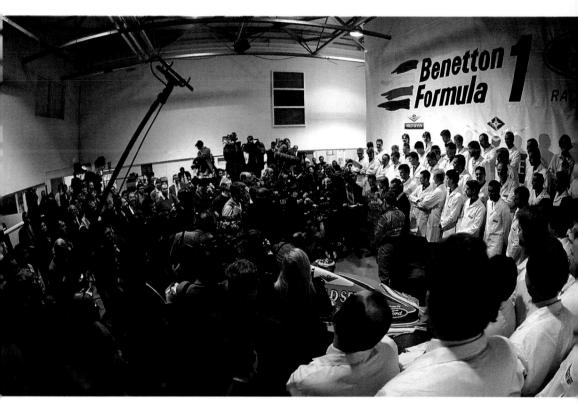

Fleet Street's finest.

The steering rack is 'shimmed' to lock the steering in the straight-ahead position prior to checking the 'toes'. Notice Bob is nearly asleep.

Setting the 'flat patch' with Dave Redding.

Silverstone.

Removing the tyre blankets before Michael takes the B194 onto the
Barcelona circuit.

Jos climbs aboard–also at the Barcelona test.

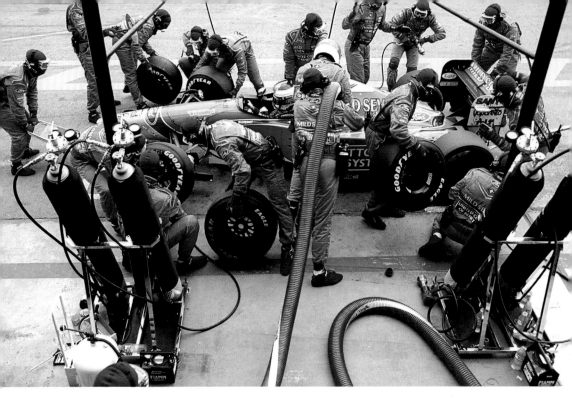

Our first 'live' refuelling pitstop in Brazil.

The first race, the first victory in Brazil.

be on our way back to the hotel for a hot shower, a change of clothes and maybe even a drink in the bar by around 9.00 p.m.

Sadly though, when testing this is very much the exception to the rule, as we will normally be changing or modifying, one or several other components and this can easily add three or four hours to the length of the working day.

The team's catering staff cook dinner for us at the circuit, and we will stop for a half hour break at around 7.30 p.m., the first time we are able to sit down and relax since breakfast, over twelve hours before.

After dinner the work continues until the car is completely finished, and ready to run when the pit lane opens the next day. No work is ever left to be finished off the following morning, as we never know what extra work we will be asked to carry out when we arrive back at the circuit, remembering that the car must be ready to run the second the pit lane opens. At last, the dust cover is fitted to the car, the sign to the world that the work is complete. As long as the other car, or cars, are finished (depending how many we have brought to the test), it is time to lock the garages, climb aboard the minibuses and see if they can reach ninety-five on the way back to the hotel.

Back in the room, the shower feels like heaven, and after twenty minutes under the hot spray, you even begin to feel the blood circulating in the feet again. The bed is the softest, most comfortable bed in the world. As you lie there, reflecting over the day's events, the eyelids grow very heavy, very quickly. You drift off into a deep sleep, with a final wish that you'll wake up before the telephone rings, with someone hurling abuse at you, yelling 'It's seven fifteen. Are you bloody coming, or not?!' That is how an average winter test at Silverstone might go.

On this occasion, however, there was so much snow around that we couldn't do any useful running at all. We sat about hoping against hope that the snow would melt. It was pointless though. We couldn't risk writing off a '94 chassis at this stage of the game. In the end it was Schumacher who called it a day for us all. After a couple of exploratory laps he returned to the pits complaining that it was so cold he had lost all feeling in his hands.

For two days we had defiantly stared at the snowman we had made and for two days the snowman had defiantly stared back. We packed up and returned to the factory.

Forty-eight hours later, on Sunday the 20th, the transporters headed down to the south coast to catch the 5.30 p.m. ferry from Dover to Calais. We were off to Spain and Portugal in search of warmer weather. We were taking chassis 01 and 02, with as usual Dave, Bobby and me crewing 02. Paul Howard, Lee Calcut and Carl Gibson – one of the Test Team mechanics – were to run chassis 01. Carl was standing in for Paul Seaby, who had been granted a week off to get married, and take a whirlwind honeymoon in Scotland. It was now or never really for Paul, as time off during the season is more or less out of the question.

This time there wouldn't be a '93 chassis attending the test. Jos had made a good initial impression with Ross at the Barcelona test, and proved himself worthy to drive one of our new cars.

We left the factory for Heathrow, at a very reasonable 11.45 a.m. the following Wednesday. I noticed as I walked through the race bay that chassis 03 was being assembled by the other three Race Team mechanics, Max, Kenny and Jon. They hadn't been to any of the tests so far, due to the fact that their chassis had only just been delivered to them from the composite department. At least we would have three cars complete for Brazil, providing, of course, we didn't write any of them off during testing.

A local coach company – Jeff's Coaches of Witney – has the contract to take us all to and from the airport. In the five years I have worked at Benetton neither I, nor any members of the race team, have recognized the same coach driver twice, in well over a hundred and fifty trips. Where do all his drivers come from? Where do they all go to?

We were at Heathrow with an hour to spare and yet again found ourselves ambling around Duty Free. This time, however, I was sorely tempted to buy. Not a souvenir London Teddy bear. No, no. My interest had been caught by bottle of wine. And not just any bottle of wine either.

What had grabbed my attention was a bottle of *Chateau Mouton-Rothschild*. I'm no wine expert, by any means, and I get immensely bored when people drone on about what you should and shouldn't like. To me, you either like a wine or you don't. Personally I would love a bottle of Mouton-Rothschild. However, in the end I decided to leave it. Mouton-Rothschild has never been cheap and the price was just a little too reassuringly expensive.

The second I boarded the plane I regretted not buying it. I did exactly the same, when I was in Bordeaux last winter. Judd and I had driven down to the Medoc and Pauillac for a few days holiday. We had driven to the Chateau, where I had strolled around the *Mouton-Rothschild* vines. Of course, winter isn't really the best time to see the area at its most colourful, but I was still enchanted.

I wanted to know more about the history of their great wine and the magnificent Chateau. *Mouton-Rothschild* is the only producer ever to be promoted to First Growth since the 'Great Classification of 1855'. Each year a different artist has been commissioned to design the label for the following vintage. Artists such as Warhol, Miro, Dali and even Picasso have all produced work for their labels.

However, when I was offered the chance to purchase a bottle of the '88 I fought with myself for over an hour before deciding not to buy. 'Where will you store it?' I asked myself. 'What if you drop it?' and 'This is a work of art, you could never bring yourself to drink it.' (Actually that argument wasn't very sound. I could always bring myself to drink it.)

The moment we started to drive away I regretted not buying it. Next time the chance arose I would buy a bottle and be done with it. Well the chance had arisen and yet again I had let it pass. Next time. Definitely next time.

We landed at Seville at a little after 6.00 p.m., loaded everything into the minibuses and drove straight to the hotel. The Don Tico is a relatively new hotel, built I presume in what is considered to be the traditional style, right in the middle of the famous sherry producing region of Jerez.

It is a large building, consisting of four wings joined together in a square with a big lawn and a pond in the centre. All the floors are paved with terracotta tiles and the whole place reeks of strong soap. In the reception, in the restaurant, the hall-ways, the bars and in the rooms. The pungent smell of soap follows you everywhere. That first night we thought the smell was a 'one-off'.

Perhaps they had just carried out a huge spring cleaning programme prior to our arrival but the smell was just as bad the second day. We tried leaving the windows open before we went to work and left notes asking the maid not to clean the room, just make the beds. The maid reacted to this request by closing the windows and apparently using more of the bizarre cleaner than ever. I tried ringing reception and telling them about it. They were very polite and apologetic but didn't seem to actually do anything about the smell. In the end we just gave in and put up with it. After all, by this time we only had one more night to stay there.

Jerez circuit is no longer used for Formula One races. The last time we raced there was in 1990. It was the final race of the European stage of the World Championship and the second part of a double-header, following on from the Portuguese Grand Prix at Estoril. The circuit has very good, large garages for us to work in and is fairly well protected from the wind, as it is set in natural hills right amongst the vines of the sherry producers.

All of which is fine as far as I am concerned. The problem as far as Grands Prix go is that no one turned up to watch them. It was so bad during the 1990 race weekend that the organizers erected fences and positioned large trees in barrels in front of the empty grandstands, so when the cameras panned around the circuit the viewers watching at home couldn't tell what a sparse crowd there was. There was a joke going around the pits that if any locals were arrested for speeding over the race weekend the Judge would sentence them to go and watch the race. It was that bad.

The first day of the test was spent setting up the garage. The truckies erected the banners, adorned with Benetton emblems, and bolted together the 'climbing frame', the stand for the pit-wall, where the engineers ponder over monitors and telemetry screens, and shelter from either the sun or rain. We duly carried out our usual pre-running checks and prepared the flat patch ready for the next day's testing program.

We couldn't do any actual running on that day as the circuit was being used by several of the FIM Grand Prix motor cycle teams, and for obvious safety reasons, bikes and cars never use the track at the same time.

We tested at Jerez for the following four days. Michael in our car and Jos in 01. Jos had been told to take it steady and 'just get a feel for the new car'. There was no need for him to try to break any records. No one expected him to be close to Michael. Indeed we would have been more than a little concerned for the safety of the new car if he had been. Jos did a fine job. He didn't push the car and his feed-back, about the various set-up changes impressed our engineer Frank Dernie and Ross and they were both pleased with his performance. Michael himself was sent out to try to put a race distance on the new car.

We had the same engine in the chassis that had been fitted for the Silverstone test, as apart from the two laps put on it by Michael before his hands started to freeze, the engine was 'brand new'. After half distance, though, the engine developed a fault and Cosworth made the decision to change it. The next day we attempted another race distance but this time we suffered with transmission failure and it took the rest of the day to repair it.

When the car was going, it went well and Michael managed to break the old lap record with ease. We were just not yet able to get a full race distance out of it. It would come, we all knew that. It was just a matter of time, and it's far better to have these faults develop during testing than during the qualifying sessions in Brazil. That, after all, is what we go testing for.

The next two days saw us putting more miles on the engines for Cosworth and although they were far from happy, you could sense an air of optimism creeping into their conversations.

On the final night of our stay in Jerez, Michael took the whole team out to dinner. This was a nice gesture and is something that he likes to do quite often. He sees it as a way of thanking everyone for the effort put into preparing the car for him and is appreciated by us all I think.

'Order whatever you would like,' he told us, 'the bill will be kept open all night!' We were still there, lounging back in the chairs, drinking and chatting long after Michael had gone to bed. As we sat there I noticed that the restaurant had an impressive number of bottles behind the bar and I asked to see the wine list, which our waiter quickly produced.

'Do you happen to have any *Mouton-Rothschild*?' I asked.

'No Sir, I'm afraid we don't. We do have some very nice locally produced sherry. It's very good!' he informed me.

'No thank you,' I told him. 'I'm sure it is good. The best in the world in fact. Unfortunately, sherry, however good, is not what I'm after.'

# MARCH

March began with another migration. This time we were flying west to Portugal, taking in a brief stop at Madrid to change aircraft. We had to check in at Jerez domestic airport at 7.15 a.m. and were planning to leave the Don Tico and its surplus of soap at seven o'clock. We reckoned that fifteen minutes would allow ample time for the short drive to the departure terminal.

It had grown into another late night the previous evening when eventually we had managed to extricate everyone from the restaurant, and most of us were feeling rather delicate, myself included. By the time we had managed to wake everyone, by ringing round and banging on bedroom doors, it was well past seven o'clock when we finally left the hotel.

While waiting for the stragglers to surface and climb aboard the minibuses, we noticed that Greg Field, our Race Team Co-ordinator, had gone missing. 'Where's Greg disappeared to, Mick?' I asked the Chief Mechanic. 'Back to the restaurant we were at last night,' he replied. 'He's lost his wallet and can't finalize the hotel bill. The company credit cards are in it!' A loud cheer went up. 'Good old Greg!' someone shouted and we all burst out laughing.

Formula One mechanics are, on the whole, a sore bunch and can seldom resist the opportunity to exploit a chink in a team mate's armour. Greg had only rejoined Benetton at the beginning of February and we doubted that this was the sort of start he was looking for.

He had been our Travelling Parts man when he was last with us, but had left some years ago to further his career. He had been offered the position of Team Manager, first with the now-defunct Onyx Grand Prix outfit and later with

Team Lotus.

In fact, it was at Onyx that I first met Greg. He interviewed me for a position on their Race Team, back at the end of '89, when I was trying to get into Formula One. He didn't give me the job!

Greg had now returned to Benetton to help replace Gordon Message who was one of the most calm and relaxed men I have ever known. He has earned great respect, although never demanding it, from everyone he has worked with. But now, after fourteen years of continuous service with first Toleman and then Benetton, he has finally decided to call it a day, and has left in order to pursue a life long passion for sailing boats. He has certainly given enough of his life to Formula One to deserve some peace and pleasure in his retirement, and I wished him every success in the world.

Gordon's extensive duties had now been divided between Greg and our Team Operations Manager, Joan Villadelprat (pronounced Jo-ann). Joan would continue with his own job while at the factory, as well as the sporting – as opposed to technical – issues, at the circuits. Greg was responsible for the race and test team logistics, and generally making sure everybody was where they were supposed to be when we were travelling abroad.

Anyway, it transpired that Greg had been trying to telephone the restaurant for the last thirty minutes, to see if his wallet was there, but could get no reply. Which as it was only 6.15 a.m. when he rang, and since we were in Spain – where early mornings, as far as the locals are concerned have been banned – was no great surprise to anybody.

He had found out from the receptionist at the Don Tico that the restaurant opened at ten o'clock to serve morning sherry, but as our flight was due to take off for Madrid nearly two hours before this, he had decided to drive back to the restaurant and attempt to wake someone up.

Fortunately Greg had managed to wake the owner, and his wallet was waiting safe and sound behind the bar, retrieved from underneath the table by the cleaning staff. Thus it was a greatly relieved Race Team Co-ordinator who screeched back into the hotel car park, quickly paying the bill before speeding off to the airport.

'You can't miss the airport,' we had been told. 'Turn right, out of the hotel and just keep going. It's only about five minutes away.' So we turned right at the hotel exit and headed off down the main road, soon getting the maximum possible speed out of the minibus. After about ten minutes we began to wonder why we couldn't see anything slightly airport shaped. There were lots of fields, most of them planted with old, gnarled vines, but no runway of any description.

After fifteen minutes we turned around and headed back towards the hotel. Someone had tricked us. We were sure of it. After all, airports, even small ones, are normally visible to the naked eye, and surely at least one of us would have noticed it as we drove past, even with a hangover.

When we arrived back at the Don Tico we realized what we had done. We found that there were two exits, both leading onto different roads. Up until now we had only been using the exit leading towards the circuit and the international airport, we were unaware that the other one even existed.

We set off again. The truckies were just pulling out of the hotel car park.

They planned an overland trip to Portugal of about nine hours, intending to be in Estoril by late afternoon. If we missed our flight they stood a good chance of being in the hotel bar of the Estoril Eden before us.

This time, though, we sighted the airport within two minutes of setting off, and within five the minibus was standing deserted, with all the doors left swinging open, half on the kerb, half on the road, outside the departure terminal.

As it turned out, we were in plenty of time to catch the flight to Madrid. For some reason it had been delayed by forty minutes. I can't imagine why, but it certainly wasn't due to air traffic congestion over the airport. As we looked out of the huge plate glass window that overlooked the apron and runway network, our plane was the only one in sight.

There were no other flights landing, none taking off and none taxiing on the tarmac. One could only assume the reason for the delay was either a mechanical problem with the aircraft, or that our drivers had invited the pilot to dinner with us the evening before and consequently, like the rest of us, he was at this very moment searching the departure building for Neurofen, Evian and strong black coffee.

When eventually we did take off, the flight to Madrid took less than an hour, and by midday we had changed aircraft, landed at Lisbon, cleared customs, loaded the bags into two minibuses and were speeding west, towards Estoril and the hotel.

There are a couple of large and well kept golf courses close to the circuit. As soon as we checked into the Estoril Eden the golfers amongst us quickly changed, jumped back into a minibus and disappeared. I was feeling very tired after the four day test and the only thing I had any inclination to do was sleep.

I woke at around six o'clock. After a shower, I called Bat's room to see what he had in mind for dinner. The west coast of Portugal is famed for its fish restaurants, which, with great justification, rank amongst the world's best. Therefore, after a brief discussion we decided to stroll down the Cascais coast road to an Italian restaurant we had been to on several occasions in the past, for garlic mushrooms and a pizza.

It is an odd feeling to walk into a restaurant, in a foreign land, thousands of miles from home, and the waiters remember you from previous visits, chatting to you like old friends. I have been to the local Italian in Chipping Norton far more times than I have visited the one in Cascais, but the staff in England simply refuse to recognize me from Adam, even though we will nod at each other when our paths cross in the newsagent's.

Bat had also been asleep most of the afternoon, and it was well into the early hours of the next day before we felt tired enough to return to the hotel. When we had arrived, the restaurant staff had seemed pleased to see us. They seemed even more pleased when eventually we paid the bill and left them to get off to bed.

We left for the circuit at seven the next morning. As in Spain, we weren't running on the first day. We had to thoroughly check the cars over after the Jerez test, replacing any worn components and spherical joints etc. We changed the set-up for the different circuit and fitted different springs and brakes.

Michael Jakeman is the gearbox mechanic on our car. His name was shortened to Jakey the day he joined us from Williams, back in '91. He had the transmission apart, and gave everything a thorough inspection. As we were working on our car, Paul, Carl and Lee were rebuilding 01, and Dave Butterworth, the gearbox mechanic who during the season normally works on car number five, was busy carrying out the same inspection work to their transmission.

During the rebuild Greg told us to expect J.J. to show up. He was coming out to Portugal to see the cars in action, and have a seat fitting in the B194, in preparation for the forthcoming Italian test at Imola, due to happen immediately after this one finished. J.J. turned up later that afternoon. It was good to see him, and I was amazed at how well he looked. It was difficult to believe that it was less than six weeks since his accident. He had lost a little weight, but on the whole, he looked in remarkably good health. He was keen to climb into the new car and impatient to have the seat made.

This is a fairly straightforward process, thanks to the invention of 'two part foam'. We have a carbon 'bucket seat', that is made to the largest size that will fit inside the chassis. Inside this is laid a large black plastic bin liner, on which the driver sits.

The two 'parts' of the foam are measured into separate containers, to ensure that precise amounts of each chemical are used (too much catalyst and the result is like an erupting volcano). When the driver is sitting comfortably the two chemicals are thoroughly mixed together and gently poured into the open end of the bin liner.

This has to be done quickly, but carefully, as the chemicals will start to react after about ten seconds of being brought together. When they do react, the resulting foam expands in the bin liner, looking similar to the froth from a well-shaken can of Coke. The foam fills the bag, copying the shape of the bucket-seat on one side and the exact shape of the driver's body on the other.

It is most important at this stage that the driver doesn't move, or the impression will be ruined. After a minute or two the reaction slows to a stop, and there in its basic form is the new seat. The bin liner, complete with the solidified foam, is then lifted out of the chassis, and trimmed to detail with a sharp scalpel.

After a final check that the driver is still happy, which is achieved by putting him and the seat back in the car, it is then covered with Tessa tape (a very strong and sticky fabric-based tape which has a million and one uses in Formula One) to give the fairly brittle foam a chance to survive.

The seat is now ready for use. If, after a few laps in the car, the driver remains satisfied, the composite department back at the factory will use it to make a mould and a proper carbon seat is produced that will precisely match the contours of the driver's body, fitting him like a glove.

With some drivers one attempt at this is enough. With others it can take four, five, or even more attempts before the driver declares himself happy. Fortunately J.J. was happy with the first. A big relief for Tim Baston, our fabricator cum composite specialist, who had been assigned to do these two tests with us.

Tim had been brought close to breaking point at Jerez, constantly having to repair the car's floor and diffuser, after the low ride height we had been running, combined with the uneven track, had repeatedly worn it through to the honeycomb core. It was extremely distressing for him to see the car tearing along the pit straight to the accompaniment of spectacular showers of titanium sparks spraying high into the air as the skid plates crashed against the tarmac.

The sparking skids weren't the problem, however, as these are designed to protect the floor from contact with the track. However, on an uneven surface it isn't just the skids that are in contact with the track, and Tim's long hours of night-time repair work were undone.

The following day Michael Schumacher was sent out in our car intending to run a full race distance, but at roughly the halfway point he again suffered engine failure. He had backed off the throttle as he approached the right-hander at the end of the start/finish straight, when there was a huge cloud of smoke out of the exhausts.

Yet again the car had been running well, but not for long enough. The next day we tried again, but still with no luck. With only nine laps of the race distance to go, the gearbox failed. Despite these setbacks, however, optimism was building. We were getting closer and closer to the required level of reliability, and I felt sure it would come. We would try again tomorrow.

That evening Jos took us all out to dinner. The new driver was learning quick. Obviously he had been taking lessons from Michael, who must have told him that it is always wise to look after the mechanics. We are, after all, the last people to touch the cars before they are let loose on the circuit. Of course, it isn't necessary to buy us dinner but everyone likes to be appreciated!

It was a good night out, made even more enjoyable for us, though certainly not for the restaurant staff, by a power cut. Not just in our restaurant but right along the coast. It must be a chef's worst nightmare to be right in the middle of preparing thirty dinners, only to find your kitchen suddenly plunged into total darkness, the situation made even worse by the laughter of the guests, who appear to display no sympathy at all.

The manager came rushing out of the kitchen, clutching bunches of candles. 'Please,' he cried 'help yourself to candles! I'll fetch some empty wine bottles to put them in.' Jos's manager, Huub Rothenburger, looked slightly alarmed at this suggestion. 'Don't bother fetching any empty bottles,' he called, 'fetch another twenty full ones. There are enough empty bottles on the table already!'

'Yes sir, immediately. Sorry. Right away.' The manager disappeared off into the gloom, shouting at somebody we couldn't see, but within two minutes we heard the unmistakable sound of a cork squeaking its way out of a bottle, followed by a loud pop!

These sounds were repeated several times and then a rather stressed looking wine waiter appeared out of the dark. He was greeted by a loud round of applause as he dispersed the wine around the long table. All due credit to the restaurant staff, as under the circumstances they did an excellent job, carrying on with only the flicker of candle light and the gas hobs to see by. All the steaks arrived, more or less at the same time, and although they were very much on the rare side, the dinner was still a most enjoyable affair!

Saturday the fifth, the final day of the test, was a wash-out. The rain began to blow in off the sea at ten o'clock in the morning. It was only a light drizzle at first, then built in strength to become a comprehensive downpour. There was no way we could go for a race distance in those sort of conditions. We stopped for an early lunch, and waited to see if the weather would improve. It didn't. At two o'clock the engineers decided to call it a day.

The Benetton transporters were once again loaded with the two race cars, the pit equipment, banners, tool cabinets, wheel rims and all the associated paraphernalia. Similarly, the Cosworth transporter was filled with engines, tools and telemetry equipment. The motor-home, which serves as our mobile kitchen, was loaded with tables, chairs, pots, pans and coffee machine (though, not before Stuart, who drives the motor-home around Europe for us, had been into the garage to see if I would like a last espresso before turning off the machine. It's an offer I never refuse).

Michael, Jos, and J.J. thanked every member of the team individually for the work we had done for them and after wishing the truckies a safe journey home, we washed our hands for the last time, climbed aboard the minibuses and set off for the airport.

Owing to the test's premature finish, we had to wait for nearly five hours at Lisbon for our flight home. Nobody felt like going into the city for a walk, we were all too tired for that. All we wanted to do was go home, and sleep.

Lisbon is a classic example of an airport with next to no facilities. There are two drab coffee bars which, given almost any alternative you would never enter. But as there was simply nothing else to do, we sat around the dingy Formica tables on hard plastic seats, watching the minute hand of the wall-clock take hours to do one revolution, too tired and irritable to make conversation.

It was just one o'clock in the morning when I opened the front door of the cottage. I dropped my suitcase on the floor, climbed the stairs, and was asleep before my head hit the pillow.

The trucks arrived back on Tuesday night, so we were back stripping the cars by Wednesday morning. While we had been away in Spain and Portugal, Max, Ken, and Jon had finished the build of chassis 03. This had been sent to Italy with the test team, to the Imola circuit for the final test, before the racing season itself got under way.

News filtered back to us that although J.J. had been passed fit enough to test the car. After a couple of runs he felt he needed more time to heal before he should drive again. Later that same week we were advised that Jos would be driving our car for the first race. I considered this a very sensible decision, as although J.J. had tried very hard to complete his recovery for Brazil, there was no point in rushing the natural healing process, and driving the car too early could delay his rehabilitation still further.

I had no problem with the idea of Jos sitting in for J.J. We had got to know him quite well during the previous tests, and everyone felt that he deserved the opportunity to drive rather than introduce a new and untried driver cold into the team in practice for the first race.

Even so, the prospect of driving the car in Brazil must have been very daunting for Jos. He had never driven in a Grand Prix before. Granted he had just won the German Formula 3 Championship, but there is a world of difference between Formula 3 and Formula 1.

Max, Ken and Jon had not accompanied chassis 03 to the Imola test, although it is normal practice for the three mechanics to stay with the car they build, as it becomes 'their' machine and they become acquainted with its every detail inside out.

All the cars are built exactly the same but everybody has their own way of doing things. I can tell my work from Jon's, or Lee's (the other two front end mechanics) just by looking. It's the way we run the wiring looms, or the positioning of ty-rap blocks and so on. All three methods are correct, simply different. It is the same with the mechanics on the rear end of the cars. We all have our own little traits.

This time, however, their car had been handed over to the test team, so they could stay at the factory and practise the new pit stop procedure with the rest of the race team.

The rules had been changed at the end of '93 in order to allow the cars to be refuelled during the race. This practice had rightly been banned for the past ten years due to the danger of a possible fire. Someone with a curious sense of logic – or an incredibly short memory – had now decided that it was now safe to be revived.

During the weeks of argument and confusion about what was, and what wasn't legal, concerning active suspension and electronic driver aids, the decision to allow refuelling had been passed almost unnoticed. The decision had certainly not gone unnoticed by the mechanics, the people who would be expected to carry out the act. Unfortunately, however, as mechanics we have no significant voice in these matters, and all we could do was try as hard as possible to make it as safe as possible. Until, that is, such time as someone in authority became brave enough to ban it again.

The refuelling equipment is the same for all teams and is supplied through the FIA's motor racing governing body. It is manufactured by a French specialist company, Intertechnique, who deal with aircraft refuelling. The system is charged with nitrogen and capable of delivering 12 litres of fuel a second. The delivery pressure is controlled by a 'pop-off' valve, set to 1.6 bar. The rigs were to be supplied, sealed and checked by the FIA at every Grand Prix.

The fuel rig itself is a huge contraption, standing nearly six feet high, and weighing close to seven hundred kilogrammes. It resembles something from the old Soviet space program, with massive solid steel walls seemingly capable of withstanding an internal nuclear explosion.  The fuel hose itself is made up of an inner and outer sleeve. The fuel is delivered down the centre tube and the car's tank then vents back up the outer section. This tank vent is vital – if it wasn't fitted, the chassis would crack and split open under the pressure of the incoming fuel.

We had been measured up by Sparco, the F1 clothing specialists, for fireproof underwear, overalls, boots, gloves, knee and elbow pads, balaclavas and goggles. All such equipment is made to the same specification as that used by the drivers and we appreciated the fact that no expense had been spared to protect us.

The local fire brigade had visited the Benetton factory and instructed us on their fire fighting techniques, as well supplying halon filled extinguishers, which should, we hoped, douse the most violent fire in seconds. This protection made everyone feel safer, of course, but if given the choice I think all of us would have voted not to refuel in the first place.

Before we could practise the pitstop, the refuelling equipment needed to be stripped down and cleaned. This was not because we doubted that Intertechnique had done a good job of building the assembly, but some teams had discovered swarf (waste material produced during machining and drilling), left inside the rigs following their manufacture.

Owing to the very small tolerance of the car's internal fuel pumps and injection system it is vital there are no contaminants in the incoming fuel. The fuel itself is 'double filtered' to ensure complete purity, so only after every component of the refuelling equipment had been thoroughly cleaned did we introduce any fuel to the rig.

We had purchased two units from Intertechnique, one for each driver. This would allow us to fill each rig with precise amounts of fuel, which might vary depending on differing driving techniques and the predetermined pitstop strategy. We might, for example, decide to refuel one car twice and the other three times, depending on tyre wear and the predicted pitstop strategy of the competition.

Having two rigs available would also allow us the safety of a back-up in case one of them failed. It would be a disaster of some magnitude if we were unable to refuel the cars due to an equipment failure, and had to watch Schumacher or Verstappen run out of fuel while leading the race.

The job of stripping, checking and servicing the rigs had been entrusted to the Sub-Assembly department. These are the people who build the various components, such as drive-shaft and upright assemblies, steering racks and dampers before handing them over to the mechanics to be installed on the individual chassis.

During the '93 season, Sub-Assembly had built and maintained the actuators and valves for the active suspension, and they are still responsible for the precision hydraulic components of the gear change mechanism on our semi-automatic transmission. As 'fluid' experts it was natural that they should be handed the duty of maintaining these new pieces of equipment. Moreover, as Simon Morley, our travelling Sub-Assembly mechanic, was to become our refueller and operate the rig during the pit stop, we could rest assured he would maintain the equipment to the highest possible standards.

Over the next few days work continued on the rebuild of the three cars bound for Brazil. Unfortunately work on chassis 03 was held up until its return from the Imola test. Hour upon hour of preparation work went into the cars. We knew, after all the testing we had carried out, that the B194 was both quick and agile. We had a fair chance of coming away from Brazil with a good result and, as mechanics, we were going to do all we could to ensure their reliability.

Every bolt was carefully inspected for manufacturing defects before being cleaned, lubricated and finally tightened to the correct torque. Wiring looms were positioned and ty-rapped into place, before being snipped loose and repositioned again and again, until we were happy with their final positioning.

We had to ensure that no cable was too tight, and eliminate any risk of the looms chaffing.

Silverstone's south circuit had been booked for the shakedown. We had to have the cars finished, transported to Silverstone, and ready to run, by 10.00 a.m. on Wednesday the 16th.

The night before the shakedown we were still waiting for several of the components which would enable us to finish building the car and, as the hours ticked by, it slowly changed from being another long day, into being another late night. We had been working an average of about fourteen hours a day during the previous week and were all starting to feel tired.

By the time we had finished the 'set-up', and the cars were ready to go, it was 4.30 in the morning. We had to be back at the factory at 7.30 in order to catch the minibus to Silverstone. Of course, nobody enjoys working these long hours, but we resign ourselves to this state of affairs and accept them as part of the demands imposed by a career in Formula 1 motor racing.

The people who live more than a short drive away from work had booked into a local hotel, thus ensuring at least a couple of hours sleep. Without this, they would be forced to turn their cars around and head back to the factory before they reached home.

I drove back to Chipping Norton, and was in the cottage at just after 5.00 a.m. I left a note on the coffee machine, asking Judd to set the alarm for 6.50 a.m. This would give me nearly two hours sleep and still leave time for a shower and be able to make it back to the factory for 7.30 a.m.

I awoke to the sound of the radio, rubbed my eyes and slowly focused on the clock. The figure of 9.20 a.m. glared back at me. I nearly died! I rubbed my eyes and refocused. Surely I hadn't seen it clearly. It now claimed the time to be 9.21 a.m.

Dammit! Judd must have forgotten to set the alarm! Not so! It had gone off alright exactly at 6.50 a.m. as I'd asked! I had just slept straight through it.

I threw my clothes on and shot down stairs. I was so angry with myself. I couldn't believe it. The answer-phone was flashing its little red light at me. Someone had called while I had been asleep. It was Mick. 'Hello Steve,' said the cassette, 'I don't know if you're awake or not, but we're just leaving for the circuit. Make your own way there, and I'll see you soon. Bye.' I hadn't heard the telephone ring any more than I had heard the alarm, and to make matters worse the message was over two hours old already!

I dashed out to the car and headed off to Silverstone. Ten minutes late wouldn't be too bad, but two and a half hours . . . I have never felt so ashamed about being asleep in my life. It wasn't the sleep itself, but the fact that I had let the team down. Someone would have to cover for my work as well as do their own, when they too would only have had a couple of hours rest. I felt terrible.

The Fiesta made record time on the trip to Silverstone. I had the windows and sun-roof wide open, and felt wide awake by the time I parked the car at the south circuit. I opened the flap of the marquee that we were using as a temporary garage to be greeted by a loud cheer and a round of applause. 'You made it then!' I heard someone say.

I was bright red with embarrassment. 'Sorry Mick,' I apologized.

'Don't worry about it Steve,' he said with a broad smile on his face, 'we're all knackered!' I kept my head down for the rest of the day, and, keeping a low profile, quietly got on with the job. The spare car crew had been sent to Silverstone with chassis 01 the day before, in order to attempt a race distance with the latest spec ZR engine.

This would be the final attempt before we flew out to Brazil for the real thing. Cosworth were in good spirits, telling us they were now completely confident of the reliability of the engine. They proved themselves correct. Michael had been assigned to drive the car and managed a complete race distance without a moment's hesitation. We were all very pleased.

The B194 had proved the quickest Formula One car on the majority of circuits we had been to. It was certainly the first definitive 1994 car ready to go testing and we had successfully completed thousands of kilometres. We were in good shape. What we had to do now was load everything into boxes, air freight it out to Brazil, and show the world what we could achieve with it.

We flew out to South America on Sunday the 20th. The freight had left two days before, on the Friday morning. We landed at Sao Paulo international airport twelve hours after leaving London, the flight passing relatively quickly as we chatted with mechanics from other Formula One teams, some of which I hadn't seen since Adelaide last year.

We duly landed in Brazil at 7.00 a.m. on Monday morning. Even at this early hour, as we stepped off the 747 the heat and humidity was like walking into a Turkish steam room. The quilted jacket I had been wearing for protection against the English weather became instantly redundant as the first beads of perspiration appeared.

Eventually we cleared passport control and customs – a time-consuming process in Brazil – loaded the bags aboard the Volkswagen Combi vans and headed towards Morrumbi and the Hotel Novotel, which would serve as our home for the next seven days.

The drive to the hotel follows a wide, slow running river which cuts straight through the centre of Sao Paulo. As you travel along, the water changes colour from dark brown to dark green, to an even darker green, and back again. It is every bit as detectable with the nose as with the eye, and every so often evil looking carpets of beige foam are released into the river, from huge concrete pipes. The scum floats down-stream to where young children, dressed in rags, play unattended on the steep, slippery slopes.

There appear to be three distinct classes of Brazilians. There are those who are very rich and have everything. Next are the people who serve the ones who have everything (the staff who run the hotels, shops and restaurants). Then there are the rest of the vast population, the ones who have nothing.

By this, I don't just mean people struggling to make ends meet or even the poor. Quite literally, they have nothing at all. They survive in their thousands, in slums and shanty towns scattered all around the city of Sao Paulo. Their houses are made from anything they can find on the streets. Pieces of corrugated iron and oddments of timber have been nailed or tied together over months and years, to become irregular tangled webs, each flimsy structure dependent on the other for support. The more ingenious residents of these permanent 'temporary housing solutions' have managed to install some form of running water and even electricity!

We were given Monday off in order to adjust to the time difference between Britain and Brazil, and to get over the long journey between the two countries. That is everybody except Mick, and the truckies, who had gone to the circuit to see if our equipment had made the journey in one piece, and to paint the garage floor, so that it would have time to dry for when we began work the following day.

The truckies travel with us to all the intercontinental races – known as 'fly-aways' – as they each have different jobs to do at the circuit, apart from driving the transporters to and from the European races, of course. They are responsible for fuel and tyres, having to produce different tyre compounds at a moment's notice at the behest of the engineers, making sure they have been pre-heated to the correct temperature in their blankets beforehand. They also adjust the cars' fuel load during the practice and qualifying sessions, depending on what quantity of fuel the engineers wish to run with.

The truckies are also responsible for the equipment, including the gantry, air-guns, bottles and hoses, as well as the front and rear jacks. All these have to be rapidly assembled and positioned in the pit lane while we are on the grid with the cars prior to the start of the race.

All these accessories must be assembled promptly and correctly, just in case an accident on the first lap results in one of the cars needing a replacement nose section or new tyres. It wouldn't go down at all well if the guns failed to work in an emergency pit stop because the air bottles hadn't been turned on.

Bat and some of the others had gone straight to bed, to get as much sleep as possible before they left for the Masque and all the bizarre offerings to be found there. I lounged around the pool for most of the day, and lounged around the bar for most of the evening.

The four-piece band played *The Girl from Ipanema*. They remembered us from previous years and knew what we expected them to perform. As soon as they had finished we shouted for more. They played it again. In fact we wouldn't let them play anything else. Eventually they gave up and either went home, or moved on to another hotel in the hope of practising another tune. I had braved a couple of Caipirinhas, and by midnight I needed my bed to make a full recovery. The lift door opened and out stepped Bat and Reggie, on their way to the Masque. 'Prawn juice and go!?' Reggie asked. 'Yes,' I replied, 'completely grizzled!' Reggie is the second fabricator cum composite specialist who travels with us during the season. His real name is David Jones but he acquired the nickname Reggie due to his uncanny resemblance to the infamous Kray twin during his sixties period. I share a room with Reggie whenever we travel away, which usually means having the room to myself most of the time, normally being fast asleep by the time he returns from an evening out.

There had been lots of rumours concerning scrutineering, circulating in the press, prior to our departure from England. The majority of the articles implied that havoc would ensue when it came to checking the cars' eligibility, with most of the teams protesting to one another about what was and was not legal.

Under the new rules, the teams were forced to do away with accessories such as active suspension, traction control, start control and fully automatic trans- misions. These functions were deemed to detract from the drivers' ability and their skill in car control. Apparently people wanted Formula One to be por- trayed as a Drivers Championship, not a Constructors Championship.

I found this argument both sad and very frustrating. To me, Formula One represents the pinnacle of mechanical engineering. It is a constant battle between the abilities of rival teams and the laws of physics, to produce the ulti- mate in engineering excellence. It is for this aim that I and many others spend so much of our lives building, testing and racing our cars.

However, the rules are the rules, and our software specialists had disarmed all the banned functions of the engine and gearbox management systems, to comply with the regulations. To Charlie Whiting (the FIA Technical Delegate, whose job it is to ensure that we all play to the rules of the game) it must have seemed an insufferable task, made even worse by the media constantly stirring the bubbling cauldron. As things transpired, scrutineering was successfully concluded without any of the tantrums and theatricals anticipated by some sections of the press.

I was very impressed at how calm and relaxed Jos seemed during the two days leading up to Friday and the first practice session. The pressure on him was obviously immense, but he seemed to take it all in his stride and it seemed incredible that only two years previously he had raced nothing bigger than a kart!

In practice and qualifying the cars were very reliable, and certainly in Schumacher's hands very quick. During Friday's sessions Ayrton Senna was the only driver quicker than Michael, with both of them being well over a second quicker than the rest of the field. Each time Ayrton drove his Williams down the pit lane and past the Benetton garage he would lift his helmet visor and look in, keeping his eyes fixed on Michael's car, or if that was out on the circuit he would watch the mechanics, scrutinizing them until he had driven slowly past.

'His eyes seem to pierce you,' said Ken, walking over for a quick word while Michael was out on the track. 'It's bloody unnerving!'

'He's damning you for Michael's speed!' I replied.

A Benetton appeared in the pit lane and Ken shot off to pull it back into the garage. This is the normal way for getting the car back inside, and all teams follow the same traditional procedure: the driver pulls up in front of the garage, he stops the car at forty five degrees to the entrance and puts the car into neu- tral. The number one mechanic then reaches into the cockpit, taking control of the steering wheel, while the other two mechanics hold onto the rear wing and pull the car backwards.

By the end of Friday's qualifying session Ayrton was on provisional pole position with a time of 1m16.386s. Michael was less than two-tenths of a second behind him in second place. We anticipated that our main opposition for the season would remain the same three teams as in recent years: Williams, McLaren, and Ferrari.

The greatest challenge would obviously come from Williams, who had claimed the World Championship for both driver and constructor for the previous two years. They had retained the very powerful Renault engine, and with Senna behind the wheel looked as formidable as ever.

McLaren, who had pipped us last year to finish second in the Constructors Championship, had suffered a fairly terrible day by their standards with all sorts of problems with the throttle mechanisms on their new Peugeot engines. Mika Hakkinen managed a respectable fifth, albeit well over a second and a half off the pace.

Jos, despite an early spin, managed 11th fastest time. Owing to the damage caused by going off the circuit, we had to replace the front wing and floor. He was very apologetic about the extra work he had caused us, and he promised to try for a better grid position on Saturday. I felt, that for a chap who had never driven around the circuit before, and who had just undergone his Baptism of fire, he had done a pretty good job already.

That night we changed the engines in both the race cars, and carried out the routine checks to the brakes, suspension and transmission. All were fine, and apart from the repair work Tim and Reg had to perform on the damaged floor and front wing, we were in good shape and managed to get away from the circuit by 10.00 p.m.

Unfortunately, this wasn't the case for all teams. As we walked towards the paddock gate I could hear several carbon cutting tools in action, small air-powered grinders which resemble and sound like a dentist's drill, as mechanics were hard at work repairing or modifying different parts of their cars. The high pitched squeal of tortured carbon followed us down to the car park, as we climbed into the minibuses and drove out of the circuit, back to the Novotel.

During qualifying on Saturday Jos was true to his word. After a good night's sleep and having some time to contemplate all that had gone on the day before, he managed to improve his grid position to ninth. He could perhaps have gone even quicker, but it started to rain and as far as improving grid positions was concerned it was all over.

Just before the heavens opened, Ayrton managed to break into the high 1m15s bracket, much to the vocal delight of the crowd. Michael had also improved on Friday's time, managing 1m16.290s, which was just under one-tenth quicker than Ayrton had achieved the day before. This time the crowd noisily disapproved.

When the rain fell I thought that would be the end of the day's running, but we heard the Williams fire up again, and with a set of rain tyres fitted, Ayrton was out, pounding round the circuit once more, getting a feel for the car in the wet, just in case of rain during the race. Michael was also despatched into the rain, the pair of them using the remaining minutes of qualifying to evaluate their cars in the wet.

There was no doubt that the race for the Brazilian Grand Prix would be between these two drivers. Neither of them was prepared to offer any advantage to the other by neglecting to glean the last possible ounce of information about the track, its changes when wet, and the handling of the car under different conditions.

Saturday night was spent preparing the cars for the race the next day. Fresh engines were fitted, and I installed a drinks bottle to help Jos replenish some of the liquid he would lose during the course of the 71 lap race, although Michael chose not to use one.

As a rule of thumb, when things are going well, and the cars are both fast and reliable, we have little additional work to do during the race preparation. Consequently we were able to finish and get back to the hotel relatively early. The engineers are loath to alter the car very much when they have found a 'quick' set-up, just in case what they ask us to change is found to be a backward step.

Once again we were one of the first teams to leave the circuit. I took this to be a good omen. Over the last couple of years Williams had always been one of the first teams to get away on Saturday night. The same went for McLaren when they were World Champions. In order to finish the race preparation, we are, of course, prepared to work for as long as necessary, but let's be honest, nobody actually wants to work all night!

We left the Novotel at 5.45 a.m., in order to guarantee access to the circuit, and avoid getting caught in the horrendous traffic. Thousands of Brazilians would soon swarm to Interlargos in the hope that their local hero, Ayrton Senna would win his home Grand Prix for the third time. Judging by the fanatical way they waved their national flags and continually shouted 'SENN-NA! SENN-NA! SENN-NA!' they wouldn't be best pleased if they were not rewarded with the outcome they so obviously desired.

As soon as we managed to get through the already swelling crowds and into the relative peace and quiet of the paddock we pushed the cars up to the scrutineering bay, which is located at the entrance of the pit lane. Here the cars are checked to make sure they are legal, as far as weight and dimensions are concerned.

The race warm up, the final half hour that the cars are allowed on the circuit prior to forming up on the grid for the actual race, started at 8.30. This is a worrying time for everybody, as we wait to see if there are any problems with the cars since their preparation the evening before.

This short session is similar to a shakedown, in the sense that it is a systems and handling check, as opposed to a true test of speed. The last thing we would want to happen at this stage would be for the driver to spin off into the guard-rail.

After the warm up both Jos and Michael declared that as far as they were concerned the cars were perfect. Cosworth on the other hand weren't so happy. They had been looking at the data acquired during the warm up and told us that everything was fine with Michael's car but that we needed to change the engine in chassis 02, our car.

By now we had carried out numerous engine changes on the B194 during the run up to the season. We were certain we could complete the job in time for the race, but nevertheless we got straight on with it, not wanting to waste any time in case we encountered any additional problems on the way.

The fresh engine was fitted with half an hour to spare, before the pit lane opened at 12.30 p.m. This gave us just enough time to change into our fireproof overalls, and have a quick espresso before strapping Jos into the car.

As soon as the green light came on at the end of the pit lane, signifying that the circuit was open, we sent Jos out to complete an installation lap to confirm that the engine was OK and wasn't suffering from oil or water leaks. Everything was fine and we despatched him to the grid.

Michael had also completed a lap and had radioed back to the pits, saying that everything was good, and proceeded straight to his grid position. As soon as the cars depart for the grid, the mechanics, engineers and tyre men leave the pits and set off to meet them there. These are the final 30 minutes before the start of the race, and the period of highest tension for the teams. If a problem occurs with the car now, there is no time to waste and the problem must be corrected quickly and methodically, with all the precision and organisation of an operating theatre.

The mechanic who works on the area of the car where the fault lies would carry out the repair, as he knows his part of the car like the back of his hand. He would receive assistance only if he requested it, so he could be certain every task had been completed and nothing had been overlooked. The mechanic carrying out the work would ask for tools when he needed them, and they would be handed to him as a scalpel would be handed to a surgeon. If both of his hands were busy, his brow would be mopped of sweat if needed.

This may sound very dramatic, but it is the way we would proceed. Remember that the sole objective of the race team is to get two cars up and running from the grid when the light turns green. Everything is subservient to that end. If one of the cars fails to start the race, we will have failed in our purpose.

Fortunately, there were no problems with either car, and both Benettons proceeded into the formation lap without incident. As soon as they had moved off, we returned to the pits, getting into position, checking the wheel-guns and jacks in case of an emergency pit stop. The lights turned green and the first Grand Prix of the year began.

As with practice and qualifying, it is not my intention to give a lap by lap description of the events during the race, as that is not the purpose of this book. Again, all those details can be found in volumes dedicated solely to that aim. Besides which I simply haven't got enough free time in between races to write it all down! I will of course give details of the Grand Prix from the mechanics' point of view.

We were proved correct in our predictions about Senna and Schumacher being the principal players in the race, and within a few laps they were both well out in front of the rest. Ayrton leading, Michael a few seconds behind, but closing all the time.

It is almost impossible to see anything of the circuit from the pits, so every time Michael and Jos had gone past the pit lane entry and we were sure they wouldn't be dashing in for tyres, I would have a quick glance at the monitors to see how we were doing. Jos was going well and had even managed to move up a couple of places. Things were looking good.

I wondered who would be the first team to stop for fuel. No one I had talked to over the last couple of days was looking forward to going first, but when the car screamed down the pit lane and into position there would be no choice in who it was. It was boiling hot in our fireproof clothing and our goggles steamed up from our breath.

We were told over the radio to expect Jos in first. He was expected to pit on around lap 17. On lap 15, however, I noticed the McLaren mechanics ripping the blankets off their tyres and jumping into position. Their refuelling man pulled the huge hose over his shoulder and got poised for action.

Like it or not, McLaren International was going to be the first Formula One team to carry out a 'live' refuelling pit stop in over 10 years. A moment later Martin Brundle's car came in. The tyres were changed well before the fuel delivery was finished, which seemed to take an extra two seconds.

Then Paul Simpson, their Chief Mechanic, lifted the 'BRAKES ON' board clear, and Brundle was off. You could almost sense the relief from McLaren that everything had gone well. A few seconds later I heard Frank Dernie over the radio telling Jos to come in for tyres, and within seconds he was in.

I operate the rear jack during the pit stop and as soon as the car had gone past me I had the jack located in the 'jacking plates' (two long hooks, located on the bottom of the rear wing mounting). I waited for Simon to attach the fuel hose before heaving the jack down, lifting the rear wheels clear of the ground.

Simultaneously Kenny was doing the same with the front jack. I watched as the rear wheels were changed, and checked to see that everybody had finished. It had been decided that Kenny and I would keep the car in the air until the fuel-hose had been removed and Simon was safely out of the way.

By keeping the car in the air we prevented the driver from pulling away with the hose still connected, which could be potentially disastrous. When Simon duly pulled the hose off, I let the car back down. Jos selected gear, increased engine revs, began to pull away, and promptly stalled the engine!

This was the first time he had ever taken part in a pit stop, so I suppose it was understandable to a degree. Thankfully, it wasn't a complete disaster. We quickly had the engine fired-up again, and Jos sped off back into the race.

Michael was now right on Ayrton's tail, with less than a few metres between them. 'In for tyres Michael! In for tyres Michael!' I heard his engineer Pat Symonds warning. We got ready, and at the same time so did Williams. We would be pitting on the same lap. We had practised pit stops over and over and over again. If we remained calm and everything went well, we felt sure we could out-pace the Williams crew, and hand Michael the lead.

Senna's Williams entered the pit lane first, then our Benetton. They must have been close to racing speed as they screamed towards us. Ayrton darted into his pit, Michael hurtled into ours. The next few seconds were incredible. The pit stop went perfectly. Simon connected the hose, the car went up, the wheels were changed, the fuel-hose was removed, and the car slammed back on the ground.

Mick pulled the 'BRAKES ON' board away, the engine screamed and Michael shot down the pit lane like a bullet. A fraction later Ayrton blasted after him in pursuit. We had done it. We had given Michael the lead. Thereafter, Michael began to pull away. He soon had the gap up to five seconds, with the rest of the field more than another 30 seconds behind. Following his slow pit stop, Jos had been doing a good job, remaining patient and carefully moving up through the field. He had managed to get into ninth place when he was involved in a huge accident.

As he pulled out from behind Irvine's Jordan, in an attempt to overtake, Irvine pulled out to try and lap Bernard's Ligier. This forced Jos to go very wide. Eventually the Jordan and Benetton tangled, flinging Jos's machine high in the air and into a terrible somersault, landing on top of Brundle's McLaren.

Thankfully no one was seriously injured. Chassis 02 wasn't so lucky. In an accident lasting a little over three seconds, the work of weeks had been completely destroyed.

Ayrton pitted again on lap 44 and Michael came in next time round. Both were very quick stops, but Michael was now leading the Williams by over nine seconds. Then, 16 laps from the end of the race, the pressure was suddenly off when Ayrton spun and stalled.

All Michael had to do was take it steady and ease the car over the finish line. We showed him 'SENNA OUT' on the pit-board, and confirmed this to him over the radio. Michael crossed the line to win the race a full lap clear of the rest of the field.

The team was ecstatic – we had proved without a shadow of doubt that we were going to be a major force to be reckoned with, and that the competition had a lot of catching up to do. We pulled off our overalls, pleased to be rid of them now that the race was over and thankful they had not been needed.

We went down to the podium where I was impressed at how happy Michael looked when presented with his trophy. He was absolutely thrilled. It came as a refreshing change when compared to some of the sombre faces we had seen accepting awards in the past.

One of the circuit trucks brought back chassis 02 which looked very sad and sorry for itself. There was a lot of damage to the suspension, but the chassis had done its job perfectly, providing a safe haven for Jos during the course of the accident. It would, nevertheless, require severe attention back at the factory if it was ever to be used again.

Dave and Bobby removed the damaged gearbox and fitted the spare, while Jon and myself bolted on new wishbones and uprights, in order to make the car a 'rolling chassis', and so be able to get it onto the cargo plane and eventually back home.

After all the cars and equipment had been packed and made ready for the return flight, we went back to the hotel, showered, changed, and went out to celebrate our win. It turned into a big night, with several of the team not returning to the Novotel until shortly before we left for the airport the following day.

However, I must make one correction. I said earlier that I could quite believe the antics of the girls from the Masque. I was wrong. After going out on Sunday night and seeing just what does go on, I agree with what Bat had told me in Barcelona: the Masque is both bizarre and quite unbelievable!

# APRIL

We managed to beat the freight on its return trek over the Atlantic and back to England by twenty-four hours, giving us a whole day off to readjust to European time and recover from the aches and cramps induced by the 20-hour journey back from South America. The trip had nearly doubled in time from the outward flight due to having to fly via Rome, and change aircraft for the connecting flight back to Heathrow.

One day off didn't seem very long, and it passed too quickly as I lounged in front of the fire, watching the video of the race which Judd had taped for me over the weekend.

'Congratulations,' she said when I walked through the door of the cottage, 'well done'. The tone of her voice didn't sound particularly sincere, but there were understandable reasons for that. After all, she does work for Williams, so I could hardly expect her to be too pleased with the result. 'Don't start worrying yet,' I reassured her, 'the season has only just started. Anything could happen between now and Adelaide.'

Some of our friends have commented on how awkward it must be, working for two rival teams. In fact it doesn't bother either of us. By mutual agreement motor racing is a banned topic of conversation and, apart from congratulating or commiserating with each other, Formula One and Grand Prix racing are never mentioned. Each of us is more than happy to enjoy the break from what otherwise is an all consuming occupation.

We had been correct in our assessment of the damage to chassis 02. It was to be withdrawn from service until a detailed evaluation of the necessary repair work could be carried out. As the time schedule for the next Grand Prix was as tight as ever, it would prove impossible to carry out the repair work, and return it to us before the freight would have to leave for Japan.

We were presented with a brand new chassis, number 04. This had travelled with us to Brazil, in a box, as the 'emergency spare', in case one of the cars had been badly damaged during Friday, Saturday, or even, heaven forbid, the Sunday morning warm-up.

As Dave, Bobby and I began to build chassis 04 into a complete car, the test team mechanics had started to prepare the next chassis, 05, to take over the job as the emergency spare. Max, Kenny, and Jon retained 03 for Michael, while Paul, Paul and Lee stayed with 01 as the spare car.

Silverstone had been booked for the shakedown, prior to the freight leaving for Japan, on Tuesday the 5th, giving ample time for what was now becoming a fairly familiar rebuild. The work was carried out at a steady pace, and the progress was so good that we even managed to have Sunday off.

J.J. drove in the shakedown and seemed to be his old self. It wouldn't be long before he would be ready to tackle a race distance again. He had been advised against driving in Japan, and although disappointed, he seemed happy for Jos to stand in, at the forthcoming Pacific Grand Prix.

All Nippon Airways flight NH202 departed Heathrow's terminal three for the 12-hour flight across Europe, Russia, Siberia, and on to Narita airport Tokyo at 6.00 p.m. Sunday evening. I had asked at the check-in desk if the man behind the counter could arrange a non-smoking window seat for me, and, if possible, with nobody sitting on the same row.

This enabled me to start scribbling notes for the March entry in this diary, without people becoming curious as to what I was doing. More to my amazement than anything else, he had obliged. He told me he had sealed the other seats on my row, so that barring the flight becoming fully booked at the last minute, nobody would be able to allocate the seats to other passengers. What a splendid chap!

Japanese cabin crew provide excellent service, genuinely going out of their way to ensure their passengers have everything they need. Nothing is too much trouble for them. Unfortunately, this – as far Reggie, Jakey and Bob are concerned – is their weak spot.

When dinner is served, normally consisting of noodles with chicken or fish, they will deny all knowledge of how to use their disposable wooden chopsticks. They wait until a stewardess walks down the aisle towards them, and then attempt to eat the noodles with the chopsticks still joined together, using them as a crude spoon, faking extreme difficulty and looking as though they need advice. Seeing their plight the girl rushes over, only too keen to show the struggling passengers how to separate them. This they do, immediately throwing one of the chopsticks away and attempting to spoon their dinner inside with the one remaining stick. This brings a look of horror over the girl, as she feels guilty for confusing her passengers still further. More chopsticks are produced, and she demonstrates the correct technique to adopt. They then try to follow her instructions by breaking their one remaining chopstick in half, creating two very under-sized items. More shocked and worried looks, followed by even more confusion. And on it goes, until they give up on dinner altogether and settle for three large gins instead.

On long haul flights it has become common practice for the airline to display a computer generated map, showing the route and position of the aircraft as it slowly circumnavigates the planet. The system highlights the various major cities below us as we cruise thousands of feet above.

It also displays air speed, outside temperature, time from departure and time to destination. I suppose all this is calculated to set the passengers at ease, and prevent them constantly irritating the crew by asking 'How long to go? Are we nearly there?', or 'Is it much further? I'm getting bored!' Not half as bored as the cabin crew, one might safely assume!

Several hours into the flight the screen announced that we were flying over Siberia, one of the most remote regions of the world. I looked out of the window and down towards the barren, snow covered, howling landscape, where it seemed incredible that human life could survive. The similarities between the frozen, bitter wasteland below me and Silverstone in early February came immediately to mind.

Eventually we landed at Narita, Tokyo's new international airport, feeling crumpled and unwashed. After clearing passport control (which in direct contrast to Brazil is both efficient and well organized) we made our way to the baggage hall. The staff were very friendly, they had obviously been briefed that the Formula One teams were entering Japan via their airport and might need assistance.

My suitcase arrived at the same time as Dave Butterworth's and we set off through the customs exit. Dave smiled politely to the customs officer. The customs officer smiled politely back. 'Excuse me Sir,' he said in perfect English, 'do you have anything to declare?'

'No, I'm afraid we don't,' replied Dave, looking slightly disappointed, 'but thank you very much for asking!'

'You're very welcome Sir' said our new friend and bowed very graciously.

'Thank you very much indeed!' added Dave and returned the bow. They gave each other a final polite smile before we departed through the exit and out into Japan.

The next leg of the journey was to Haneda International, to catch the onward flight to Okayama. Haneda is located on the opposite side of Tokyo Bay to where we had landed, so we were treated to a 90-minute coach journey to get there.

After the 12-hour flight we had just completed and the looks from the tired, stubbly faces of both team mates and mechanics from other teams, the idea of this impromptu sightseeing tour of Tokyo's vending machines, of which there are literally thousands, promising 'peace and everlasting joy in life' to the customer who invests in a can of hot, sweet and dreadful coffee was hardly a popular one.

The journey to Haneda passed in silence as everyone either dozed or read, nobody feeling sufficiently sociable to hold a conversation. We arrived and checked in with plenty of time to spare before the flight departed. The time was spent dozing or reading, with still no one feeling sociable enough to hold a conversation.

The flight to Okayama was thankfully brief, lasting just under an hour and a half, but after the length of time we had been travelling since leaving London it was more than enough. Once again we collected our bags and wearily headed towards the exit. The doors opened automatically, revealing several blinding lights. The local TV companies had turned up to film the teams arriving from Europe. Reporters and journalists ran around scribbling notes, and trying to interview as many people as possible.

It didn't seem to matter who they interviewed, just as long as they belonged to a Formula One team. Questions were fired at us in broken English, and microphones pushed towards us. Did we like Japan? Would we win? Did we like the circuit? Did we speak Japanese?

At times like this it is difficult to remember that when we are in team clothing we are representing our company, our sponsors and are all ambassadors for the sport. Whatever we said would have been preserved on video tape, and the fact that all of us were very tired and irritable would be of no relevance when the film was shown on national television, and so we answered their questions as politely (and briefly) as possible.

We were nearly at the hotel now. Just one more ninety-minute coach journey and we would be there. It was a sight for sore eyes when at last the driver pulled up in front of a large and plush looking building, announcing that we had arrived at the Bishunkaku Teranoya Hotel and, for a few days at least, home !

I was last to get off the coach, using the time to stretch my arms and legs after a journey that had lasted close to 24 hours, the equivalent of sitting in an uncomfortable chair for three full working days. I had a brief stroll around the hotel grounds, while the chaotic queue at reception died down a little.

While I was completing the registration card I sensed a bright light shining behind me, the heat beginning to warm the back of my head. One of the film crews had followed us to the hotel. Enough was enough, all I wanted was to have a shower, a change of clothes, and to be left alone. I grabbed the key from the girl behind the counter and headed for the lift.

'Steve!' I heard as I dashed away, 'Steve!' I looked behind me, and a man in a bright green jacket smiled back at me. 'What is your room number?' I couldn't understand how he knew my name, unless he had been watching me fill out the registration card. What a damn cheek! 'Go away!' I said, the art of diplomacy beginning to fail me. I jabbed at the call button on the lift, hoping the doors would slide open, allowing my escape before the camera crew caught up with me. No such luck, the indicator above the doors told me that both the lifts were up on the sixth floor, having taken the rest of the team there only minutes before.

I jabbed the call button again, desperately urging the lifts to come back, but it was no use, the three-man team was upon me. 'We want to make tea for you!' said Green Jacket, pushing the microphone under my nose. 'GO AWAY!' I implored. I knew the Japanese were fanatical about Formula One, but surely even the most ardent Grand Prix fan didn't know the name and face of everybody who worked within the sport and to want to make tea for us all was, to say the very least, bizarre!

The brightly dressed presenter beamed an enormous smile at me, and said something in Japanese into his camera. 'We wish to make tea for you!' he repeated, and smiled again. A big, broad (and I was beginning to think, almost manic) smile. 'I don't drink tea! Now GO AWAY!'

I decided that these three were a little odd, and I began to fear for my safety. Fortunately the lift arrived, and for the first time in my life I was, quite literally, saved by the bell. I jumped inside and pressed the sixth floor button, preventing 'Earl Grey For Foreigners' from following by blocking their entry with my suitcase. The doors closed, shutting out the blinding camera light and Green Jacket's beaming smile.

A few seconds later the doors opened to reveal a long corridor with bedrooms off to either side. I walked towards my room, enjoying the peace and quiet of the deserted corridor, and looking forward to a hot shower. The peace and quiet didn't last long. The doors of the second lift opened, and out bolted the camera crew.

'Steve, which is your room?' they cried, 'we wish to make tea!' I began running down the corridor. 'REG!' I yelled, 'REG, GET THE BLOODY DOOR OPEN!' Reggie popped his head out of the door. 'Come on Steve quick!' he said, urging me on, 'they're coming! Run, run!' I shot down the corridor, with Green Jacket and his camera crew in hot pursuit. I dived into the bedroom and Reggie slammed the door shut, helpless with laughter.

After a shower and a change of clothes, I told Reg about my strange experience down at reception. Reg was still laughing about it, and he had an explanation for what had happened. Greg had given the film crew my name, palming them off onto me because I'd been the last off the coach.

'Er, well I'm a bit busy right now, but see Steve, the chap just coming through the doors. I'm sure he'll give you a few minutes.' Cheers Greg! Thanks a lot! There was a polite knock, and a girl's voice asked if she could come in. We both leapt for the door. It was the girl from reception. She explained that it would be a great honour if the hotel could perform the famous tea ceremony for Reggie and myself, as a gesture of welcome to the team.

The local news crew from Yunogo, the small town close to the hotel, had asked if they could film the event. Now it all made sense! As tired and weary as we were, there was no way we could refuse the honour that was being bestowed upon us. Indeed we felt sure that it would have been a grave insult to do so.

Of course they could make tea for us, and the film crew would be more than welcome to film us. Green Jacket beamed an even bigger smile as he, his sound man, and his camera man, slipped their shoes off and joined us. The tea was prepared with great care by a girl wearing traditional costume, and we sipped it dressed in kimonos, sitting cross legged on bamboo matting. After all the confusion and misunderstanding it was difficult to stop laughing, but everybody seemed pleased as we drank the tea, smiled at the camera and did our bit for international diplomacy.

The following morning we left for the circuit at 9.30 a.m. after a 'Special Western Style Breakfast' consisting of cold fried eggs and potato salad.

As this was the first time that the Tanaka International circuit at Aida had played host to a Grand Prix, we were allowed to run the cars for two unofficial test sessions on Thursday. This was to give the drivers a chance to familiarize themselves with the circuit layout and also allow the engineers a chance to work on the set-up, prior to the normal practice and qualifying sessions on Friday and Saturday.

The circuit itself is a fairly short and winding affair, situated amongst a dramatic mountain range of heavily wooded slopes. This made the access to the track quite difficult, as the narrow roads twist and weave their way up from the valley below.

To ensure that the teams would be able to get in and out of the circuit with as little trouble as possible, the organizers had marked out a special route for us, from the main road in the valley, up through the hills and into the paddock. It was sealed off to all other traffic, with police patrols at both ends and guards posted at all road inter-sections, to prevent local farmers slowing us down with their tractors. The police, dressed in their smart blue uniforms and white military style helmets, treated us like VIPs, snapping to a rigid attention and saluting as we drove past. We couldn't believe our eyes at first. And this wasn't the action of just one over-enthusiastic young recruit – on the contrary, every policeman along the thirty minute route did exactly the same thing. Very impressive.

As we unpacked and checked the cars for Thursday, we also chatted with mechanics from other teams, finding out what had been going on since the previous race. The Ferrari mechanics told stories of the horrific hours that they had been putting in, both at the factory and while testing, in an attempt to cure the poor understeer of their new car. Jean Alesi had been replaced by Nicola Larini for both this race and the next at Imola after the Frenchman had been involved in an accident testing at Mugello. It sounded like a very similar incident to J.J.'s, and Alesi too had suffered back injuries, although fortunately not as serious as our man's.

Eddie Irvine had also been replaced, thankfully not due to injury, but as a result of his part in the accident with Jos and the others at Interlagos. The subsequent FIA inquiry had held Irvine responsible, and a one-race ban had been imposed upon him. Irvine had disagreed with the penalty and had appealed against the decision. The appeal board had met and they too had disagreed with the penalty.

Unfortunately for Irvine, the appeal board decided that the original penalty was too lenient and had immediately increased it to a three-race ban. Consequently Aguri Suzuki had been drafted in as guest driver, which considering we were in Japan was a good move by Eddie Jordan, ensuring the team instant and valuable press coverage.

Williams had been hard at work testing in Jerez in an effort to improve the FW16 while McLaren and Peugeot concentrated on trying to cure their throttle problems. Everyone it seemed had been hard at work trying to make up for lost time during winter testing. I hoped they hadn't been able to make up too much time. Thursday was known as a 'Private Testing Day', but the times of that test were made public every time a car passed the start/finish line and, I imagine, within five minutes of the session finishing, a copy of those times would have been on the fax to every motor sport publication in the world.

The one major thing that came to light during Thursday, was that everyone could use more downforce. Aida was certainly no high speed circuit, and from what I could see, by the end of the session nearly all the teams had fitted their 'high-downforce' rear wings. These have an extra 'plane' on them, mounted in front and above the standard wing.

If you study photographs of the different cars you will notice that all of these extra wings are positioned in precisely the same location. This is done in order to stay within the rules (whose planning officer clearly defines where you can and where you can't build). The only difference between the wings is the shape of the 'end plates', which, within limits, are not subject to such vigorous controls.

I think it was the Arrows team who first used this extra wing, during winter testing at Silverstone, before the start of the '93 season. There had, of course, been much bigger wings in the past, with all sorts of add-on extras, but rule changes had removed those from the cars years ago.

The new high-downforce rear wing is a good example of how designers adapt the rules to their own advantage, and how quickly that advantage is taken up by other teams, as we all watch and study each other to see what the opposition comes up with.

Michael finished the session on Thursday 1.2 s quicker than Ayrton Senna, with a time of 1m11.307s, with Hill third, less than three-hundredths of a second off his team mate. Hakkinen's McLaren was fourth, followed by Jos in fifth place. Ferrari was still suffering with their understeer problems, as the cars visibly slithered all over the place. It would be another late night for them.

We changed the engines in both the race cars. This was not due to mechanical failure but because the number of laps we had covered during the test session meant that the engines would be 'out of life' halfway through Friday and none of us relished the prospect of changing engines at that point.

We also carried out a wear check of the brakes to assess their condition and anticipated life. Reliability-wise, everything was fine with the cars, and the only other work that the engineers asked us to carry out was a spring change. Michael wanted his car a little softer, while Jos wanted to go a little stiffer. The cars had been set-up with different spring rates back at the factory, Michael electing to try the car relatively stiff and Jos comparatively softer.

The changes that we now carried out had brought the cars (in terms of spring rate) much closer together. After we had finished the set-up change the bodywork was polished, and the car covers pulled over.

During the practice sessions on Friday morning everybody seemed to have made improvements, after the evening or in some cases overnight alterations. However, it was, without doubt, Ayrton Senna who made the most dramatic improvement, as he forced the Williams to go 2.3 sec quicker and during the qualifying session demonstrated just how much the FW16 had improved by snatching provisional pole from Michael by two tenths, returning an impressive 1m10.218s.

Michael was visibly disappointed at losing pole position. It is one of the things he hasn't yet achieved, but it would come sooner or later, everyone could see that. Michael's knowledge of the car, and his ability to get the maximum out of it seemed to increase with every test and race.

On the Friday and Saturday of a Grand Prix weekend the teams are restricted to a limited number of laps, 23 in the morning, and only 12 during qualifying, and since a lap of the Tanaka International track is only 3.7 kilometres, the engines would not have been subjected to sufficient use to require changing. Providing that after a post-session check they met with Cosworth's approval, they could stay in for Saturday.

Mike Janes and Jim Brett, the two Cosworth engineers, consulted the information collected from the data loggers and Pete Hennessey, their travelling engine builder, inspected the engines for any fluid leaks or other problems. Everyone seemed happy, and the engines were given a clean bill of health.

On consultation with the drivers, however, Michael decided he preferred the engine that had been in his car on Thursday, as opposed to the one he had just qualified with, saying that it felt smoother, and gave him better throttle response. Cosworth had no objection to allowing the previous engine to be refitted, by now they were more than happy with the reliability of their new engine, so Max, Ken, and Jon set about changing it.

Saturday was much hotter than the previous two days, and there was little chance of improving on Friday's qualifying positions. Air expands with a temperature increase, resulting in a reduction of available oxygen per cubic metre of air and consequently engine power falls. This theory also works in reverse, of course, and this is the reason why some teams claim such quick lap times while testing. If they send their cars out last thing in the afternoon, as the sun begins to set, but the track is still warm, having retained the earlier heat, not only will they take advantage of enhanced grip, but the engine will also benefit from the increase in available oxygen as the air temperature drops.

Neither Michael or Ayrton made any attempt to improve their grid position on Saturday. Instead they used the remaining minutes of qualifying to 'scrub in' their sets of tyres for the race. This is done to check that the tyres have been balanced correctly and that they feel right, as well as to remove the top coating of rubber which helps to improve the initial grip of replacement sets fitted during the pit stops. The tyres are normally scrubbed late in the session, as the circuit is usually at its cleanest and this avoids impregnating the new rubber with grit.

Jos had been sent out to try to improve his time and position, but he could only get within 0.1 sec of his Friday's best. Unfortunately for us, Christian Fittipaldi had managed to improve with his Footwork and had stolen Jos's ninth place in the line-up. Jos would start the second Grand Prix of his career from tenth place on the grid. I thought there was little to be ashamed of in that.

Fresh engines were fitted on Saturday night, of course, and the usual checks were carried out to the cars. I fitted the drinks bottle in the car for Jos, and showed Jon the rough layout for the bottle and pipes, as Michael had decided to use a drinks system as well. Once more we were in good shape, and by 10.30 p.m. we were heading down through the hills back to the hotel, taking the salute from the ever-present Japanese police force.

I for one was pleased to have an early night, as by 5.00 the next morning we were heading back to the circuit. The warm up was thankfully uneventful. I spent most of it waiting to show Jos his lap times on the pit-board, and watching the other cars exit the final corner and come on to the straight. There was no doubt about it, the Benetton was, by far, the best handling chassis on the circuit.

Michael and Jos would be starting from the right-hand side of the grid, and as this side is off the 'racing line' they had been told to drive 'off-line' during the final laps of the warm-up, going straight over their grid positions, to clean the dust and grit away, and so minimize the chance of wheel spin during the start. This they did, producing billowing clouds of dust by the action of the floor and diffuser.

I was forced to leave my account of the Pacific Grand Prix at this point. I had finished the above paragraph at around midnight on Wednesday the 27th. We were leaving for Imola at 5.00 the next morning, so I had gone to bed for a few hours' sleep. I anticipated being able to complete my account of the Japanese race, and begin telling you about Imola after I returned to England on Sunday evening, when I could spend a couple of days at home, waiting for the transporters to return from Italy.

The sad and tragic events which were to unfold in Imola have prevented me from completing the final part of the Pacific race weekend. It was a race that Michael won with ease, as Ayrton was forced to retire following an unavoidable collision with Nicola Larini's Ferrari after his Williams had been nudged from behind by Hakkinen's McLaren at the first corner of the opening lap.

I had been looking forward to Imola for many weeks. The circuit is located within a few miles of the Ferrari headquarters at Maranello, and in honour and recognition of the greatest name in Grand Prix history the circuit is named after both Enzo and his son Dino. The famous Prancing Horse is set high up on the control tower which overlooks the entire circuit, and to me the whole place has a special aura about it.

Imola was the first Grand Prix I attended as an employee of Benetton back in 1990. It was a race filled with fond memories, for as the security guards waved our minibus through the paddock gates, and I walked into the pit lane as a member of the Formula One fraternity I had achieved a life-long ambition. To me Imola was a very special place.

Now, though, I shall never look forward to going there again. I had wanted to tell you about so many things, like the *tifosi* (the passionate Italian fans who worship Ferrari with all the devotion of a major religion) and how they spend all Friday and Saturday night opposite the pits, singing and shouting in support of their beloved scarlet cars as the mechanics prepare them for the following day.

I was looking forward to telling you about the atmosphere on race day, as massive crowds swarm into the circuit, all sporting a scarlet caps or waving flags adorned with that rearing black stallion. I was looking forward so much to telling you about so many exciting and wonderful events.

I returned from Imola in the early hours of Monday morning shocked and confused. Even now, five days later, I find it difficult to accept the truth of what has happened. We suffered terrible accidents at Imola of a dimension that I thought would never happen.

During Friday's qualifying, Rubens Barrichello had a big accident. His Jordan was thrown very hard against the debris fence at the *Variante Bassa* chicane, the car just clipping the tyre barrier as it was launched into the air. An accident in which, despite its appearance, he thankfully only suffered fairly minor injures. It was the sort of incident that had become all too familiar over the last few years – dramatic, unnerving, but with the driver coming out of it relatively unscathed.

The Barrichello accident was but a forewarning of the horrors that were to follow. The next afternoon, again during qualifying, Roland Ratzenberger lost his life after his Simtek-Ford suffered a terrible accident on the approach to Tosa.

The whole of the pit lane was plunged into deep shock. We had almost become to believe that our drivers were invincible. That the cars were so safe that they could survive anything. Yes, they would go off, and yes, they would be damaged, leaving us long hours of repair work, but our drivers would be untouched. How naive we had become.

As a mark of respect we took no further part in Saturday's qualifying. Neither did Williams. Other teams did run when eventually the session was restarted, each I suppose having their own reasons for doing so.

The pit lane was very quiet and subdued during the Saturday night race preparation. I don't think the reality of the situation had fully sunk in. The senses were reluctant to accept a situation that had seemed impossible to envisage.

# MAY

J.J. had rejoined us for Imola. But, at a stroke, his emotions had been transformed from bubbling enthusiasm at the prospect of starting his first Grand Prix for Benetton, to deep sadness. He had lost a close and personal friend with the passing of Roland Ratzenberger.

Come the race and J.J.'s car had stalled on the grid at the start and Pedro Lamy's Lotus collided with the back of it. This again resulted in a big accident, sending the Lotus skidding into the armco on the left of the track and back over to the other side. Pieces of debris were sent flying into the crowd opposite the pits, injuring several of the spectators. Both cars were very badly damaged. The Lotus had struck our car with considerable force, ripping the wing and the whole left rear corner off the Benetton, and I was naturally very concerned for J.J.'s safety. Thankfully both drivers got out and walked back to the pits unaided, although J.J. had injured his arm as he had held it out of the car to signify that his car had stalled.

The safety car was sent out for several laps while the debris and the damaged cars were removed from the track surface. When the safety car was recalled and the race resumed, Ayrton too suffered a colossal accident when his Williams failed to negotiate the flat-out Tamburello left-hander after the pits.

It was an accident which, I am devastated to say, also proved fatal. The race was immediately stopped as Professor Watkins rushed to try and save Ayrton's life. We were not aware of the terrible consequences of the accident until the restarted race was nearly over and the sad news began to filter down the pit lane.

Not Ayrton. Surely not Ayrton. It just didn't seem possible. It couldn't happen again. Not twice in one weekend.

I can't remember doing any fuel or tyre stops that day. The video of the race shows we did, but I can't remember doing them. I just wanted it to be over. I just wanted to go home. We all did. Then, towards the end of the race, the right rear wheel came off Michele Alboreto's Minardi as he exited the pit.

We could see the car slewing towards us, Michele fighting with the wheel, doing everything he could to avoid ourselves and the other teams further up the pit lane, the car virtually out of control. The wheel nut flew into our pit as the Minardi sped past, catching Max on the leg and leaving a cut that would require stitches. The rest of us, thank God, were unhurt, but the wheel bounced with great speed into the Ferrari pits, on to the Lotus mechanics and off down the pit lane. The car collided with several of the Ferrari mechanics before Michele managed to steer it out of the pit lane and onto the race track.

The Ferrari and Lotus pits looked like a bomb had gone off, with people lying on the ground, some calling out in pain. We ran to try and help and did all we could before the medics arrived. The whole weekend was a horrible and hideous nightmare. So many terrible things had occurred that I wasn't able to take them all in, and it wasn't until I eventually got home and tried to comfort Judd that the safety veil of shock began to lift and I began to realise what had happened and what we had lost.

I drank a large scotch, quickly poured myself another, and like millions of others around the world quietly cried myself to sleep.

Monday and Tuesday, May 2/3, were quiet days spent at home, slowly coming to terms with the loss we had all suffered. In a little over 24 hours, Formula One had lost both one of its newest and most eager drivers, as well as its elder statesman and arguably the greatest driver of all time. Brazil, quite understandably, was in deep shock and the Government had announced a three day period of mourning. To the Brazilians, Ayrton had been much more than a Grand Prix World Champion. He was a national hero, a role model for the young and a statesman for the country.

Ayrton was the perfect Brazilian: passionate, ambitious and fiercely proud of his country and his origins. It had become his trade mark to display his country's flag when driving his lap of honour after a victory showing to the watching millions all over the world, that Brazil had done it again.

Through his ever-present determination to succeed, he had been an inspiration to thousands of people. He proved that if you really want something and are prepared to devote yourself to it, then anything is possible. Indeed even myself, in my own small way, had learnt the lesson from Ayrton, that determination can lead to success, when I was writing letters of application to Formula One teams back in the late eighties in the hope of being granted an interview, which eventually led to employment.

Judd had gone into work on Tuesday. She too was obviously very upset, and I thought it might help her to be with work colleagues for a while. I asked her to pass on my deepest sympathy to everyone. It didn't seem anywhere near sufficient but what else was there to say?

She returned later that day and told of hundreds of flowers that people had left at the factory gates, and pages of fax messages from people the world over, from as far away as South America, Japan, New Zealand and Australia, all expressing their sympathy at the loss of such a respected and talented man.

It frightened me to think that the actions that transpire on the Grand Prix circuits go to have such an effect on people throughout the world. It genuinely frightened me. Many thoughts have gone through my mind since the Imola weekend, not least that maybe I should stop racing. That it isn't worth the injuries and the terrible loss of life that can and have been incurred. After hours of quiet discussion, both Judd and myself came to the conclusion that it would do no good to stop.

After all is said and done, what good could it do? What had happened had happened, and no amount of people leaving Formula One could change that. We felt sure that giving up wouldn't be the wish of either Roland or Ayrton. Indeed Ayrton never knew the meaning of the words 'give up'.

I returned to work on Wednesday the 4th, and we began the preparations for Monaco. Due to the start line accident between Pedro Lamy and J.J. we needed to send chassis 04 to the inspection department. Following the severe shunt to the box and back end of the car we needed to confirm if there was any damage to the engine mountings, a situation which would effectively render the chassis useless.

As this would take a couple of days to complete, we couldn't afford the time to wait and see whether 04 had been damaged or not, and so we started to build chassis 06 into a complete car. Michael had driven chassis 05 at Imola and this, like his previous chassis, 03, had been a race winner. Nobody had celebrated this win and his victory in Italy had almost gone unnoticed. His old chassis, 03, had been transferred to the spare car crew, while their chassis, the original 01, that had been used for the press launch back in January, had been handed over to the test team.

Our new chassis 06 was now carefully transformed into our next race car. Once again I carried out the methodical and painstaking process of attaching the hundred or so ty-rap blocks and began the installation of the wiring loom.

This involved gently persuading the spaghetti-like mass that it *does* want to fit and that it *will* lie there and that it *must not* move when it is there. This is achieved with the aid of hundreds of ty-raps, which are pulled tight, snipped back off and replaced, again and again until eventually the loom stops struggling and resigns itself to becoming part of the car.

At the same time that I was installing the chassis loom, Dave was fitting the fuel system into the tank and Bobby and Jakey began to prepare and build a new gearbox, as the Lotus had completely destroyed the one we used in Imola.

The turn-around proceeded well and without problems. At least it did until we fired-up the engine and discovered a water leak from the cooling system. Cosworth quite rightly said that they would need the engine taken out and returned to their factory in Northampton in order to ensure its correct repair, and a replacement engine was dispatched to us, to allow us to finish the build of the car, and enable us to carry out the set-up and run the car at a shakedown before we left for Monaco.

We had difficulty in finding a circuit to shake the cars down at, as everywhere seemed to have a race meeting on, of one sort or another. Eventually Greg announced that he had located a circuit for us. Well not so much a circuit as such, more a strip really. We were going to Santa Pod Raceway, 'Britain's Premier Drag Racing Venue'. We had visited Santa Pod last year, when once again we had struggled to locate a vacant circuit to shakedown at. No one seemed over-keen at the prospect of a return visit.

I used to be a regular visitor to Santa Pod in my teens, and it was there that I had my first real exposure to motor sport. My friends and I would go and watch in awe, as the 'nitro' burning dragsters, with their massive eight litre V8s would dash, in pairs, down the quarter mile strip. I thought even then that the place must have seen better days, but when we arrived for the shakedown the place looked even worse than I remembered it.

No money seemed to have been spent on it for years, and I felt disappointed that it had fallen into such a state of disrepair. The once pristine tarmac had now become cracked and crazed, resembling a dry river bed, more than a racing surface, and the sad looking control tower made the shanty towns of Sao Paulo look well constructed in comparison.

J.J. had drawn the short straw and had been assigned to drive. I have never seen a shakedown carried out quicker, and I have never seen a driver so keen to leave afterwards. The cars were fired-up one at a time, and driven through the drizzle, once up and once down the drag strip.

'It's fine!' declared J.J. 'No problems at all. Let's do the next one!' After the three cars had been given their brief test, he changed out of his overalls, and his hire car shot off to Heathrow. I was left with the distinct feeling that he wasn't very impressed with 'Britain's Premier Drag Racing Venue'. Neither was I.

We flew out to Nice on Tuesday the 10th, leaving the factory at a very civilised 9.30 in the morning. Allowing for the trip to Heathrow, the flight to Nice, the hour time difference between England and France and the coach transfer between the airport and Monaco, we were actually in the city of Monte Carlo by late that afternoon.

Monaco is renowned as a tax haven, and is well known as the playground of the wealthy. Never more so than when the Formula One circus hits town. During the week leading up to the Grand Prix, Monaco is the place where the rich flaunt their money. They drive high performance Ferrari and Porsche sports cars around the streets of the tiny principality at a stylish 30mph, with an arm draped out of the open window making their gold and diamond encrusted Rolexes sparkle in the sunshine.

The rich park outside Loews Hotel, desperately hoping that theirs is the most expensive car on parade, as they go off to eat in the most expensive place money can buy. The rich talk loudly in restaurants, and complain even more loudly when they are told that the restaurants are fully booked. Meanwhile, the Enormously Rich (the people who have long since lost the need to display their wealth) quietly ask to see the wine list, and are politely served dinner, before they retire for the night to their yachts which, unlike their gold-laden counterparts, won't be told to weigh anchor and leave the harbour by Saturday night.

Monaco is without doubt the most famous street circuit in the world, and the most prestigious Grand Prix of the season. It is at Monaco that the hospitality and treatment of sponsors is at its peak. Everybody is out to impress their guests. It is the jewel in the Formula One crown. The media love it, the sponsors love it, the fans love it. The mechanics hate it.

From the second we arrive, to the second we leave, the Monaco race is a pain. There are no garages, which means we have to work in awnings fixed to the side of the race trucks. These large tents are either sauna-like beneath the hot *Cote d'Azur* sun or, if the weather decides to play up, the tents flap and blow about, offering no protection against wet feet as the rain trickles underneath the sides, making the working area resemble the bottom of a drained-out swimming pool.

The race trucks are parked along the harbour road, opposite the *Rascasse* restaurant and not, as some people might think, in the pit lane. Far from it! On the Thursday, Saturday and Sunday of the Monaco Grand Prix (we don't run on Friday due to the Formula Three meeting) the cars have to be pushed out of the awnings, down the harbour road, up the circuit past the *Rascasse*, round into the pit lane entrance and down into positions marked out for us next to temporary garages.

These garages aren't big enough to get the cars into but are used as storage space for all the tools and equipment that are needed during the sessions. Like the cars, the equipment we use has to be brought up to the pit lane from down on the harbour road, most of it being loaded into hire vans last thing at night ready for an early start in the morning.

Everything is taken up there for Thursday morning and, when qualifying is over, the whole process is reversed, and everything is reloaded and taken down to the harbour, and the cars are pushed back again. On Saturday morning we take everything back up, and on Saturday night we take everything back down.

On Sunday morning we get the cars out of the awnings, and along with the equipment we push everything back up to the pit lane again, stay there for the race, and as soon as the flag falls we load everything and take it back down again.

As we work on the cars both inside the awnings and at the pit lane we have to set two flat patches. This requires two different sets of shims, that have to be labelled and kept separate to avoid confusion. The whole process of working at Monaco is very time consuming and immensely irritating.

Because of the water leak from the engine we had fitted at the factory, and the resulting engine change we had carried out, the first job following our arrival in Monaco was to remove the spare engine we had fitted and swap it for the repaired engine that we had originally installed. The only problem was that we didn't have the original engine with us, as the trucks had left for France before it was ready.

Consequently, it had been sent on later by means of a courier service, which had promised it would be with us no later than 2.00 p.m. on Wednesday. By 1.00 p.m. we had the spare engine off the chassis, in case the courier arrived ahead of schedule, allowing us to make an early start on the installation.

By 6.00 p.m. we had serious doubts that the courier would be with us by Wednesday afternoon, and by ten o'clock that evening I began to doubt he would be with us on Wednesday at all! The van eventually turned up at

11.00 p.m., loaded not only with our engine but also parts for several other teams.

The driver didn't receive the friendly, appreciative welcome he had expected. It was gone one o'clock Thursday morning before we had the engine installed and fired up, with the car back on the ground and the dust cover pulled over. We loaded our tool cabinets into the hire vans in preparation for the morning hike up to the pit lane, and headed back to the hotel.

The Hotel Terminus is about five minutes walk from the harbour. Up the hill and past the old market place, to where it is situated just outside the train station. All the rooms seem to be decorated in the same drab brown and contain two small single beds which, due to the somewhat compact size of the rooms, makes it necessary to climb over one of the beds to get to the wardrobe.

The showers work, supplying copious amounts of warm (though seldom hot) water. It is important to remember to take your own soap, as the postage stamp size bars they leave in the bathroom are completely useless for anything except giving a reason to argue with the manager. I find it very hard to believe that the manager uses these microscopic pieces of soap in his own bathroom, so why does he expect us to use them? Why not put normal size bars of soap in the rooms and charge a few francs more for them?

Every year we go there I have the same conversation with him. 'There isn't enough soap in the rooms. We will need some more for the morning.'

'The maid will leave more when she cleans the room tomorrow.'

'Yes, I'm sure she will but we will have left the hotel before she brings the new soap!'

'You will have new soap in the morning!'

'But we will need to wash before she brings the bloody soap!'

'OK, I'll give you more soap now!'

'Thank you!' He drops a small bar of soap on the reception, which he has retrieved from a room behind the desk. 'There are *two* of us,' I remind him, 'we will need *two* extra pieces of soap!' He stares at me. I stare at him. Moments tick by. Slowly he produces another piece of soap from underneath his desk and without taking his eyes off me, pushes it towards me.

'*Merci*,' I say, still keeping my eyes fixed on him.

'*Bon soir*,' he replies. We continue to watch each other, neither of us sure who has won this annual confrontation. Is it me for managing to acquire the extra soap? Or is it him for making me come down to his reception and argue with him about it?

I lie in bed, staring out of the window, tired but kept wide awake by the late night trains, their brakes squealing to a standstill, as they bring the thousands of less-wealthy Grand Prix fans (who are unable to afford the exorbitant hotel prices) into Monaco from Nice and the surrounding towns.

We left for the circuit at 7.00 a.m. Even at this early hour the streets were busy, with people jostling around souvenir stalls, buying hats and helmet badges. There were even more Brazilian flags and Senna shirts around than I had ever seen outside of Brazil itself.

Williams and Simtek had both made the decision to attend the Monaco race. Both teams had entered only one car, and of course, neither of them had announced plans regarding replacement drivers at this early stage.

As I walked past the Williams pit I noticed that they were flying the Brazilian flag at half mast, in respect and sympathy for the world's sad loss. It had been decided that the first two positions on the grid would be kept vacant on Sunday, as a tribute to Senna and Ratzenberger, with their national flags carefully painted onto the tarmac. Over the past few years Ayrton had made the Monaco Grand Prix his own, winning for the last five years in succession. I thought it a touching gesture to reserve pole position for him, and run the Grand Prix in their honour.

I walked down to our pit, which was located between McLaren and Ferrari, taking time out to have a quick chat with Nigel Stepney, the Ferrari Chief Mechanic. Nigel used to work for Benetton as Chief Mechanic, and in fact it was he who offered me a position within the company and a start within Formula One back in 1990.

He had taken to working in Italy like a fish to water, and in true Italian tradition he had developed a passion for pasta, which judging by the incredible size of him he had consumed huge quantities of. He had been a large man during his time with Benetton, but following his move to Ferrari he appeared to have nearly doubled in size.

I asked him about the injured mechanics, and thankfully he had good news. All but one should be fit and back at work by the Barcelona Grand Prix. Jean Alesi had been passed fit, following his testing accident in Mugello and had returned to replace Larini in car 27. Maurizio Barbieri, however, their travelling composite specialist, had suffered a broken leg in Imola and unfortunately it would be several weeks before he would be able to return.

In an attempt to improve the safety for all of us during the race, and in the wake of the Imola accident, there had been two important changes made to the pit stop procedure by the FIA. There was to be a 50mph speed limit for all cars while in the pit lane, which had been modified by having a chicane built at both the entrance and the exit. Speeding was to be punished with a 10 sec penalty, but as all the drivers were deeply concerned for our safety following recent events, I doubted that anybody would willingly transgress this new rule.

The other change, that was also to take immediate effect, was that we and the other teams' mechanics were not allowed to stand out in the pit lane during the race, except when carrying out the actual pit stop. This was designed to keep the pit lane as clear as possible, an obvious benefit, especially at Monaco, where it is little wider than a supermarket aisle.

Michael suffered an engine failure on his first flying lap during Thursday's practice session and it wasn't until the short fifteen minute break, half way through the session, that the marshals were able to retrieve and return the stranded car to our custody.

Max, Kenny and Jon now set about changing the engine, right at the side of the pit lane, as once the sessions are under way it isn't possible to get the car back down to the harbour road and into the race truck awning, where, although far from perfect, the working conditions are infinitely more tolerable than being out in the open, exposed to the elements and less than a foot away from over 20 screaming Grand Prix cars.

The noise generated by a Formula One engine is, to say the very least, extremely loud, even when we are simply running them up, to get some heat into them, prior to handing the cars over to the drivers (at this stage the engine is only being revved to around 4,000 rpm).

On the circuit the engines are running close to 15,000 rpm, and the noise becomes inconceivably loud. The exhaust note changes from a low growling thunder to that of a high-pitched banshee wail.

On most of the tracks we visit, this sound is free to dissipate around an open expanse, but at Monaco the noise simply echoes off the walls of the apartment blocks and hotels, making normal speech an impossible form of communication.

I glanced over and managed to catch Kenny's eye. He looked back with an expression that said everything. He didn't need words to describe his views on having to change a Grand Prix engine at the side of a narrow and busy road in a small French town, during the holiday season. I shrugged my shoulders back at him. There was nothing to say. It was just unfortunate, and I reminded Kenny of one of our old expressions later that night: 'Monaco is simply a test of patience, and the whole weekend must be treated as a character-building exercise!'

Because Michael's engine had failed so early in the session he hadn't been able to get a feel for the circuit, or gauge the set up of the chassis. Consequently, once J.J. had completed several laps he was called in, and we fitted Michael's spare seat, changed the pedal and belt settings, and sent him out in our car. I think J.J. was pleased to have a rest from driving, his neck was suffering from all the on/off throttle work and constant left/right G-loadings that the Monaco circuit induces, certainly lack of fitness was affecting his driving. Within a few laps Michael had managed to make the car circulate close to four seconds quicker than his best. He stayed in our car for the rest of the morning, and with a time of 1m 21.822s he was quickest in that first session.

In the closing minutes of practice the red flags began to wave, and the pit lane exit was closed. There had been an accident. After Imola all of us were concerned at the sight of a red flag. I walked over to the monitors on the pit wall, and asked Joan, our Team Manager, if he knew what had happened. 'It's Wendlinger,' he told me, 'he's hit the armco coming out of the tunnel. Sid Watkins is with him now, but it was a big shunt.'

I didn't stay to watch a replay of the accident, so am unable to describe first hand what happened to his Sauber as it exited the tunnel, but apparently the car slewed broadside into the water filled barriers placed in front of the armco. His helmet sustained a big impact during the accident. The medical attendants carefully lifted him out of the car, and immediately took him to the Princess Grace hospital.

Sauber later issued a press statement, stating that Wendlinger was in a critical but, thankfully, stable condition, and that he had been moved to the Saint Roche hospital in Nice for specialist attention. The news came as another sad blow for everyone, but there was hope, and we all prayed for a full recovery. Understandably, Sauber decided that they would prefer to take no further part in the Monaco Grand Prix and proceeded to pack their equipment and wait for more news.

During the qualifying session later in the afternoon J.J. hit the guard rail. Thankfully he quickly confirmed on the radio that he was fine and uninjured. 'It's not a big shunt,' he informed us, 'I've just 'kissed' the barrier, but the right-front may need a little attention.'

After the qualifying had finished and we had taken all the equipment back down to the harbour, the marshals returned the car on the back of a recovery truck. We got it back inside the awning, up onto high stands and began an inspection of the damage.

My initial impression was that J.J.'s claim that the car had merely 'kissed' the barrier had been a classic piece of understatement. Judging by the damage to the right-hand front suspension, the car must have contacted the barrier in a long and passionate embrace!

 The brake duct had been smashed to pieces. The top and bottom wishbones were bent in half, and the pushrod had suffered a similar fate. This damage was all unfortunate, but fairly straightforward to replace. It was the condition of the suspension mounting that gave most cause for concern. The point on the chassis where the 'front leg' of the top wishbone is attached had been damaged. Not by very much but there were definite 'witness marks' on the titanium insert, suggesting that the mounting might have moved slightly or that the core of the chassis might have suffered slight internal damage.

We reported our findings to Frank and Ross, and took ten minutes off for lunch while they decided what they wanted us to do. There was really only one course of action to take, and deep-down we already knew what the outcome of their meeting would be. Ross came over and confirmed the inevitable: 'Sorry chaps but we're going to have to change chassis!'

Following its Imola shunt, the inspection department had thoroughly checked 04, and, finding no damage, it had been brought with us to Monaco as the emergency spare.

Now it was our turn to experience an exercise in character building, as we began to dismantle the chassis that less than six days ago we had been assembling in the hope that it would remain with us for the rest of the season.

However, things were not as bad as they could have been. We had an extra day to complete the rebirth of 04, remembering that we don't run on Friday in Monaco. It is known as 'The Day Off'. I've been going to Monaco for the last five years running, and neither I, or indeed any of us, can ever remember having the day off!

In fact, three years ago, due to gearbox problems with our Benetton B191, we even managed to turn 'The Day Off' into an 'All-Nighter', completing the preparation for Saturday's practice and qualifying with just enough time to return to the Terminus for a shower and change of clothes before walking back down to the pits and starting work again 15 minutes later.

Because the spare car hadn't been used, and therefore required little work, Lee (its front end mechanic) was able to lend a hand in the build of 04. The majority of parts, such as pedals, master cylinders, steering rack and column were already fitted. Mick had replaced these back at the factory, after they had been inspected and rebuilt, and the wiring loom had remained installed from when I had originally fitted it prior to the Pacific Grand Prix.

Dave, Bobby and Jakey removed the engine and gearbox from 06, and after checking them over, refitted them onto 04. Wayne, our car's representative from the electronics department, swapped over the control modules from the damaged chassis, and helped to install the engine and gearbox looms. With time on our side it was actually a fairly relaxed build, and the three cars were down on the ground with dust covers fitted by 9.30 p.m. All in all, by Formula One standards, not a bad day off really.

While we had been working on the chassis change, a press release from the FIA had been issued to the teams. In a three page document, the president, Max Mosley, outlined massive changes he intended to be made to the cars in an attempt to increase driver safety.

For the following Grand Prix in Barcelona, Mosley had decreed that the diffuser was to be drastically decreased in size, and he had written a ruling which effectively removed the 'vortex generators' from the front wings. These are the long carbon 'end-plates' designed to swirl the 'dirty air' coming off the front wing away from the floor, preventing it from going underneath the car, and affecting the performance of the diffuser.

For the Canadian Grand Prix, there were to be further and even more dramatic changes to be made, including a weight increase of 25 kilogrammes and a longer cockpit opening. The latter change would require the teams to design, manufacture and safety-test a new chassis in less than a month!

I suspected that there would be some very bewildered engineers trying to understand the logic behind these new regulations, which had been imposed on the teams by the FIA '. . . as a matter of *force majeure*, it having proved impossible to obtain all the consents required by the Concord Agreement notwithstanding extensive discussions with the parties concerned'. I doubted that it would be as simple as that, but time would tell.

During the qualifying session on Saturday, Michael's driving was perfection to watch, and as he drove around the tight, demanding circuit, his skill in car control was second to none. He secured his first ever pole position by being just under a second clear of Hakkinen's McLaren.

With a time of 1m18.560s, Michael Schumacher and the Benetton B194 had qualified for the 52nd Monaco Grand Prix, with a quicker time than anybody had ever achieved in the history of the event. That in itself is a great achievement. I felt very pleased for Michael and very proud to be a member of our team.

J.J. had continued to suffer with his neck muscles, and unfortunately had been unable to hold onto his qualifying position from Thursday. As the other teams continued to improve, he slipped from 12th to 17th.

He was obviously disappointed. So were we, but it couldn't be helped. A stiff and aching neck is painful enough when you're sitting in a comfortable armchair. It is impossible to imagine the agony and discomfort there must be while trying to drive a 200mph race car. Before the start of the race on Sunday afternoon, there was a minute's silence in remembrance of Ayrton and Roland. We remained with our cars, the drivers gathered at the front row of the grid. We all hoped that this and all future races would pass without incident. Thankfully the Monaco Grand Prix did. Michael led from the green light to the chequered flag, in a perfect demonstration of his talent and the Benetton's performance. Both Michael and J.J. pitted twice, with all four pit stops being carried out quickly and smoothly. It seemed strange to see the cars leaving the pits at a trundling 50mph as the new rules decreed.

Furthermore, it must have been very difficult for the drivers to adjust to this, and override their instincts to reach racing speeds as soon as possible, but despite the odd – and I think excusable – burst of speed by some drivers, all of them complied with the new requirement.

J.J. managed to complete the race distance, and despite finishing just outside the points, in seventh place, his result gave reason for our car to rejoice. It was, after all, the first race of the season that we had actually finished!

When eventually the crowds had subsided we managed to get the cars back down to the harbour road, and carry out the post-race checks for oil and water consumption, as well as a set-up check to see if the ride-height and/or tracking had changed during the race.

The awning had been taken down and loaded into the trucks during the course of the day. All we had to do now was to load the cars, tools and any other equipment that kept arriving back from the pit lane. By 9.30 we had finished. After a quick trip to the Terminus for a shower, we headed for 'Stars and Bars', a new American style bar/restaurant located on the harbour road, next to Riva Boat Services, and just opposite the point where our awning had been erected.

The best tables in the house had been reserved for us, and with everything being charged to the company credit card it turned into a late night as we celebrated our success. Michael had just won the first four races of the season, and was 30 points clear of Gerhard Berger in the Drivers' Championship. As a team we were leading the Constructors' Championship from Ferrari by a margin of 18 points.

We left Monaco and headed back to Nice the following morning. Some of us were late getting up, and most of us wore dark glasses, either to keep the bright sunshine out or to make it harder for others to notice the tired, bloodshot eyes hiding behind them.

While I was waiting in the airport departure lounge, I browsed through my copy of *Alf Francis, Racing Mechanic*. This is the biography of a mechanic who worked with Stirling Moss and Jack Brabham during the 1950s. It's an excellent book, and one which I often read for inspiration as I try to update the story of a race mechanic 40 years later.

Believe me when I tell you that in some ways nothing has changed in over four decades, especially the long hours and the late night parties. I was reading the closing pages, telling of Alf working on Brabham's Cooper during the 1957 Monaco Grand Prix and when I looked up from the page, sitting in the seat directly opposite me was Sir Jack himself!

Like me, he was patiently waiting for the flight to begin boarding. I could hardly believe what a coincidence it was. I lent over, and politely asked if he would mind signing the book for me. He seemed pleased to oblige, and I thanked him very much.

Most of Monday had gone by the time I was home, and I spent the remaining hours of the day chatting with Judd, and writing up the notes of the race weekend. We had Tuesday off as we waited for the transporters to return. A day which I spent watching the video of the race, trying to catch up with unpaid bills and replying to week old answer-phone messages.

On Wednesday morning Joan called us together for a meeting to explain the situation regarding the regulation and legality changes, decreed by Max Mosley a few days earlier.

'It's going to be a lot of work,' he told us, 'Rory and Willem (our two aero-dynamics experts) have been in the wind tunnel all night, trying to calculate the effect the changes will have on the car. It isn't good news. They predict that we could lose over thirty percent of the car's downforce. We may be able to get some of it back, but it will take time.'

'I'm asking you all to remain patient and have broad shoulders. What we must do is to make sure that the cars are safe, and that the modified parts are thoroughly tested before Barcelona. We are going to Jerez before the race to give us some test time.'

'I will ask some of you to go out to Barcelona on the Wednesday, this will give us an extra day to prepare for the race. Flavio is working with Ron (Dennis) and Frank (Williams) to reach a sensible political solution. I'm sure all of us are in favour of increasing safety, that goes without saying, but we must be very careful. We have more or less been asked to take a hacksaw to the cars, and we must give very careful consideration to the effect that these changes may have.'

After the meeting had finished we began to strip the cars, and carry out the routine service work. The new changes were aerodynamic, and they wouldn't affect the basic mechanical components that needed to be rebuilt, such as the steering rack, uprights, gearbox and fuel system. While we worked on the chassis the wind tunnel tests on the diffuser and front wing continued for the rest of the day and, indeed, late into the night.

Some of the other teams had gone testing at Silverstone, and it wasn't long before stories began to filter back about cars spinning off the circuit, due to the decrease in downforce they were experiencing. Several teams, including Williams, Ligier, Minardi, and ourselves were having problems with their rear wing mountings. Some had been cracking, and in extreme cases the mounting had failed altogether. These failures were later diagnosed as coming from new loads and vibrations, induced into the wing mountings following the modifica-tions to the diffusers. All the teams had lost the ability to attach 'supports' between the rear wing and the floor, because the area of the floor used for anchorage points had been removed to comply with the new regulations.

On Tuesday the 24th, and as a result of a rear wing failure, Pedro Lamy had a big accident at Silverstone. The engine and gearbox were ripped off the Lotus in the resulting impact and the chassis was catapulted over the safety fence into a spectator area. Lamy was rushed to hospital suffering from leg injuries, but thankfully he was not in a critical condition. He had been very lucky.

In order to evaluate the changes, as much work as possible was conducted in the wind tunnel, while Ross and the engineering department carried out load and structural tests on the rear wings. As I mentioned at the beginning of the book, Benetton has one of the most advanced facilities in the world, with access to 'state of the art' technology and equipment, and we have staff who have been correctly trained to use that equipment.

We are one of the lucky teams. I wondered how much testing work the less wealthy teams would be able to carry out. I am certain they would do their utmost to ensure their cars were as safe as possible before the Spanish Grand Prix, but the cost of running a Formula One car involves massive financial outlay, so it stands to reason that there is only so much that can be undertaken and achieved when working to a limited budget and tight schedule.

On the Wednesday before the Barcelona race Flavio wrote an open two page letter to Max Mosley, in which he criticized the changes that had been made to the cars, and questioned their safety in the 'Barcelona specification'.

'Despite these concerns (on safety),' wrote Flavio, '. . . you continue to insist on these ill conceived measures. It is our opinion that the ability of yourself and your advisers to judge technical and safety issues in Formula One must be questioned.'

McLaren's managing director Ron Dennis had also written to Mosley, expressing his views on the new regulations. 'The prospect of further ill-considered decisions from the governing body in an attempt to resolve the crisis, is of the gravest concern to us. We therefore respectfully require that the teams are allowed to restore the appropriate control and discipline to the management of F1.' Things eventually came to a head on the Friday morning of the Barcelona race weekend.

I had flown out to Spain on Thursday morning with about half the team. The rest had either flown out on Wednesday, as Joan had requested, or were flying into Barcelona from Jerez, following the test they had just completed. Tim and Reggie had been asked to attend the test because of their carbon and fabrication skills. When I met up with them on Thursday they both looked tired, telling of long nights spent working on the diffusers and wings in preparation for the race. Every night they had rebuilt the diffusers, only to modify them again as Rory and Willem faxed through their latest designs from base, as they fought to regain the missing downforce.

By Thursday night the three race cars sat in the garage with their dust covers fitted. Built and ready to run in the requested 'Barcelona specification'.

On Friday morning, our technical director, Tom Walkinshaw, explained the situation to us. Most of the teams had decided that they wouldn't run their cars until the situation was resolved. The feeling was that Formula One cars are too precise an instrument to alter without very careful consideration, and that any alterations should be handled by the people who know the cars best, that's to say the teams and their engineers.

A handful of teams did run in the morning practice, Ferrari included, but the majority took no part in the proceedings. We pulled the doors down and waited to hear the outcome of the emergency meeting that was taking place in Frank Williams's motor home. I took a walk over to our motor home for an espresso, and to pass the time I had a stroll around the paddock. There were several classes of cars competing during the weekend including Formula 3000, and some old Ferrari sports cars from the 1950s and 60s.

As I looked around I thought about the time I had worked at Graypaul in

Loughborough (the Ferrari dealership for central England), remembering the years with some fond memories. A Ferrari dealership provides an excellent training ground for an enthusiastic mechanic, and the arts of patience and attention to detail are quickly absorbed.

If you are keen and willing to get involved, then Ferrari can be very rewarding, but get it wrong or dither about and they can become a nightmare. I have seen mechanics reduced to tears simply attempting to change the ancillary drive belts on a 400 V12 engine (the procedure is a little like a Rubik's cube, one wrong move and you have to start all over again!)

I have seen others tremble with anxiety because they have been asked to work on a car that is said to be worth five or ten million dollars. To me a Ferrari is worth its engineering, not what a salesman (and I have met several sad and pretentious examples in my time) claims it to be worth.

Life had seemed a lot easier then, working nine to five and maybe even the odd Saturday, but never ever was I asked or expected to work all night. The road car industry simply didn't require it. I have always loved the Ferrari marque, and I enjoyed my time working with Enzo's cars a great deal. I could have stayed within his road car division for many years, eventually becoming a dealership manager, I suppose. Certainly the work was pleasurable and easy enough, but for me it lacked challenge, and would only ever have served as second best. It was without doubt Enzo's race team, Scuderia Ferrari, that I was most interested in. It was the race team that gave me the desire to work within Formula One, and as it appeared almost impossible to join them I felt I could at least work in the same field and formula as them, even if this would mean competing against them.

It was the sight of Stirling Moss walking around the old sports cars, dressed in traditional white overalls, that brought me back to the present. He was obviously taking part in the historic race over the weekend. 'Excuse me Mr Moss,' I said, 'would you do me the honour of signing a book for me?'

'Certainly, where is it?' he asked. I shot off to the garage, quickly returning with my Alf Francis volume. I asked him to sign it on the page showing a photograph of Stirling and Alf standing side by side, with copies of their autographs underneath.

'I'll have to sign it on the photo of Alf, so you can see it, and,' he added, 'it won't look like the copy of it you've got there! That was done years ago, when I could write!'

He duly signed the book for me, and after thanking him and wishing him good luck for his race I returned to the garage to see if there was any news from the meeting. There wasn't. I nipped out for another coffee.

At 12.30 p.m. Tom Walkinshaw reappeared from the meeting, and updated us on current events. A solution had been found, the details of which would become clear when all the rumours had died down. All the teams would attempt to qualify their cars in the afternoon session.

We would remain in the current, revised specification for the rest of the weekend, as although we and the other major teams would be able to revert back to the old specification, the smaller teams were not able to do so. They would require additional parts from their factories to convert the cars back, and there simply wasn't enough time to do that.

Common ground had been reached. The doors were lifted open, and the hot Catalan sunshine streamed back inside the garage. We warmed the engines up, strapped the drivers inside the cars, and the first qualifying session for the Spanish Grand Prix began.

Michael was once again very quick, and dominated the qualifying session. On his tenth lap he crossed the timing beam with a provisional pole time of 1m23.426s, over a second ahead of Mika Hakkinen who was second quickest. J.J. was feeling much stronger than he had at Monaco, and with a time of 1m25.587s he was provisionally seventh on the grid.

Three new drivers joined the Formula One scene at Barcelona. Alessandro Zanardi was driving Lamy's Lotus, standing in for Pedro following the Silverstone shunt. Alessandro is a very likeable chap who we got to know while he was test driving for us a couple of years ago. He had left us after Peter Colins had offered him the seat at Lotus alongside Johnny Herbert. He was quite upset about leaving us, but the seat at Lotus was obviously preferable to the test drive at Benetton. He had made us promise to keep talking to him and remain friends after he had left the team. We promised!

He had suffered a bad accident at Spa last year, and he was forced to give up his drive as a result. He had, however, been retained by Lotus as their test driver. It seemed slightly ironic that it was due to Pedro's accident that he had been given the opportunity to rejoin the race team again.

Andrea Montermini was driving the second Simtek, alongside David Brabham. Like Zanardi, Montermini had also driven a Benetton test car. I had been on the test when he had driven. He always reminded me of a mischievous elf, and although he had been very keen to drive, my lasting memory of the test is that he kept going off a lot.

The third new driver was David Coulthard, the Williams test driver. He, like Damon, had been promoted from the test team. I believe this is good, sound policy, as he would be familiar with the team, he would know how they work, and he wouldn't be looked on as a stranger. All of this can only build confidence, which is a vital ingredient in a driver.

Sauber had returned to take part in the Barcelona Grand Prix, but had made the decision to field only one car. Wendlinger's car, number 29, would remain withdrawn from the Championship until such time as Karl's return to good health could be confirmed. He was still at the Saint Roche in Nice, where he lay in a stable and controlled coma.

This had been induced to allow Karl's internal injuries time to subside before the doctors gradually began to reduce the medication, and bring him round to a state of consciousness. It was still early days, but the news of his stability was an encouraging sign of recovery.

After studying the data that had been collected during Friday's sessions, and having talked to both drivers, the engineers concluded that the cars could benefit from being slightly stiffer, and running a little closer to the track. The floors hadn't been wearing very much through grounding on the circuit, and it seemed safe enough to drop the ride-height by a couple of millimetres. Overnight we fitted 10 per cent stiffer springs, and lowered both J.J.'s and

Michael's cars. In Saturday's free practice this was found to be an advantage.

During the last few minutes of the morning session, while I was leaning on the pit wall, waiting to hang the board out to J.J., and watching the cars exit the final bend, and correct themselves for the start/finish straight, I saw one of the Simteks run wide. It was the cloud of dust thrown up from the outside of the track that caught my eye, my attention momentarily diverted as I glanced at Frank Dernie's stop-watch to gauge how far J.J. was from completing his lap.

A split second later the Simtek hit the wall. The whole front end of the car disintegrated on impact, and the pedal-box area of the chassis was missing when it finally stopped spinning, coming to rest in front of the pits on the main straight. It was Montermini. His helmet lolled forward, his feet clearly visible through the hole in the front. Steam, smoke, oil and water gushed from the engine bay. It looked disastrous, and we stared in horror at what we had just witnessed, unable to believe that such an accident could happen again. Frank reacted first, switching on his radio, immediately telling J.J. to abort his lap and return to the pits. 'There's been a massive shunt on the main straight J.J. Forget the lap and come in. I repeat. Forget the lap and come in. There is a red flag! There is a red flag!'

Within seconds Sid Watkins was at Montermini's side, and the marshals had an ambulance and fire engine ready to assist if needed. I was impressed at the speed with which everybody reacted to the accident, and very relieved to see Andrea's helmet begin to move again. That in itself was a reassuring sight.

Slowly the medical team removed him from the car, and shortly afterwards I heard the familiar sound of helicopter rotors chopping through the sky as the doctors carefully transported Andrea to the *Hospital General de Catalunya* in Barcelona.

J.J. slowly drove down the pit lane, and we pulled the car back inside the garage. Following the accident there were only two minutes of free practice left, so the officials decreed the session to have finished.

We began to check the cars over and prepare them for qualifying. Joan had gone off to discover more about Montermini's condition. He returned with good news. Despite his colossal accident (which had been at well over 140mph) Andrea had escaped with relatively minor injuries: a black eye, minor concussion and a cracked heel bone.

It seemed unbelievable. You could injure yourself more than that by falling off a bicycle! We were all pleased and very relieved to hear the news, but I now feel more than ever that (if there ever was such a thing) Montermini has the luck of an Italian leprechaun!

Saturday afternoon was much cooler than Friday, and in a reversal to the qualifying sessions of the Pacific Grand Prix, everybody improved their times during the second session. J.J. moved up from seventh to fourth on the grid and Michael secured his second career pole with a time of 1m21.908s In between the two B194 cars, in second and third position on the grid, were Damon's Williams FW16 and Mika's McLaren MP4/9. Ferrari had managed sixth and seventh while David Coulthard had done an impressive job to get the other Williams to ninth place on the grid.

During practice and qualifying both Benettons had been running well and quick, despite fears that the regulation changes regarding wings and diffusers might well affect us more than others. It was no secret, for example, that Ferrari had been struggling with handling problems, and that the enforced aero-dynamic changes might well be of little detrimental consequence to the performance of the 412 T1, which could lead to them having an unintentional advantage if other teams found their cars going slower due to the changes.

However, from what I had seen during practice and qualifying it appeared to me that the handling of the Ferrari had neither deteriorated or improved, as both Berger and Alesi fought with their cars through everywhere bar the straights. If they ever got the thing to go around the corners, Ferrari would become a very competitive force.

The warm-up on Sunday morning had gone well, and had seen J.J. with the quickest time of the session. Michael was close behind in second place, and everything looked good for the afternoon. However, during the race, and unlike the previous two days both cars ran into problems, although nowhere near as soon as Beretta's Larrousse, whose engine failed in a cloud of steam during the formation lap.

I felt sorry for his mechanics. They would have spent hours preparing the car during Saturday night, only to see their efforts go up in smoke before the race had even started!

The race began and, as the new regulations decreed, we stayed inside the garages, watching the race develop on the monitors. Michael made a good start, immediately pulling away from the rest of the field, and at this stage it looked like being another commanding drive, from green light to chequered flag.

Alesi had made a blistering start in the Ferrari, and had managed to get from sixth to fourth by the first corner, overtaking J.J. in the process. This was very frustrating for us, as it became impossible for J.J. to get past Alesi as the race began to settle down. The immense power of the Ferrari V12 pulled Alesi away from J.J. on the straights, only to be caught up again at the corners, as Alesi struggled to make his car change direction.

Ross made the decision to call J.J. in for an early pit stop. If we couldn't overtake the Ferrari on the circuit, then we would overtake it in the pits. We didn't know when Ferrari intended to call Alesi in, but as I looked out of the garage I could see the immensity of Nigel Stepney waving the mechanics out of their garage, a definite sign that a Ferrari pit stop was imminent, but whether it was for Alesi or Berger we didn't know.

Ross wasn't prepared to wait and find out, immediately calling J.J. to pit for tyres and fuel. If we pitted at the same time as Alesi it was imperative that J.J. got under-way and back into the race first. If we pitted a lap before them the pressure would be off slightly, but we would have to make use of the advantage, carry out the stop quickly and cleanly, and dispatch J.J. back into the race as soon as possible to give him a chance to build up as much lead on Alesi as he could.

Ferrari have always had the reputation for being very quick at pit stops. Providing everything goes well, they are a pure delight to watch. If, however, things go wrong, then the pit stop can turn disastrous, and it can take the mechanics precious seconds to recover the situation. In recent years, though, they seem better than ever, and they have become incredibly fast. We knew that to beat them we would have to operate very efficiently.

'Stand by chaps, he's 40 seconds away,' Frank informed us. I heard the air-guns being given one last check, a quick pull on the trigger to make sure the sockets are travelling the right way. The wheel nuts are 'handed' (right hand thread on the left wheels, left hand thread on the right), this is so they will 'self-tighten' as the wheels rotate when the car is running on the circuit.

These nuts are also colour coded to avoid confusion, red on the left, green on the right (port and starboard), in case we need to change one due to a damaged thread.

'Ten seconds chaps . . .', and then J.J. was in. He slowed to a stop, the front wing coming to rest on the front jack. I followed behind, throwing the rear jack into the lifting mounts. As soon as Simon had connected the refuelling hose, Kenny and I lifted the car. I kept an eye on the rear wheels, making sure that they had been cleanly changed, and waited for Max and Dave to put their guns in the air (the signal that they had finished).

At the same time I was watching Simon, and waiting for him to disconnect the fuel hose. It had been decided that we would leave the car in the air until all the work had been finished. This would stop the drivers (in all their race eagerness) trying to pull away before we had finished.

Kenny was doing the same thing with the front of the car, and after a final glance at each other to confirm that all was well, we pulled the release mechanisms on the jacks, Mick lifted the 'BRAKES ON' board clear, and J.J. was on his way. The whole stop had taken seven and a half seconds, we could be happy with that. Alesi pitted on the following lap. Ferrari lived up to their reputation, and carried out another good stop, but it wasn't good enough. We had taken the advantage. The Benetton was in front of the Ferrari. We had done well and our spirits were high. The feeling didn't last long.

Michael's voice suddenly came over the radio link, 'I have a problem. The car will not change gear. I repeat, the car will not change gear. I am stuck in fifth. What should I do?' There was no sign of stress in Michael's voice, and he seemed completely calm as he asked for advice. His engineer, Pat Symonds, reacted very quickly. 'Keep going Michael. Give us a few seconds to look at the data. Stay out. I repeat, stay out.'

'OK,' replied Michael. Within a few moments Pat was back on the radio. 'Michael, we have looked at the data, and there is nothing we can do. It is a hydraulic failure. You have lost pressure to the gear selector. I repeat, there is nothing we can do. You are on your own. Do what you think best.'

'OK, Pat. Should I come in for fuel?' he inquired.

'You need to, yes.'

'OK. I'm coming in this lap.' As soon as I heard this I thought, as I think we all did, that Michael's race was over. He had to pit for fuel, and it seemed impossible that he would be able to come to a standstill and drive off again with the car stuck in fifth.

I checked to see that we had a 'starter' handy, as there was a strong possibility that Michael would stall the engine as he tried to leave. I should mention that there is no 'on board' starter on a Formula One car. Its additional weight, coupled with that of the extra loom, and either a battery or an air bottle to power it would prove too great a penalty to justify its existence. The idea is that we start the engine with a remote starter, temporarily connected to the gearbox, and hopefully the driver manages to keep the engine running, until he turns the ignition off after his return to the garage.

Anyway, back to the pit stop. Michael came in. We carried out the refuelling, changed the tyres, and off he went. As soon as I released him off the jack, I prepared to give him a shove on the rear wing, to help him nurse the car away, but he didn't need any help, and he slowly trundled off down the pit lane. I was amazed. If I hadn't seen it for myself I wouldn't have thought it possible.

There then followed a drive that must surely go down in the history books as one of the best ever. Michael had lost the lead to Hakkinen during the pit stop, and then second place to Hill, as he struggled around the circuit in fifth gear.

After a few laps, however, we saw Michael's times start to improve again, and he managed to hold onto third place. He later explained that he had been trying different racing lines, going wider around the corners to enable him to keep his speed up. This was a skill he had learnt in his sports car days, when trying to conserve fuel. Indeed, our telemetry showed that his fuel consumption had decreased during the course of the race!

Michael's second pit stop was carried out with the same apparent ease as the first, leaving the pits with just a slight stutter. In the closing stages of the race both McLarens suffered engine failure, and unfortunately so did J.J., which sadly ended the possibility of him scoring his first Benetton points.

Damon went on to win the race, and Michael finished an incredible second, with all due credit to his incredible driving skill, and the most impressive tractability of the Zetec-R V8. Of course, luck had played its part, for if the gearbox had been in any other gear than fifth, it is extremely unlikely that the engine could have coped, or that the car would have remained competitive, but, without doubt, luck will always play its part in Grand Prix racing.

The Williams camp was understandably very pleased with the result. As I made my way down to the podium I shook hands with a delighted Patrick Head, and congratulated him on their victory.

'Very well done Patrick.'

'Thank you,' he said, 'we needed that.'

# JUNE

It had been six months since I had started to decorate the bathroom, and it had been six months since there had been any progress. I had got used to seeing the half-stripped window frame, and only having hardboard as a floor covering isn't much of a problem if you place a towel on the floor.

The door, propped up against the wall since coming back from the pine strippers in December added, I thought, a somewhat rustic charm to the cottage. Judd didn't agree, and indeed made it quite clear that it would be altogether safer for me if the bathroom restoration was swiftly brought to a conclusion.

It was time to seek professional help, and in that respect I was very lucky. My neighbour, John Guy, is by trade a painter and decorator, and judging by the excellent renovation he and his wife Sue (who has the most enviable ability to grow superb vines at will) had carried out on their half of the old barn he is very skilled at his profession.

After explaining that unless the bathroom quickly progressed I would soon be living alone, he was more than happy to help, and I immediately had a spare set of house keys cut to leave with him. 'Don't worry,' he reassured me, 'It's as good as done!' Good old John I thought, and promptly washed my hands of the whole affair.

By Wednesday, the first of June, the cars had been stripped, and we had started the rebuild for the next race, the Canadian Grand Prix, which would take place in Montreal at the Circuit Gilles Villeneuve on Sunday the twelfth.

We had several modifications to carry out to the cars, to keep in line with the new safety regulations. The subject of the new regulations had become clearer since our return from Barcelona. A special committee of Formula One engineers had been appointed to oversee any proposed changes, and evaluate them from the point of view of safety. Max Mosley had conceded that as long as all the teams were in agreement, Formula One could implement its own changes and carry them out whenever the committee deemed correct to do so.

The changes that we were going to make for Canada would be a modification to the front push-rods, which would allow them to break free of the upright assembly when they were stressed in tension in the event of an accident, instead of arching round and possibly striking the driver. This would assist the front wheel to pass clear of the cockpit. With the car running, the push-rod would only work in compression, so there could be no danger of it failing under normal circumstances.

We were also going to modify the air induction system, in an attempt to reduce engine power. It had been agreed that the teams would remove the advantage of the 'ram-air' effect from the air-box.

The air inlet to the engine is located on the inside of the roll-hoop, above the driver's helmet. As the car builds up speed, air is forced through the roll-hoop and down inside the air-box. This increases the air pressure inside the air-box by approximately 1.5 psi, resulting in a mild, but quite legal, form of super-charging. Legal, that is, until now.

The new regulations require that air-box pressure must equal atmospheric pressure. The actual figure for atmospheric pressure will change depending on the height of the circuit we happen to be running at (as atmospheric pressure drops as altitude increases), but as long as the two figures, from inside and outside the air-box, were equal, FIA Technical Delegate Charlie Whiting would be happy.

The reduction was to be achieved by cutting vents into both the bodywork and the air-box, which would effectively bleed the pressure of the incoming air. The ruling was that we could have the vents any shape we liked but that their area should be one and a half times the area of the air-box inlet.

This freedom to choose the shape and position of the vents once again ensured that Rory and Willem were in their element and they rushed off to try various prototype shapes in the wind tunnel before committing themselves to a definite design.

We were also going to have to use standard 'pump' fuel, as the various chemical cocktails that the fuel companies had been supplying up until now had been outlawed. Some of the smaller teams had already been using pump fuel, as their limited budgets or sponsorship deals did not allow them the luxury of the specialized brews, and the new regulation would only affect the top four or five teams.

The idea was to reduce engine power and presumably make the smaller teams more competitive, but as the power loss had been estimated to be in the region of two per cent I doubted that the difference would be very noticeable.

The final change for Canada was an increase in the weight of the cars. The original statement made in Monaco had demanded 25 kilogrammes more, but this had been reduced to 10kg, thus making the new minimum weight for the cars 515kg. This extra mass was achieved by two additional ballast trays attached to the floor, each loaded with five kilogrammes of lead sheet.

Because the Canadian Grand Prix is an Intercontinental race, while we were busy working on the cars, the truckies were busy unloading all the equipment and tools from the transporters, and reloading them into the 'fly-away' boxes (known as pack-horses). Our travelling-parts man, Oz (actually his name is Andrew, but I have never heard anyone refer to him as that), did exactly the same thing with his 'spares' and everything else we might need to prepare, run, repair, qualify and race our cars. The list would include nuts, bolts, washers, thousands of ty-raps, glues, resins, twin pack foam (just in case J.J. or Michael decide they don't like their seats any more), bin-liners, garage banners, car stickers and floor stickers. Wayne and Bat packed all their electronics and radio equipment, and the sub-assembly department loaded the various specification brakes and callipers, along with spare steering racks, uprights and drive shafts. Loading everything for a 'fly-away' is a long, unpopular process, and this one coming in the middle of the season is most inconvenient. Brazil was fine, as it was the first race of the year, and everybody was keen to get going.

With the Pacific race coming straight after, everything remained packed and ready to go. No one minds packing for Japan and Australia. They are the two final races of the year, and when the season draws to a close everybody starts to get into party mood.

Time is a precious commodity in Formula One and the schedule between the finish of the Spanish Grand Prix and the first practice session of the Canadian race was as tight as ever. We had to have the cars finished and the 'pack-up' completed by Thursday evening.

By arrangement with the Formula One Constructors Association, the British based teams send their freight all together, in an agreement designed to reduce transport costs. Indeed the top teams have a percentage of their costs met by FOCA. The freight had to be at Heathrow first thing on Friday morning, to allow time for it to clear customs and be loaded aboard the cargo plane for its journey over the Atlantic. From there it would have to be unloaded, clear Canadian customs and be transported to the circuit, where hopefully it would be waiting for us when we arrived on the following Tuesday morning.

We worked late into Wednesday night to ensure we could have everything finished for the next day, and at eleven o'clock the following evening the 'pack-up' was complete. The cars were ready to go, fitted with their wooden travel-floors, waterproof covers and 'travel' steering wheels.

These are old steering wheels, without the electronic gear change paddles fitted (we fit these to dissuade souvenir hunters from liberating them while the cars are in transit). I use a Martin Brundle wheel, from his time with us in '92.

I think Jon has an old Roberto Moreno wheel, from the days before Michael arrived. Lee, in a moment of 'off season' enthusiasm (or boredom) has gone to the trouble of cutting one out of a sheet of plyboard which he stained with wood dye and even varnished.

The majority of us were flying out to Montreal on Monday morning, although the truckies were going out a day earlier in order to paint the garage floor and allow it time to dry before we arrived. This meant that I had three days off, and it was in this time that I wrote about the events of the Barcelona race and even managed to spend the weekend at home with Judd.

During Saturday evening we listened to the radio, sank back into the settee and relaxed with a bottle of *Chateauneuf-du-Pape*. At ten o'clock Mozart was replaced by the announcer's voice, and we prepared ourselves to be told of everything that had gone wrong with the world during the course of the day.

What we heard, however, was the welcome and reassuring news that Karl Wendlinger had regained consciousness. Initial signs looked promising, and he would soon be returning to Austria where he could continue his recovery in more familiar surroundings. This was tremendously good to hear and to celebrate we pulled the cork on another bottle, filled our glasses, and drank to his good health.

The flight to Montreal takes a little over 7 hours which, when compared to the 14 it takes to get to Brazil, or the 20-odd it took to reach Japan, is quite bearable. Eight hours is about my tolerance limit. After that I'm bored. My legs ache, my eyes are too tired to keep reading, and my ears become sore from using a Walkman. Maybe it becomes easier and more tolerable in First Class. I would certainly expect so, but as I've never flown First Class – and am never likely to – I wouldn't know. I have flown Club occasionally, but other than on a long-haul flight there appears to be little difference (not that I'd ever turn it down if offered an upgrade of course).

On a 747, however, Club Class is a definite improvement. Last year, on the way home from Canada, Dave and I were fortunate enough to be upgraded to Club, and relished every minute of it, stretching out almost horizontal in seats actually made for comfort. The cabin crew issued us with bags containing odd and interesting things for the flight.

There was even a small aerosol of natural spring water to spray on the face. The label proclaimed it was 'To reduce the risk of skin dehydration from the drying effect of the cabin air' (a problem which presumably doesn't occur in Economy). The wine list offered by the steward is exactly that, a list to choose from, not a sheet that tells you what you are getting.

Seven hours, however, is easy enough to pass without the need to be pampered, and it wasn't long after lunch, a read and a quick nap that the pilot informed us of his intention to land at Montreal's Mirabel International. The airport is located quite a way from the centre of Montreal, and it took us just under an hour, from the time we had cleared customs, and loaded everything and everyone into the minibuses, to the time we reached the middle of Downtown Montreal.

I'm not particularly keen on cities, having spent the majority of my life in the country, where the air is cleaner, and the sight of green fields and woodlands are far more appealing than tower-blocks and indignant traffic wardens will ever be. However, if I ever had to choose a city to live in, I think Montreal would feature high on the list.

The streets are clean and wide, and the buildings on either side of them vary greatly in design, and are not just mammoth blocks of concrete repeated over and over. In the centre of the city is an old church. People are welcome to eat lunch on the large grassy area which surrounds it, on picnic tables which have been built to accommodate them.

Just down the hill from the church is a large square, where local artists gather to talk and paint. The food is inexpensive and good, and the fresh lobster is even better. French is the first language of Montreal. It is normal to be greeted with 'Bonjour, hello!', and the majority of road signs are written in French and English. It has a clean, bright and efficient metro system, a large university, several art galleries, concert halls, and the whole place appears very cosmopolitan. It is a city that Canada should be very proud of.

Montreal is five hours behind London, and allowing for the flight, we had effectively only lost two hours since leaving England earlier in the day. By the time we had checked into the hotel, unpacked, showered and changed, it was still early afternoon.

Reggie, Bat and some of the others were keen to visit the 'Orange Box Clubs', the dubious 'girlie bars' that along with the art galleries can also be found in Montreal. However, by comparison, these clubs are far tamer than the Masque in Sao Paulo. Here the strict house policy is 'look but definitely DO NOT TOUCH!'

For a few dollars, one of the girls will dance for her paying customer. She stands on a low stool or box (hence the rather odd nickname for the clubs), as she slowly gyrates to the music, inevitably finishing the dance bereft of clothing, which she duly puts back on, only to take off again during the next dance.

The girls can apparently make quite a lot of money during the course of an evening. When asked, they all seem to have the same use for the money they earn: 'Oh, I only do this part-time, to get me through college. I'm actually going to be an accountant when I graduate.'

Within twenty minutes of checking in, Reggie had washed, changed and departed with Bat to discuss foreign exchange rates with some of the trainee bankers. I suspected it would be the early hours of the next day before their negotiations would be completed.

During the drive from the airport the radio had informed us that Montreal's baseball team, the Expos, were playing at home against the Houston Astros, 'Start time 7.30 p.m. Be there!' I had never seen a live baseball game before, and so, driven by curiosity I decided to go and take a look.

Jon decided to come along as well, so we caught the metro to the huge and quite spectacular stadium, spending the evening drinking 'Genuine Draft' (which rather curiously came in a bottle), and eating slices of 'Double Hot Pepperoni Pizza', while we watched in silent confusion. The fans cheered when apparently nothing had happened, and booed and hissed when yet again apparently nothing had happened.

At one point the entire crowd rose to its feet and began to stretch and shake their arms in unison. 'It's all part of an old baseball tradition,' a chap in the next seat told us. 'It's known as "The Seventh Innings Stretch."' We stood up and stretched too, not wanting to offend anyone. When in Rome . . .

On Tuesday morning we set off on the brief ten minute journey to the circuit and began to prepare for Friday's practice. The circuit is rather odd and its squashed-looking shape is due to it having been built around the perimeter of a small man-made island, the Ile Notre Dame, constructed right in the middle of the St Lawrence river.

A deep canal runs along the back of the pit straight to allow cargo ships access to and from the Atlantic. It's quite a sight to look out of the back of the garage and see an ocean-going vessel the size of a housing estate gliding silently past. The only thing to separate the canal from the circuit is the old Olympic rowing lake, which is a long and fairly narrow strip of water.

On Thursday afternoon of the Montreal meeting, the rowing lake plays host to the 'Annual Formula One Raft Race'. This, for some people, is the most important race of the weekend, with the Grand Prix itself being of purely superficial interest by comparison. The competition is fierce, and the will to win immense. It is only teams that either sink or give up half way that claim the race to be just for fun.

The rules for the event seem at first glance to be relatively simple: the raft must be constructed out of packing material that has been used by the teams to transport their cars and equipment to Canada, and when built it must only carry a maximum of four people at any one time.

The raft must cross the rowing lake, pick up a rear wheel and tyre, and return to the other side. The first raft to return wins the race. It may sound simple, but you must remember that this is Formula One. Controversy and political wrangling are as rife in Thursday's raft race as they are in Sunday's Grand Prix.

The memory is all to clear, for example, of Ferrari's ingenuity when a couple of years ago they produced their raft, which until just prior to the start of the race had remained out of sight in the back of the garage. When the command 'READY . . . GO!' was shouted from the bank, and the rest of the field began to frantically paddle across the lake, Ferrari calmly fired up their outboard motor and shot off, the bow of their rather boat-like raft standing proud of the water, leaving the rest, quite literally, floundering in their wake. It was shortly after this incident that the rules were rewritten, to make it quite clear that engines of any description were banned.

As far as controversy goes, this year was no exception. Jordan have won the race for the last three years, with a craft which resembles a canoe far more than it does a raft, and it is here that the problem lies. What actually distinguishes a canoe from a raft?

Stuart Prattley, one of the Williams mechanics, had written a letter of complaint to the Raft Race Chief Scrutineer, in an attempt to force Jordan to change their design. 'This is an official protest,' he wrote, 'against any team entering a canoe-style craft in the Montreal Formula One Raft Race, as we believe that it contravenes the regulations, as it is not a raft, it is a canoe. We would like to remind all competitors that the definition of a raft is a buoyant platform of logs, planks etc. used as a vessel or moored platform, and that the canoe-style crafts entered by various teams do not conform to this definition, and should be excluded from the event.'

However, Stuart wasn't prepared to come up with the fee needed to lodge the complaint officially (in this instance not $10,000 but a race shirt or team issue jacket), and so his letter had to be disregarded. Yet again Jordan's craft and crew went on to take the first place honours. Steve Cotes (the Williams truckie, who deputizes as Raft Race Scrutineer during the event), promises a further review of the regulations for next year which will incorporate a definite shape and dimensions for the rafts. He says this will make it much fairer and easier for everyone to compete on more equal terms!

As for as the race meeting, it was a mixed weekend of success and frustration. From the second the pit lane opened for business on Friday morning, Michael appeared confident of coming away from Canada with more points, and maybe even finishing with a podium position.

He and Pat soon found a set-up they were happy with and, despite the much improved performance of Ferrari during the first qualifying session, Michael felt sure that another pole position was feasible. Alesi was really flying, and at times the performance of his Ferrari seemed almost unbelievable, but every time he put in a quick lap Michael managed to go just a fraction quicker. Alesi had pole. Michael had pole. Alesi reclaimed it. Michael snatched it back. Alesi went out again, and threw the Ferrari around the circuit with a passion. He seemed desperate to put car number 27 at the top of the grid, especially here at the circuit named after one of its greatest drivers. He crossed the line with a time of 1m 26.277s.

Michael then set off in an attempt to beat it, but in the final minutes of the session, during his quick lap, the engine let go amidst a cloud of smoke and steam and, overnight at least, Alesi held on to his provisional pole.

Michael was a comfortable second and his mood remained confident that Saturday would see him once more at the head of the grid. J.J. on the other hand was having a terrible time, complaining that the car had no grip, and that whatever we tried to cure it with made no difference. We fitted softer springs. No good. Stiffer springs. No good. Roll bars, less ride height, more ride height, more wing, less wing, all no good.

We tried everything we possibly could to improve J.J.'s performance but all to no avail. In the end, as qualifying was drawing to a close, Frank and Ross asked Pat for a list of Michael's set-up, and we quickly copied it onto our car. This, we thought, must surely improve his time and grid position, which at the moment was a disappointing sixteenth. However, it wasn't to be, and J.J. returned to the pits still complaining that whatever we did made no difference.

That night we checked every component on the car: suspension joints, wishbone movement, dampers, we could find nothing wrong. We checked the set-up, but everything was perfect. We checked our set-up equipment against the other cars just in case we were being misled by a faulty camber gauge or digital vernier, but everybody's equipment gave the same readings.

We had all retained the same chassis we had used in Spain. Michael's crew had 05. Paul, Paul and Lee had kept 03 for the spare car, and we had kept 04. All three chassis were tried and tested, and as far as we were concerned all three were identical. We could do no more but go back to the hotel and try again tomorrow.

J.J. hadn't mentioned to me about any discomfort, but I think driving here may have been hurting his neck. There is certainly a lot of on/off throttle work and heavy braking at Canada (in this respect the circuit is similar to Monaco, which had also troubled him). It is possible that this was playing a part in the car's lack of performance, and not wanting to worry anybody about his injury

J.J. was keeping quiet, driving through the pain and putting a brave face on the matter.

We finished work early enough to be able to have dinner away from the circuit which, providing we don't have to eat too late is a good thing, as it allows the team to split up and get away from each other for a few hours.

Jon and I decided to take the short stroll down to 'Jazz and Ribs'. A small and always busy restaurant, which rather predictably specializes in barbecued pork ribs, while its patrons suffer live jazz performed by authentically loud, large, and profusely sweating musicians.

Jazz, as a music form, has always baffled me. I personally don't like it, but would never question the views of anybody who says they do just as I would never question anybody's views on what is and what isn't art. In my experience if you question an artist on whether or not their work is artistic, the artist will claim to have won the argument already.

I suppose, like a particular wine, you either like jazz or you don't. I don't, but it doesn't put me off going to a restaurant that specializes in it. After all, I may one day hear something that completely changes my thoughts on it. It wasn't to be on that Friday night, though, and I left 'Jazz and Ribs' (or 'Noise and Lard' as it became known) with the thought that if the 'musicians' performed their 'art' in the street they would be politely asked to shut up and leave, or forcefully silenced and removed for disturbing the peace.

During Saturday's qualifying session Michael finally managed to take and retain possession of pole position, beating the time Alesi set on Friday by just less than a tenth of a second. Indeed the majority of teams improved their times. Both days were hot and sunny, but I think the circuit had improved, being 'cleaned' by the cars the previous day, and from the rubber they had left behind.

There had also been slight set-up changes overnight, and, of course, the drivers had become familiar with the circuit layout. Unfortunately for Ferrari, Alesi was amongst only four drivers not to improve on his Friday's time. However, that time was still good enough for second place on the grid, and Berger had grappled the other Ferrari up to third position.

The handling of the 412-T1 was obviously improving, probably helped by the abundance of straight sections on the circuit. No such luck existed for our car, though, for despite an improvement in time, J.J. had slipped from sixteenth to twentieth on the grid. Some part of the car/driver combination simply wasn't working correctly. We had thoroughly checked the car and couldn't fault it. Ross decided J.J. should race the spare car, to completely eliminate any mechanical aspect from the equation. As soon as we returned to England 04 would be sent to Silverstone, to carry out a 'back to back' test with another B194 to discover whether they reacted differently.

I took J.J.s seat out of the car and gave it to Lee, along with measurements for the seat belts and the push-rod lengths for the clutch and brake master-cylinders (which would alter the pedal positions) in order to 'set' 03 for J.J. He handed the two spare seats over to me. One for J.J., one for Michael. These seats, although perfectly servicable, are second best as far as the drivers are concerned. 'Yes it's fine,' they will say, 'but let's save it for the spare car.'

We would now be swapping roles with the spare car during Sunday, remaining in the garage prior to the start of the race, and listening to the radio communication between Ross, Frank, Pat and Mick, just in case a last minute problem occurred with one of the other cars that couldn't be fixed on the grid, and we needed to send either driver out in 04.

This does happen from time to time, and if there is one thing I have learnt about Formula One cars, it is if they are going to fail they will always do it at the most inconvenient time. In Hockenheim last year, for example, Michael's car, which had behaved impeccably all weekend, developed an active electronic fault during his reconnaissance lap on the way to the grid. Fortunately he felt the car handling erratically before he reached the pit lane entrance, and managed to come back in, quickly jump into the spare car, and return to the circuit before the pit lane closed. There was some fairly frantic action to finalize the car on the grid, but everything went well, and Michael finished the race in second place.

This time, fortunately, there was no such untoward occurrence, and both cars set off on the formation lap without a hitch. When the race began it was another completely dominating drive by Michael.

Unhindered by gearbox problems he quickly pulled away from the pack to lead the race from start to finish. We had planned for one pit stop, which on lap forty we carried out calmly and methodically. There was no need to rush, as Michael had nearly a full-minute lead over the opposition when Ross called him in. We changed tyres and refuelled the car in a sedate ten seconds, sending Michael back into the race well ahead of Damon's second placed Williams.

J.J. had a good day too, and had driven the spare car from his lowly twentieth grid placing to a creditable seventh by the end of the race. In the warm up he had been twenty-first quickest, and things didn't bode well for the afternoon, but after a long meeting with the engineers he returned to the pits determined that the race would go well. Fortunately, it did.

Christian Fittipaldi managed to get his Arrows/Footwork across the line ahead of J.J. to claim the final Championship point of the meeting, but later when his car was scrutineered it was found to be underweight, and he and his car were disqualified from the event. His one Championship point for sixth place was immediately snatched back and awarded to J.J.

We were well into the pack-up for the journey home when confirmation of J.J.'s score was announced. The news came as a very pleasant and welcome surprise for the crew of the spare car. 'Well done boys!' I congratulated them. I was actually a little envious of them, as their result meant it was only car six out of the Benetton stable that had failed to score.

'Think positive,' I told myself, 'it's still early days, the season is only six races old. There are another 10 rounds to go, and lots of time to score yet!' Bobby wasn't so sure, and he told me the year was fated for us to go the whole season simply writing off and rebuilding new chassis, without scoring a single point to show for our efforts.

'Bobby should know,' Dave said, 'after all, he is the personification of global evil. He knows all about bad luck and ill omens.' Oz walked past carrying one of the garage banners. He stopped and joined us as we looked Bobby up and down. Bobby said nothing, he just looked slightly hurt. Oz walked on, 'Kraken!' he accused, shouting over his shoulder.

In the middle of Downtown Montreal is a large bar called 'Thursdays'. It's a popular place with the locals, and during Grand Prix week it's a popular place with the teams also. On each bar and every table there are bowls of complimentary peanuts, still in shells, for the customers to break open and eat while they drink ice cold beer straight out of the bottle. I've noticed in recent years that it's become almost impolite to offer people a glass to drink out of.

There aren't any waste bins to put the empty shells into, and the reason for this soon becomes clear. Everyone simply drops the shells on the floor. This action isn't frowned upon by the waiters and management, indeed it's positively encouraged. The floor is covered in shells, and around the bar they are sometimes four or five inches deep.

Above the bar on the next floor is Thursdays Restaurant. A smart, elegant place, where the throwing of peanut shells would most definitely be frowned upon, and it was here that our post race celebration dinner was held. In Canada it has become a Benetton tradition to have a party, regardless of the race results, but when we win, the celebration climbs to new heights.

Joan had called the restaurant manager to one side, told him who we were, and informed him that we had just won the Canadian Grand Prix. The manager seemed pleased to see us. Joan then told the manager that we were here to 'push the boat out a little,' as he put it, and the manager seemed even more pleased to see us.

Joan then told the manager that there was 'effectively no limit to the proposed budget for this little get together' and Joan would appreciate it if the manager's staff would 'supply whatever my boys would like'. At this the manager beamed an enormous smile, and gave his solemn oath that he could rest assured of the best quality and service money could buy.

The evening started quietly enough, and as people arrived they began to gather around the reserved tables and ponder the menu. I found myself sitting next to Jon and Jos, who despite not actually having raced for us since Japan had attended every race, being told by Flavio to 'watch and learn.'

He had duly removed his driver's overalls, donned a race shirt and radio, and observed and learned. Jos said he fancied a glass of champagne, and asked the manager what he recommended. Dom Perignon seemed to be the order of the day, and at two hundred dollars a bottle I suppose it was always going to be. 'Fine,' said Jos, 'we'd better have five bottles.'

'Certainly sir.'

'No, better make it ten, and scatter them around the tables!'

'A very wise and thoughtful decision sir, if I may say so,' enthused the manager.

'And Steve likes red wine,' Jos informed him.

'Of course sir. We have an excellent wine list, that I'm sure will have something to interest you.'

A quick scan through the list, and the name I was looking for jumped out of the page at me: CHATEAU MOUTON-ROTHSCHILD. Then my eyes glanced over at the price column. There were a lot of fine wines on the list, many of them costing several hundred dollars.

There was, however, only one wine, a Premier Class Grand Cru Bordeaux, with a four figure price tag. Weighing in at a cool one thousand one hundred dollars and apparently only available in magnums, it was the Mouton-Rothschild.

'Ah the Mouton,' cooed the manager 'it is a beautiful wine! A truly exceptional year, when the sun shone its splendour upon Pauillac, and the vines nurtured majestic grapes, whose efforts were destined to be written about and recorded for all time in the books of vinicultural history!

'We managed to obtain a few magnums. Not many bottles are left now of course. Only a privileged few will still be able to tell of its seductive and beauteous charm . . .' He left his description to drift gently on the breeze, sighed and looking wistfully upwards seemed to be remembering a time when he too had sampled a seductive and beauteous charm.

Sales patter normally has no effect on me whatsoever, but this man was a pure genius.

'Good gracious!' I said, turning to Jos 'the sun's splendour, seduction and vinicultural history! Imagine, all that for just over a grand!'

'What about Joan?' Jos said, pinching some of my lobster, and getting instantly jabbed with a fork for his trouble. Eleven hundred dollars! A rough calculation – and even giving sterling the advantage in the exchange rate – still made it over five hundred pounds a bottle. I didn't think Joan would see ordering wine at that price as merely pushing the boat out a little, but more the launching of a major ocean going liner. It was, nevertheless, very tempting. Jon saw me mulling the idea over, and decided to investigate exactly what Joan's idea of boat pushing might include. He called over to the Team Manager's table. 'Joan!'

'Yes Jon?'

'You remember saying we can order whatever we liked?'

'Within reason Jon, yes of course!'

'Well Steve was just wondering if . . .' Jon was stopped in mid sentence, as Joan pre-empted the question. 'If either you or Steve order that thousand dollar wine, it will be the last thing you ever do!'

'Thank you for clarifying that point with us Joan,' said Jon, politely.

'No problem boys, enjoy yourselves.' Then as an after thought he added, 'Oh, and the bit about the wine goes for the driver too.'

'It wasn't me! I wasn't going to order it!' exclaimed Jos.

'Good. Make sure you don't!' After a final warning to the driver, Joan returned to his own conversation. 'And don't get drunk! Watch him you two!'

I lost sight of Jos at around 2.00 a.m. We had finished dinner, and returned downstairs to the bar. The last I saw of him, Tim and Bobby were grappling Jos to the floor, while Jon poured a large Bacardi and Coke into him. Joan, while leaning against the bar and orchestrating the affair, reminded the driver that he wasn't to drink too much, the reminder coming a little too late, I think.

All five of them were beginning to look the worse for wear, and for me it was definitely time for bed. The flight back to England left Mirabel International on Monday evening, which was fortunate, as some of the team didn't make it back to the hotel until late Monday afternoon.

It was the middle of Tuesday afternoon by the time I arrived home, and we had Wednesday off as we waited for the freight to catch up with us. By Thursday morning it too had arrived home, and we began to unpack and the trucks were reloaded with everything we had taken off for the Canadian race.

On Tuesday the 21st there was to be a four-day test at Silverstone. All the Formula One teams were invited to take part. This would allow them to gain familiarity with the revised circuit layout which had been altered to try and slow the cars down during the forthcoming British Grand Prix. We were going to send 03 and 04 to the test, let Michael drive both cars and see if he could feel any difference between them.

Irrespective of the results from the Silverstone test we were going to have to build a new B194 for the next race. It had been decided that for this race, the French Grand Prix at Magny Cours, all teams would increase the side-load strength of their chassis. This would hopefully increase driver safety in the event of an accident, and could only be seen as a worthwhile and welcome modification.

The extra strength was to be achieved by bonding additional layers of carbon to the chassis, to the outside and the inside of the cockpit area. To ensure that all teams had complied with this new ruling, and that the extra carbon they had added created sufficient strength, Charlie Whiting would carry out a side-load test on every current chassis.

This involves loading the cockpit sides, via a hydraulic ram, to a pressure of three thousand kilos, and measuring the deformation of the chassis. When the pressure is removed, Charlie could then check with ultra-sound equipment for any cracks within the core of the carbon structure.

Each new chassis that is made has an electronic security tag bonded to it, which prevents the possibility of any team 'cheating' by building only one 'strong' chassis which will pass the FIA tests, while the others they build are not as strong, but are much lighter. I'm not saying any team is guilty of this despicable action, but the security system allows complete confidence and peace of mind.

The next new chassis to be constructed by our composite department was number 07. This was our first chassis to be modified to the new strength regulation, as it was still in the composite department being finalized when the new ruling was announced. The plan was that Dave, Bobby and I should take over and build 07 into our next race car. If everything proved correct with 04 following the Silverstone test, then it too would receive the strength modification and be handed over to the test team to replace the relatively old and tired 01.

While I stayed behind and began to build our new chassis, Dave and Bobby accompanied 04 to Silverstone, along with 03 and the spare car crew. Max, Kenny and Jon stripped 05, and handed it over to the composite department to modify, while they began the service and rebuild of the mechanical components.

These new chassis builds were, to say the least, becoming very familiar. Including this one and helping with the build of 01 (as the crew of car six) the three of us had built six complete cars. An average of one chassis change for each race we had attended! I hoped that 07 would become 'lucky 7', stay with us until the end of the year, and, hopefully, score some points for us along the way.

I began the necessarily steady, detailed and painstaking work that a new chassis build demands. Each time I have built a chassis I have found some way of improving on the last, making the installation of the various components seem more orderly for example, by running sections of the loom a slightly different way from before, and so avoiding possible contact and chafing with one of the control modules. Or from previous experience knowing when to fit 'spiral-wrap' (the hard plastic sheath that is wrapped like a coil spring around parts of the loom that are particularly prone to potential damage).

There are, however, no corners to be cut, and each chassis must be assembled with great care and diligence. Each one we prepare is assembled with the knowledge that it could (and the expectation that it will) last the entire season. The carbon experts in the composite department toil for over a thousand hours in the birth of each Benetton chassis.

The fabricators and machinists spend days making the wishbones, uprights, exhausts, radiators etc. They carry out their work knowing that nothing has been overlooked, and that each component has been built to the same exacting standards. If it would take the mechanics two weeks to prepare and build a new car, it would be but a small fraction of the time others have devoted to its creation.

It would therefore be a grave injustice to everybody's efforts if we didn't build the car with the same care and precision. I began the installation of the ty-rap blocks, the wiring loom, ty-raps, the brake-bias cable, more ty-raps, anti-vibration mounts for the dash and control boxes, more ty-raps, the fire extinguishers, the throttle cable, more ty-raps, the gear change display, more ty-raps, the steering column and steering rack, the master cylinders, throttle, clutch and brake pedals and even more ty-raps. Slowly our new car began to take shape.

There were three weeks in between the Canadian and French races, allowing plenty of time to carry out the evaluation of 04 at Silverstone, and complete the build of the new car. Most days I managed to finish work at 5.30 p.m., but was unable to spend much time with Judd, as she too had gone to Silverstone with the Williams test team.

Williams had apparently been busy testing and developing the FW16, and rumours were around that Frank himself had been occupied in trying to tempt Nigel Mansell away from America, and back into Formula One, by offering him Coulthard's car (and an unfeasibly large amount of money) to drive for him in Magny-Cours.

As far as I could see, the rumours seemed reasonable enough, and they had a certain amount of substance to them. Mansell had not been having the success in Indycars he had experienced last year and he could well be looking for a full time drive in Formula One for the '95 season.

Indeed, I think that if it wasn't for his commitment to Newman-Hass (his Indycar team) he would have jumped at the chance of driving the Williams during the remaining ten races of this year. It is undeniable that Mansell has a massive following which guarantees media interest and press coverage. Not only the motoring publications either, but also the daily press, radio and television would be full of stories of 'OUR NIGE, BACK TO DO IT FOR ENGLAND! As I have said before, the sport survives on media coverage, and Mansell's return (even if only for one race) would be a most welcome event for many people.

My personal feeling was that if Mansell returned, he would find Formula One a very different world to the one he abandoned in '92, and I would be interested to see how he would react to the changes he would find.

While I was working on our new car, Oz strolled out of his office with news from the Silverstone test. Michael had been sent out in the spare car, and had spun off the circuit. He was perfectly alright and the incident wasn't really big enough to warrant the label 'accident', but, nevertheless, it resulted in the car receiving quite a hefty bang as it slid over the kerbing before finally coming to rest in the gravel trap.

When the car had been recovered and returned to the garage, however, a damage inspection revealed that the impact with the kerb had cracked the underside of the fuel tank area which would require some fairly extensive composite work to correct.

After the test had finished, Bobby and Dave returned to the factory. Michael hadn't been able to fault 04, following the 'back to back' comparison, so we temporarily moved our new chassis out of the race bay while we stripped 04, and sent it to the composite department for the side-load modification. 03 was sent for repair, where the damaged bottom section of the chassis was replaced. However, despite the repair work being a success, it was decided to withdraw it from service with the Race Team, and after a brief spell with the Test Team, 03 (with both the Brazilian and Pacific Grands Prix wins to its credit) was allowed to retire.

Paul, Paul and Lee were presented with 06 to be built as the next spare car. This was the chassis we had built for the Monaco race, and had swapped for 04 after J.J.'s shunt. When we returned to England it had been sent to the composite department, where the slight damage to the suspension mount had been corrected.

It had then travelled with us to Spain and Canada, as the emergency spare. Due to the retirement of 03, the Test Team had no choice but remained with 01 as 04 was now required to take over the role as the emergency spare chassis.

Two days before the transporters left for Magny Cours, Joan called us together for a meeting. He informed us that by mutual agreement it had been decided that it would be better for all concerned if J.J. gave his injured neck time to heal completely before attempting to drive in another Grand Prix. It is undeniable that he had tried very hard to recover as soon as possible, but despite his bravery, his neck muscles needed more time to recuperate and return to full strength.

At the moment, driving the B194 was doing J.J. more harm than good, but Flavio had made it clear to J.J. that as soon as he was physically fit and able, his drive at Benetton was assured. Jos had once more been asked to stand-in, and he had readily agreed to help. I changed the seatbelt settings and the pedal positions in our car and Tim brought over Jos's seat and two VERSTAPPEN

Alessandro Benetton chats with Flavio Briatore in Aida, Japan.

Michael with Ayrton Senna, 1994 Pacific GP.

Jos eats a good lunch...

...to build his strength for his long walk home. Aida, Japan.

Four pretty girls.

Ayrton and Michael.

Roland Ratzenberger driving the Simtek in Japan.

The tifosi at Imola.

Reg at work in the Monaco pit lane.

Parc Ferme at Monaco. Notice Charlie Whiting (the FIA Technical Delegate) at the front of the Minardi.

Andrea Montermini's Simtek has just come to rest, following his accident in Spain. He suffered only light injuries in the shunt. Notice the tribute to Roland Ratzenberger painted on the roll hoop and bodywork. The red and white design is a copy of Roland's helmet.

JJ rejoined the team at Imola. Jos came to all the races, and when he was not driving, he would learn as much as he could.

Flavio and Niki Lauda chat in Spain.

The Benetton entry for the Annual Formula One Raft Race – Canada.

Michael, Pat Symonds (centre) and Christian Silk.

Damon, Michael and Jean on the podium in Canada.

name stickers for the sides of the chassis.

The shakedown was carried out on Monday the 27th. Jos had been assigned to drive, everything went well, and the transporters headed off to Dover. As a summary to all of these comings and goings, the line up for the French Grand Prix was as follows: Car 5, chassis 05 (Michael); Car 6, chassis 07 (Jos); spare car, chassis 06; emergency spare, chassis 04.

Fine. Well now that's all clear, off we go to France.

# JULY

If you took a map of France and stuck a pin in where you calculated the exact centre of the country to be the chances are it would stick right in the middle of the *Circuit de Nevers Magny-Cours*. The area around Magny-Cours is very quiet and peaceful. Most of the land seems to be either owned by small family-run farms, or simply abandoned altogether as the older generations have died and their offspring have moved to find alternative and better paid employment in Paris.

If your idea of relaxation is sitting outside a small café, and, while sipping a chilled glass of *Pouilly-Fumé* under the shade of a tree, wishing there were a few more people about so that you could watch the world go by, then Magny-Cours is ideal, but if you want night-life, night clubs and non-stop action then go to Sao Paulo.

The circuit itself is located on the outskirts of town. A few years ago it was treated to a complete face-lift, and a small industrial park was built at the side of it in an attempt to attract new business, and hopefully reduce the local unemployment figures slightly. Ligier have their headquarters there, but despite the attractive new facilities on offer few other companies were tempted to relocate.

The flight from England to France was only an hour long, but the coach journey from the Benetton factory to Luton airport was twice that duration, as was the trip in the minibus from Clermont Ferrand (the small regional airport where the FOCA charter flight lands) to the circuit. However, the journey through the French countryside was infinitely more pleasing to the eye than the miles of red cones and traffic jams we had crawled through back in England.

We left the factory at 5.30 a.m. Thursday morning. After three weeks of starting work at 8.30 a.m., the espresso machine had to deliver three strong cups before I started to wake up and get ready to leave. The alarm had been set for 4.30 a.m., but, as usual, it was a good fifteen minutes after that until Judd's persistent nudging forced me out of bed.

With the dawning of the French Grand Prix, we had reached the main European stage of our world tour, and this, unfortunately, normally means leaving home only a few hours after midnight. Over the last few weeks the weather in England had been surprisingly hot, and it felt as though we might be treated to four individual seasons, instead of the British tradition of the winter sleet warming up just enough to become rain, and, with the grey spring deciding to give summer a miss, turn straight into a grey autumn and have plenty of time to prepare itself to become winter again.

However, the pleasant weather we had been experiencing in Oxfordshire was nothing in comparison to the heat-wave currently underway in France. When we arrived at the circuit at a little after one o'clock in the afternoon the sun (beating down with no breeze to disguise its heat) was causing Cosworth's thermometers to show close to 100°F.

It actually felt much hotter than that, for when we changed out of our travel clothes I decided, for the first time this year, to go for shorts instead of long trousers. I tend to feel the cold a lot more than others, and it is fairly normal for me to be seen wearing trousers and one of our warm fleece jackets, while the other mechanics are down to the bare minimum.

On this occasion, however, I succumbed to the heat, and even hoped it would cool down a little before Sunday. The idea of wearing the thick fireproof overalls, gloves and balaclava for the duration of the race in this temperature wasn't very appealing, despite the obvious necessity for us to do so.

After a drink and a sandwich we set the flat-patch, and fired up the engines to confirm everything was still working correctly. Then we pushed the cars down to the FIA scrutineer's flat-patch to check the cars for minimum weight and wing legality. This is most important, as although we weigh the cars at our factory and in the pit lane garage, and keep a record of exactly what that weight is (as well as the dimensions of the wings and bodywork), it is the figures using the FIA scales and equipment that will decide if the car is legal or not.

There is little sympathy from the FIA for any team which claims their car to be legal on their own scales, when the scrutineers find it to be underweight. Of course, if our figures and those found on the FIA equipment are vastly different then we will inform Charlie Whiting, and all of us will investigate as to whose equipment is at fault.

As we pushed the car back down the pit lane I noticed a large crowd gathering outside the Williams garage, as photographers jostled for prime position, and then the reason for all the media activity walked out of the garage and into the bright sunlight. Frank had succeeded in his negotiations with all the relevant sponsors, engine suppliers, teams and most importantly the man himself. Nigel Mansell had returned to Formula One.

In a deal rumoured to be worth close to one million pounds, Mansell had agreed to return to Williams for this one race, as guest driver and partner to Damon. Mansell had driven the FW16 for the first time a few days before at Brands Hatch, and even then several thousand of his fans had turned up to watch as the car was put through its paces. I have heard many people say that to pay someone so much for a weekend's work is ridiculous, and to an extent I agree.

After all, whether the actual figure involved was a million pounds, or only half that amount, it is still a colossal sum of money, but what must be remember-ed is that Mansell is a massive audience attraction, and his appearance is guar-anteed to instantly boost ticket sales and TV ratings. Thousands of Americans who may never have watched a Grand Prix before would tune in to see their current Indycar World Champion fight it out with the young stars of Formula One. I would imagine that advertising space during the American broadcasts of the French Grand Prix had become a very valuable commodity.

The tickets for the German Grand Prix had sold out weeks ago, and as many journalists had written that Mansell had been signed-up simply to beat Schumacher, the tickets were now changing hands for up to ten times their face value. The fact that Mansell wouldn't be at Hockenheim was of no relevance, the German fans still wanted to turn out and support their potential Cham-pion. In Britain too, just the mere chance that Mansell might drive at Silver-stone had sent ticket sales soaring. All of this extra business is worth millions of dollars, and makes Mansell's salary pale into insignificance by comparison. We left the photographers to it, and pulled the car back inside. Bobby and Dave fitted the dust cover, I pulled the garage door down, and when the others had finished we climbed aboard the mini-buses and left for the hotel.

We stay at the Hotel Campanile, one of a large chain of basic but clean stop-over type places which are located all over France. It is normally used by truck drivers on their constant journeys up and down the country, and is more a motel than a hotel as all the rooms are housed in a separate block to the recep-tion area.

There is one important thing to remember about the Campanile hotels – all the rooms have a shower, but they don't have any way of hanging the shower-spray above your head. This turns what should be both a simple and refreshing morning task into an irritating and frustrating pain, as you have to hold the spray and wash your hair at the same time.

Surely it would make more sense to have a hook for the shower-head, and thus leave both hands free for washing? To me it's like having to keep your finger constantly on a light switch to stop the light going out. I find it far more convenient to be able to switch the light on and then simply walk away. It baffles me why some people seem to go out of their way to make life difficult for themselves.

To get around this somewhat bizarre design flaw Reggie had fabricated a small wall mounted bracket for the shower by riveting two ty-rap blocks to a piece of aluminium plate. He fastened this to the wall with a strip of 'double-sided' Tessa tape, secured the shower-head to the bracket with two ty-raps, and there it was, a normal no-hands-required shower. Easy!

Reg could possibly become a millionaire by patenting his design and selling the shower brackets to the thousands of truck drivers who are forced to put up with this daily inconvenience. During Friday morning's practice sessions we carried out a lot of set-up changes on 07 (mainly springs) until eventually Frank and Jos found the optimum settings that suited both car and driver. By now Michael knew the handling characteristics of the B194 very well, and before long he and Pat achieved a good workable balance, finishing the session 0.8 seconds ahead of Alesi's second placed Ferrari.

In between practice and qualifying we changed the gearbox on our car as the internal oil pump had lost pressure. We fitted a new pump at first and although this cured the pressure fault, we had no idea of the damage, if any, that may have been caused to the internals.

Philippe Troivaux, our quietly spoken and instantly likeable Elf fuel and lubricants specialist, carried out a 'spectrum analysis' of the gearbox oil to evaluate the wear of the various components of the 'box. Too much iron in the oil would indicate gear or bearing wear, an excess of magnesium could warn of damage to the casing due to a bearing-race spinning in its housing.

After an initial inspection Jakey thought everything looked fine and Philippe's oil analysis backed him up. We would, nevertheless, need to strip the box and have a close look to be thoroughly convinced. This would take much longer than the time we had available before qualifying began at one o'clock, and so we fitted the spare.

The one we took off could then be stripped and if necessary repaired later that night. Mick and the spare car crew helped with the gearbox change, and we managed to get Jos out in plenty of time to qualify. I walked over from the garage to the pit wall with Frank in order to show Jos his lap times as he drove past the pits.

Magny-Cours is one of the few circuits in the world where we can see the cars approaching well before the need to show them the pit board. At most circuits the cars tear round the last corner, and are upon us and gone again literally within a couple of seconds. At Benetton it has become traditional for the front-end mechanics to operate the pit-boards when the cars are running (with the exception of the actual race, when our services are required for the pit stops).

One of the responsibilities of the front-end mechanics is to deal with the driver's comfort and any necessary adjustments while he is in the car. Because we are constantly dealing with the drivers in this way it has somehow become natural that the front-end mechanics should extend that interconnection between the driver and crew via the pit-wall communication.

It is important to maintain a calm and relaxed relationship with the drivers, as the pressures they are under can sometimes make them appear a little vexing in their requests. If the mechanics become irritated with them it can become difficult to build the relationship of trust between us that is vital to a driver's confidence in the car.

'Steve, could you lengthen my lap straps a little?'

'How much?' I enquire.

'Oh, only a little but they're too tight!' I lean in, give the straps a heave and move the tuck in his overalls. 'How's that?' I ask. 'Perfect, thanks.' Or 'I need the brake pedal a little closer to me'. I move it a fraction.

'How's that?' already sensing what the answer will be.

'Er no, too far, back just a bit,' and moving it back to where it was, 'Yes, that's perfect, just there!'

'No problem,' I reply and re-tighten the lock-nut. I don't tell them it's back in the same place, they probably feel a little more comfortable for moving around a bit, and if that translates to confidence with the car then so be it.

I don't believe they ask for these adjustments out of devilment, it's just that some drivers like to fidget as they wait to go out. Michael shows great attention to detail in his cockpit settings, he doesn't ask for changes merely for the sake of change, but he will ask for things to be exactly as he wants them.

Everything, even down to the 'density rating' of the foam used for elbow and knee protection receives close scrutiny. He is always looking for ways to improve the car's performance, and if he thinks Jon needs to add more padding here, or take it away from there, then Michael will have a good reason for saying so.

Jos, on the other hand, operates differently. He likes the chassis interior to be left fairly sparse. He won't directly ask me for any padding to be put in the chassis, he'll just point out that his elbow or knee keeps hitting this or that. He knows that if we can fix the problem it will be solved, if we can't he will drive the car as it is and never mention the problem again.

Different drivers work with us in different ways, and I have found that when a driver gets to know his mechanics well and the relationship of trust has formed between us he will confide his feelings (about the car, the team, who he thinks is right, who he thinks is wrong, and who he thinks he can trust) probably more with us than with anybody else.

When dealing with the media, for example, the drivers have to portray their public image, and apart from occasional outbursts of temper which tell of nothing but frustration they very rarely talk of any genuine problems within the team.

Once the day's running is over, while we are working on the cars the drivers come into the garage and chat about how the day has gone. I think they enjoy the freedom to talk openly to their mechanics, knowing that anything they say to us will go no further. They appear thankful for the chance to be treated like normal people, and are pleased to leave their public relations duties until tomorrow.

By the end of the day's running Michael was on provisional pole with Jos in eighth place, only one position behind Mansell's FW16. Both Jos and ourselves were pleased with the day's results. The new chassis had performed well, and the situation looked promising for an even better grid position on Saturday.

We carried out our usual checks of brake wear and the condition of all the mechanical components, and it wasn't too long after dinner before the cars were being polished and having their dust covers fitted. We returned to the Campanile for a refreshing shower, a quick drink at one of the local cafés and an early night.

I had set the alarm for 6.00 a.m. This gave us an hour before we left for the circuit, plenty of time for me to shower and make a fairly terrible instant coffee before jolting Reg into life with a quick yell to remind him of the time. I drank my coffee outside while leaning on the balcony. Even at this early hour the sun (who like us was just getting ready for the business of the day) was warming Magny-Cours with sufficient enthusiasm to ensure that it turned into another fiercely hot afternoon.

The free practice sessions during the morning had finished with Mansell at the top of the page. Overnight he and the Williams engineers had studied the data they had collected from Friday's running, and together they had made good progress. I have never worked with Mansell but he always appears to me to be very confident about what changes he thinks will help the balance of the car, and if a driver feels confident then that is 90 per cent of the battle in achieving a quick lap. I don't know on what areas of the FW16 they had been working but the monitor screens told everyone in the pit lane that he had improved his time from Friday morning by just short of 1.6 seconds.

Jos had also improved, and he finished the practice sessions nearly half a second quicker than his Friday's qualifying time. The car had once again been running very well, we had encountered no problems during the morning and, apart from changes to wing angles, and ride-height settings (as Frank fine-tuned the balance of the car) we had a fairly easy morning.

We pulled the cars back into the garage, and as Jos and Michael discussed the practice sessions with Ross and the engineers we began the preparation for qualifying. We fired-up and ran the engines for ten seconds to stabilize the oil-level before 'dipping' the tank and informing Cosworth of the engine's consumption.

Philippe took a sample of both engine and gear oil to analyse and report on any potential internal damage. The fuel tank was pumped out, the remaining quantity was carefully measured, and the figures given to both Cosworth and our engineers to confirm that everybody agreed on their calculations for fuel consumption.

The cars haven't got a 'fuel gauge' as such, but by measuring exactly how much fuel has been pumped into the tank and metering the flow rate through the injection system we can keep track of precisely how much fuel we have on board.

When we are qualifying it is important to run with as little fuel on board as possible and so avoid carrying an unnecessary weight penalty, but run with too little fuel or underestimate the consumption of the engine, and the car may splutter to a halt in the middle of what could be the pole setting lap.

This is also true during the race, of course, and there have been several cases during the final lap of a Grand Prix when the leader has dramatically slowed, weaving from side-to-side in an attempt to squeeze the last drop of fuel from the tank, only to grind to a thoroughly demoralizing standstill within sight of the chequered flag. Hundreds of hours of work and thousands of pounds of precious budget coming to nothing all for the sake of half-a-litre of fuel!

Both the B194's were prepared and ready to qualify by 1.00 p.m. As the first cars took to the circuit, and the lap times began to appear on the monitors it was obvious that Williams, Renault, and their two drivers had all been busy improving their cars, and their efforts were being rewarded.

It wasn't long before Michael's provisional pole time of 1m 17.085s had been beaten by both Mansell and Hill. Michael and Jos had gone for their first run, and had both returned to the pits to wait and watch what times everybody else was achieving before leaving for their second attempt.

Once the initial surge of cars had returned to the pits Frank decided it was time to send Jos for his second run. 'You have fuel for three flying laps Jos,' Frank informed him over the radio. 'We'll show you the arrow to come in.'

'OK Frank. Three laps,' replied Jos, more to confirm he had heard the radio message than the need to say anything. I walked over to the pit-wall, watching the cars come down the hill, thread their way through the chicane and exit the tight right-hand bend which leads onto the start/finish straight.

Jos came into view, weaved through the chicane and disappeared down the straight to commence his first flying lap. After a couple of attempts he managed a time of 1m 17.645s, over a second quicker than his Friday's best. (Unfortunately, however, that lap-time was destined to be the quickest that chassis 07 would ever know.)

Jos came into view tearing down the hill, I hung the pit-board over the wall, watching him fight with the car as it sped through the chicane. As he approached the tight right-hand bend he changed down and threw the steering to the right, but the car was going too fast to respond, his speed forcing the car to understeer.

My initial reaction was that if he got away with it then this was going to be a very quick lap. Eventually the car did start to turn-in, but this was caused more by the rear starting to oversteer than the front correcting itself. There was a loud metallic SMACK as the left-rear wheel smashed into the pit-wall, quickly followed by a shower of carbon wings, bodywork and McLaren monitors as the rear of the car buried itself into the concrete.

This action pulled the front of the car into the wall, and there was suddenly a front wheel, wing and nose flying down the circuit to join the debris from the rear.

'Bloody hell, look out!' someone shouted. We dropped down behind the pit wall to avoid being hit by flying shrapnel. The car clung to the wall as it scraped and squealed to a standstill further down the main straight. When it had all gone quiet I stood up and saw Jos climb out the wreckage and scramble over the wall.

Although visibly shaken he seemed unhurt, and he walked slowly back to the garage. The McLaren chaps brushed themselves down and breathed a huge sigh of relief, they had been very lucky that it was only TV monitors they had lost!

I looked over at our new car to survey the damage. It lay amongst a pool of water and gear oil, a cloud of steam hissing from underneath the damaged bodywork. The entire left-hand suspension and wheels were missing. On impact with the wall the left-lower wishbone on the front of the car had been driven into the chassis with enough force to fracture the mounting and damage the carbon structure around it. Having covered a mere 209km since we built it a few days ago chassis 07 was history.

I looked over at Dave and Bobby, standing in the pit lane, and shook my head in confirmation of their own suspicions. The car was returned to us on the back of a recovery truck. We pushed and pulled it back inside, and there it lay, a broken and twisted mess. The truckies unloaded 04 (our emergency spare chassis) out of the transporter and carried it into the garage.

I walked back outside to ponder the situation. As I saw it, there were two ways of looking at it. On the one hand you could say that this is all part of the intrinsic and intense excitement of being a Formula One mechanic. There is never a dull moment, and there is always something to be getting involved with. Tomorrow is another day, and who knows, maybe after we have spent the long hours ahead of us rebuilding Good Old 04 into a complete car again we could score some points with it, maybe even win the race.

On the other hand I felt an intense temptation to walk off down the pit lane, exchange my race shirt for a one-way ticket to Bordeaux, and seek employment in the peace and solitude of the vineyards.

However, after an espresso, a few minutes of silent contemplation and a few words of encouragement from Joan reminding me that life within Formula One is never easy and that it's only the frustrations and disappointments that make the eventual results worthwhile, I decided that the Bordeaux option would be the action of an individual, not that of a team player. And so, with my commitment to team spirit reaffirmed, I walked back inside to reacquaint myself with chassis 04 although it was still difficult to shake the visions of ancient, tranquil vineyards from my mind.

Lee came over and helped me with the front of the car, and with Mick, Paul Seaby and Paul Howard helping Bobby and Dave at the rear it wasn't long before 07 had been stripped and loaded aboard one of the trucks. We lifted 04 up onto the high stands, and began its assembly. The garage was baking hot as the intense sun beat down, and our shirts clung to us as though we had been sprayed with water. We worked on 04 until around 2.00 a.m. Sunday morning, when at last we had it built, set-up and ready to run for the warm-up at 9.30 a.m. I didn't seem to be asleep for longer than ten minutes before the alarm clock told us to get up again. We quickly packed, threw the bags into the minibuses and set off for the circuit.

Michael had been unable to match the speed of the Williams during qualifying and had to settle for third place on the grid, with Mansell ahead of him and Damon on pole. He spent the majority of the warm-up session out on the circuit, getting a feel for his car in race-trim, and as his grid position was off the racing line he kept running over (and so cleaning) the right hand side of the circuit.

Jos had been out in 04, and although the car was handling well and the brakes etc. were working correctly he complained of a slight vibration from the rear end. Ross decided to take no chances, so once the warm-up was over we changed the entire rear suspension and gearbox assembly.

This sudden extra work kept all three of us occupied during the rest of the morning, but we managed to have the car finished by one o'clock, giving us ample time to change into our fireproof shoes and overalls. As soon as they were zipped up our body temperature dramatically increased, and it felt like wearing Arctic survival clothes in the heat of the Australian outback.

The pit lane opened at 1.30 p.m., and we sent Jos straight out to confirm that the vibration had gone. If for some obscure reason the vibration still persisted we would have to call Jos back in and send him to the grid in the spare car before the pit lane closed again fifteen minutes later. 'How's the car now?' Frank inquired as Jos drove carefully into the pit lane. 'Has the vibration gone?'

We heard Jos switch his radio on as we anxiously waited to see if we needed to change cars. 'It's,' he deliberately paused for a few seconds, letting the tension build (Jos is never one to let an opportunity slip past) 'fine, no problems, I'll go through and straight to the grid, yes?'

'Yes, straight to the grid, we'll see you there!' laughed Frank. At two o'clock the race began. Michael made a good start, just managing to get ahead of both the FW16s by the first corner, and he and Damon set off into the distance in what promised to be the best fight for the lead we had seen in several races.

As the race settled down and began to sort itself out I stood just inside the garage, taking advantage of the shade and while leaning on the rear jack I chatted to Ken, and watched the cars come down the hill and through the chicane. Suddenly we saw a huge cloud of gravel take to the air, we couldn't see who it was but someone had gone straight through the gravel-trap and had even managed to drive back out, rejoining the circuit just in front of the pit lane entrance.

As the dust settled I was able to recognize the car, and a fraction later I heard Jos on the radio. 'I need a new nose, the front wing is damaged. I repeat, the front wing is damaged. I am in the pit lane now!' Ken cursed and ran to the front of the pit, Jakey and Wayne shot past me, and others frantically rushed into position. Jos darted in. As soon as he had brought the car to a halt the front was physically lifted onto a low stand. (Ken couldn't use the jack as the main-plane where he would locate it had been ripped off.)

The procedure for lifting the car onto the stand is something we practice over and over for just such an eventuality. The damaged nose and wing assembly was swiftly removed, and mounds of gravel were swept from the radiator ducts. When the new nose was fitted Ken was once again able to lift the car with the jack, and the stand was removed.

Ken jumped clear and Mick waved Jos out into the pit lane. We managed to change the nose and get the car back into the race within half a minute of his message. I didn't think that was too bad considering we only had three seconds to prepare for his arrival!

We didn't manage to score any points with Jos and 04 during the race, however, as a few laps later he spun off and became stranded in the huge gravel-trap at the fastest corner on the circuit.

Michael, on the other hand, gained for himself and the team a full ten points, crossing the line 12.6 seconds ahead of Damon's FW16 and Berger's third placed Ferrari. Mansell had dropped out with mechanical failure just after the halfway stage, and had disappeared back to the States even before the race had finished.

Later that night Tim and myself sat on the pavement outside the Clermont Ferrand airport, taking advantage of the slight breeze to be found there. We had arrived at about 6.30 p.m. The check-in hall had felt more like a sauna than a departure terminal, and either the air-conditioning had failed or it was going to be the next feature to be installed. We visited the bar at first, but as it seemed to be taking the barman ten minutes to pour a small glass of pure froth, coupled with the glass roof increasing the sun's heat like a magnifying-glass we decided to abandoned the building altogether.

We sat and chatted about how the season had gone so far, the events we had seen and the changes that had resulted. We were only one race away from the halfway point and the first seven races had seemed to have come and gone very quickly. However, a lot of things had happened in that time and we had witnessed some terribly sad events. We both expressed the desire felt by everyone that the second half of the season would unfold into a much happier affair. On the plus side, though, Benetton had experienced tremendous success during the first seven races. We had won six of them, and if it wasn't for transmission problems in Barcelona we might well have made it seven out of seven, but no one was complaining with Michael's six wins and a second place.

When coupled with J.J.'s single point that the spare car had scored in Canada we had a total of 67 points in the Constructors Championship, 31 clear of Ferrari and 35 ahead of Williams. Poor old McLaren, whom I had assumed would be one of our closest rivals, were experiencing their worst season for many years, scoring only ten points so far, as engine after engine had failed them.

Some people may say that it's bad luck to discuss whether we might become World Champions by the end of the year, but it was inevitable that we should ponder the idea sooner or later. We both agreed that despite our commanding lead at present, our points advantage could easily dwindle away as both Williams and Ferrari improved.

After all, it would only take either of them to come home first and second at the next Grand Prix, while we dropped out, for whatever reason, and we would loose sixteen points of our safety-margin. If Ferrari achieved that result during the next two races then they could be leading the World Championship by Hungary! We needed both drivers in the points to consolidate our position, for not only would the extra points add to our score, which is all well and good, but more importantly it would stop other teams scoring them.

One flight home, one rebuild and a few days later we were at Silverstone. The British Grand Prix is exactly one week after the French race, and consequently we had been in another race against time to have everything ready for the first practice session on Friday morning. The teams based outside the UK had sent their trucks straight from Magny-Cours to Northampton, where the mechanics (having flown ahead) were waiting to meet them and carry out their rebuilds in the pit lane garages. The British teams are more fortunate, and are able to return to their factories and work on the cars there.

We arrived at Silverstone on Thursday morning, and already the adjoining fields were filling up with tents and caravans as the British fans began to descend on the circuit.

During our trip to France the sunny weather had remained in England, and the temperate climate had transformed Silverstone out of all recognition. The howling, bitterly cold blizzards of the winter tests had relented for a few weeks, and as I surveyed the green landscape the scene was reminiscent of the dawning of a new world.

The meadows grew tall and lush, bird songs trilled through the air and, following the demise of the Annual Northampton Ice Age, life had been reborn. I would even have to describe conditions as being 'pleasantly warm'.

Indeed over the next four days we would see hundreds of people (wearing football shorts, and carrying the compulsory tartan car blanket and cooler-box) transform in colour, from an almost translucent white to the traditional lobster pink by Sunday morning.

On our return to England the composite department had confirmed that the damage to 07 had rendered it beyond repair. They had been working around the clock to manufacture a replacement, but there are only so many hours in a day, and 08 wouldn't be finished until after the German Grand Prix.

The loss of 07 and the subsequent rebirth of 04 into a race car had left us without an emergency spare chassis for Silverstone and Hockenheim, so we were forced to commandeer 01 from the test team until 08 was completed. Meanwhile, 04 had survived its two excursions into the French gravel traps without damage, and like a bad penny you can't get rid of, it had been assigned to stay with us.

Jos had been told he would be expected to drive the car, and so it appeared that fate was going to keep all of us together (04, Jos and ourselves) until we finally managed to score some points. We did, however, have one new addition. Christian Silk, the team's Data Analysis Engineer, had replaced Frank Dernie as Jos's race engineer, Frank having departed for France to rejoin Ligier as Technical Director.

As I mentioned in June, there had been several changes made to the circuit layout in order to slow the cars down. The work had cost Silverstone several million pounds, and had been swiftly carried out and completed in plenty of time for the Grand Prix. After the pre-race test the drivers had declared the alterations a success, commenting that despite the improved safety measures Silverstone had managed to retain its reputation for being both a quick and demanding circuit.

The two days leading up to the actual race on Sunday had seen the closest qualifying sessions of the season so far, with Ferrari, Williams and Benetton fighting it out for pole position, separated by time and performance margins that it seemed impossible to differentiate between. At the end of Saturday's qualifying, Damon had secured pole from Michael by a mere three-thousandths of a second!

To be able to produce equipment that is capable of accurately measuring, recording and separating such minuscule periods of time and speed is an incredible feat of technology in its own right. And when those figures were collected and converted into distance, it equated to Damon beating Michael to the pole position by a scant ten centimetres. Gerhard too was incredibly close, but with a time 0.02 sec slower than the FW16 he had to settle for third position on the grid.

It had become very clear that the opposition had been rapidly improving on their initial designs, and were closing the gap (on any advantage we had gained from our extensive pre-season testing) very quickly.

A little further down the field, Jos had just managed to get 04 into the top ten, and with a time of 1m 26.841s was just behind Martin Brundle's ninth placed McLaren.

The Saturday night race preparation had gone smoothly enough, and we had left the circuit and returned to our hotel by 11.00 p.m. The warm-up had also been carried out without drama. Both drivers had reported no problems with the cars. Michael had also driven the spare car for a few laps, and that too was running without fault.

Because of the trouble free warm-up we had little work to do after the session, so to make good use of the time before we sent the cars to the grid we lifted all three of them onto the high-stands, removed the floors and carried out a final check to ensure that everything was as it should be.

We looked to see that nothing had been chafing and that no wiring had been trapped. Bobby and Dave 'spanner-checked' the rear suspension, and I did the same with the front. The Cosworth engineers checked the data collected during the warm-up and confirmed that the engine-management systems were working correctly.

Jakey and Dave Butterworth inspected the gearboxes for any oil leaks. Philippe had taken oil samples from the transmissions and engines of all three cars, and had confirmed that there was no evidence of any internal problems. All was fine. No problems at all. It looked like being a nice and easy afternoon's work.

It was now 12.30 p.m., an hour to go before the pit lane opened. I had been cleaning the master cylinders, giving them a final check and making sure the seals between the reservoirs and cylinders were still dry when I saw the first drop of water splash onto the garage floor. Dave saw it too, and if Bobby hadn't gone to fetch the floor, as we were just about to refit it, I'm sure he would have noticed it as well. Drips of any fluid around a Formula One car are a terribly bad omen, and it becomes a sixth sense for mechanics to watch for and notice them. We looked where it had fallen and climbed underneath. A few seconds later there came a second drop, that too splashed on the floor to join the first. Bobby reappeared and joined us below the car.

'What is it?' he asked.

'A water leak I think. I'm not sure where from, we've just spotted it,' Dave told him. Then the third drop fell and all was revealed, the water pump housing had started to seep.

Bobby showed Mick, and Mick duly showed Cosworth, who quickly confirmed that it was the water pump housing that was at fault and that the only solution would be to change the engine, but with less than an hour to go before the pit lane opened there simply wasn't enough time.

We couldn't believe it! The engine had run without fault when we had installed it the night before. It would have been thoroughly checked at Cosworth, and it would have been run on their dyno before leaving the factory. The car had just completed several trouble free laps during the warm-up, we had checked it for oil and water leaks after the installation lap and checked it again as soon as the session was over, everything had been perfect!

As I have said before, if a Formula One car fails, it always fails at the most inopportune times. This may be because during a Grand Prix weekend we are always working to precise deadlines, and consequently any time is not the moment for a problem. I suppose it could have been worse, it could have started to leak when we were on the grid, and Jos would have had to start the race from the pit lane in the spare car. Or worse still it could have started to leak two laps into the race, and we would never have finished at all. At least now the spare car crew had plenty of time to change the settings for Jos, and he would be able to start the race from his grid position.

The leak was just one of those odd things that happen from time to time, it's just the law of averages that one out of a thousand castings may have a thin or porous case (problems that are almost impossible to detect), and another thousand-to-one chance that the leak didn't occur either on the dyno or when we ran the engine on Saturday night or during the warm-up.

Nobody's fault, by any means, just a reminder that none of us, particularly those within Formula One, live in a perfect world. 'It's this chassis, possessed 04! It's cursed never to score a single bloody point!' I exclaimed. I was beginning to believe Bobby had been right when he had said something similar in Canada.

I'm actually writing this report about the Silverstone race a couple of weeks after the event and looking back. I'm sure I said 'cursed' more out of frustration than genuine belief. However, it must be said that 04 has had a bit of a dogged history, for if you recall, it was 04 that the Lotus smashed into at the start of the Imola race. It came back to us during the Monaco weekend (after 06 had 'kissed the armco'), but finished outside the points in seventh place.

We had it again in Spain when J.J. suffered engine failure. We had it in Canada when J.J. complained of handling problems, and had to race the spare car. We got it back again in France (following the brief existence of 'lucky 7') where it ended up spinning off into the gravel-trap, and now here we were in Britain, and once more it didn't race. This was certainly not the most auspicious and glory-filled history a Grand Prix chassis could have, but it must be remembered that Silverstone is only halfway through the season, and with another eight races to go there was still plenty of time for 04 to redeem itself.

The real problems for us began during the formation lap, just prior to the start of the race. The cars were shown the green flag, Michael set off and accelerated towards Copse Corner. He was quicker away from his second place on the grid than Damon was from pole, and in his eagerness to check that everything was working correctly and to give a final check of the engine's throttle response he overtook the Williams and found himself leading the field as they exited the bend and drove down towards Hanger Straight.

Michael backed off and Damon took his lead position back as they exited Club Corner to begin the gradual climb up the circuit, through Abbey and along the short Farm Straight, but in another quick burst of speed he once again overtook Damon's FW16. Michael slowed as he exited Bridge, allowing Damon to lead the cars onto the grid in readiness for the actual start.

However the start had to be delayed as, a little further down the field, David Coulthard had stalled the other Williams. He frantically waved his arms above his helmet and the marshals began to wave their red flags. The 'FIVE MINUTES' board was shown, the drivers switched their engines off, and the engineers and mechanics returned to the grid, jacked the cars up and wrapped the tyres to retain their heat while the situation was sorted out.

Charlie Whiting walked over to Coulthard, and explained to him and David Brown (his race engineer) that he would have to start the race from the back of the grid, and when the cars were once again allowed to commence the second parade lap a marshal would stand in front of the Williams until the rest of the field had driven past, at which point Coulthard would be allowed to rejoin at the rear of the field.

As the cars duly departed for their second formation lap Michael again found himself ahead of Damon as he shot off towards Copse. He backed off further around the circuit, Damon drove past him and the field resumed its correct order as they rounded Woodcote and once again formed up for the start of the race. The lights changed from red to green and the cars screamed off to commence the first lap of the Grand Prix.

Unfortunately Martin Brundle's race finished before it even had started. The back of his McLaren had been emitting ominous whiffs of smoke as it waited on the grid, and as he tried to accelerate away a large cloud of smoke and flame burst from the exhaust, and for Martin and car number eight the Silverstone race was over.

He immediately pulled off the circuit, and walked back to the pit lane looking very depressed by the whole affair. I felt sorry for Martin, he had waited a long time to be offered the drive at McLaren (a drive which he had fought for and genuinely deserved), and now when at last the chance had arrived McLaren was enduring their worst season for reliability in many years, allowing neither the team nor the driver to take full advantage of their partnership.

The race got under way, and as we had seen in France, Michael and Damon began to pull away from the others and fight for the lead in a race all of their own. While everyone had been on the grid Dave and Bobby had been assisting Simon manoeuvre the fuel rigs into position, and I had been helping Kris (one of our truckies and the man responsible for the pit stop equipment) move the air-line gantries and wheel-guns in front of the garage.

As people arrived back they pulled on their balaclavas while watching lap-times and positions flash up on the monitors, waiting for the pit stops to begin.

As in France I stood just inside the garage, leaning on the rear jack and watching the activity in the pit lane. About 30 minutes into the race I noticed Joan holding a piece of paper he had received from one of the marshals. The paper turned out to be a copy of the 'Stewards' Decision N°2', and the contents of it had caused some fairly urgent discussions to take place on the pit wall. The message said: 'You are herewith advised that the stewards have decided to impose a penalty of five seconds (on) Michael Schumacher, car N°5.'

The message did not describe the details of any apparent misdemeanour or tell of any specific way that the stewards intended to administer their penalty, so we had no idea what Michael had done or how the officials expected us to react. However, for reasons I shall go into later, the assumption was made that the five seconds would be added on to Michael's time at the end of the race.

This was no time for a discussion with the driver as to why he had been penalized – that would come later. What Michael needed to do now was to remain calm and concentrate on making up the five seconds that would later be added to his time, and we informed him of this via the radio.

He did just that and, as Damon pitted on lap 15, Michael took the lead which he kept until he himself pitted two laps later. We worked as swiftly as we could, keen to reduce the effect of his penalty as much as possible. The pit stop went well, and Michael's car was back on the ground refuelled and with new tyres in 6.8 sec.

Three laps later Jos came in, he too benefited from a quick stop, and rejoined the race in tenth place, nowhere near as high as Michael of course but at least he was still going!

Then, nearly 40 minutes into the race, a marshal arrived at the pit wall brandishing another message. It had been jotted down following a telephone call to the pit lane marshals from the stewards' office. It was a reminder about the five second penalty and included a little more information.

It claimed that the penalty was being imposed for 'overtaking on the warm-up lap'. This piece of information caused several quizzical looks. 'The warm-up lap?' said Joan, 'the warm-up was hours ago! Anyone can overtake during the warm-up, it's a practice session! Let me go and ask Roland what it means and what they want us to do.' He rushed off to find Roland Bruynseraede, the Race Director, to get the situation sorted out.

As Joan approached the Start/Finish line he was surprised to see an official holding out the black flag, he was even more surprised to see the number 5 being held out as well. The sight of the black flag was a severe shock and we had no idea why it was being displayed. Joan quickly found Roland, and returned with him to the pit wall.

The Race Director told us that the black flag was being shown to Michael because he hadn't complied with the requirements of his 'Time Penalty', and explained that the penalty wasn't for overtaking in the warm-up (that was obviously a mistake and a misunderstanding by someone), but for overtaking during the formation lap!

This was the first we had heard of the punishment being a time penalty! The Stewards Decision had never stipulated that, it had merely talked of a penalty of five seconds. These are two entirely different things! If the message had said time penalty then we could have referred to the regulations, called Michael into the pit lane and got it over with.

An agreement was reached with Roland and the black flag was withdrawn. We radioed to Michael, explained the situation, showed him the 'IN' sign on the pit-board and informed him of what he had to do. He came in, drove through to the end of the pit lane to where an FIA official was waiting with a 'STOP' sign and stayed there for the required five seconds.

He was then released by the official and rejoined the race in third place behind Alesi. The Ferrari pitted on the next lap, elevating Michael to second place where he remained until the end of the race. During all the confusion Damon had managed to pull away a twenty-second lead over Michael. He had led the race from lap twenty-two onwards, and it was an ecstatic Williams driver who took the chequered flag.

In winning the British Grand Prix he had achieved something his father had been unable to do during the whole of his illustrious career and it was a very proud Damon Hill who accepted the winner's trophy, holding it aloft for the thousands of fans to see. I felt very pleased for him, as he had been under a lot of media pressure recently. Certain members of the press refused to give him the respect he thought he deserved, so he had set out from the beginning of the race weekend to prove himself worthy of the Williams drive.

He had vowed to win the race and silence his critics at the same time. Now he had done just that. Jos crossed the line one lap down, in ninth place. Although he hadn't scored any points we were still more than pleased with his efforts. This was the first time he had completed a Grand Prix distance, and for a young driver that is an important milestone.

Jos, however, looked disappointed, and said he was annoyed with himself for not finishing in the points. Tom Walkinshaw (our Technical Director) came over to congratulate him. 'Cheer up lad!' he told him, and he gave Jos a hefty slap on the back. 'You've done well today, you can't run before you can walk! First you learn to drive the car, then you learn to finish. Only after mastering these first two stages do you learn to score points!'

Trying to get out of Silverstone after the Grand Prix is a nightmare. The only certain way to beat the endless traffic jams and avoid the impromptu rally stages (as campers career and slither across farm tracks in an attempt to find a short-cut to the M1) is to fly over the top of them, and leave the circuit by helicopter.

Indeed over the course of the race weekend Silverstone becomes the busiest airport in the country, and the sky is permanently full of aircraft. The scene is reminiscent of a huge beehive as the helicopters form into a continuous line, stretching way off into the distance bringing people and supplies into the circuit. Another orderly line forms up in parallel to the first and takes people away again.

We aren't fortunate enough to be able to leave this way and so after all the banners, equipment and cars have been loaded aboard the transporters we have to wait for the traffic to die down before the trucks and minibuses stand a chance of driving out the paddock and heading back to the factory. The constant stream of traffic can crawl along at less than walking pace for anything up to four or five hours after the end of the race.

Consequently, to pass the time, most of the British based teams organize a barbecue, both for the Race Teams and their factory based staff (who are invited to Silverstone to see the end results of their hard work in action). These individual barbecues have grown over the years to become a traditional event, and have now amalgamated into one big party, used as an excuse to celebrate the halfway-point in the season.

Williams bring in professional barbecue caterers especially for the event, while the Jordan personnel resist the temptation to take the five minute walk back to their factory (located just opposite the Silverstone gates), and instead organize a live band to add to the occasion. This gives Mr Jordan the opportunity to indulge himself in his passion for playing his drum-kit too loudly, and everybody else suffers for his art.

It was well past 10.00 p.m. when we had finally run out of excuses not to attempt to leave the circuit, and it was another hour by the time everybody had been rounded up from the various motorhomes. I eventually got back to Chipping Norton at about the same time as if I'd returned from a race in mainland Europe.

I would like to talk a little about the time penalty and the black flag incident that befell us during the Grand Prix. Like the lap-by-lap details of individual races I'm sure there will be more than ample coverage and discussion of the politics of this year in the 'end-of-season annuals', but they won't be able to tell you what we as team members think about the various decisions that were made.

A few hours after the Grand Prix had finished, while we were packing the equipment away and preparing to join the other teams at the barbecue, Joan and Michael were asked to present themselves before the Stewards of the Meeting. They were asked to explain what had happened during the formation laps and why we hadn't originally complied with the requirements of the time penalty.

Joan told them of the confusion caused by the poor phrasing of the two messages we had received. He apologized for what had happened, but asked the stewards to bear in mind the necessity for clarity of communication. The general consensus was that there had been a complete misunderstanding, and everyone had become confused. Michael explained that he wasn't aware that his actions during the formation laps had breached any rules, and that it certainly wasn't his intention to infringe any regulations.

The stewards retired to discuss and deliberate the situation, and at six o'clock they issued 'Stewards' Decision N°3', the contents of which told of Benetton being fined $25,000 and receiving a reprimand not to transgress the regulations in future. We had been at fault, the officials had been at fault, the resulting confusion had been cleared up, the stewards had fined us accordingly and we had accepted that fine. Justice had been seen to be done.

The whole episode had been a regrettable series of events but the situation had been settled and the matter was closed. Michael appeared very surprised when he had been told about the problems prior to the start of the race and the ensuing confusion that had arisen. He had no idea that he wasn't allowed to sprint ahead and drop back during the formation lap, and although ignorance of the rule is no real defence against his actions it does explain the repetition of them.

The rule itself is a little ambiguous and, like so many of the Formula One regulations it is open to several interpretations. In my opinion the rule that Michael fell foul of was written for an entirely different reason to the one that the stewards took it to mean.

The rule says, 'Any car which fails to maintain starting order during the entire formation lap must start the race behind the last line of the grid.' I believe it was written so that if a car begins to suffer from a misfire or some other problem during the formation lap, then the cars behind it can overtake, and allow the stricken car to drop back through the field, preventing a traffic jam occurring as it chugs around the circuit at 5mph, or even worse, grinds to a standstill.

If there was no facility in the rules to allow others to overtake the stalled car then the entire field would have to stop and wait for it to be recovered, resulting in a situation which would clearly be very impractical. Indeed I'm sure that the fundamental reason for the formation lap's existence is to allow the cars to be given a final 'systems check' prior to the start of the race. The dangers of a misfire or a stalled engine when the lights turn green and the cars are fighting for improved positions are obvious, and without doubt the safest place for a car to be when suffering a misfire is definitely at the back of the grid.

Some people may argue that the purpose of the formation lap is to work the tyres and warm them prior to the actual start of the race, and although I agree that this does occur, the possibility to work the tyres is only an advantage of the formation lap, not the fundamental reason for it.

However, if the rule was to be taken word for word and applied literally, then I believe it ought to have been enforced in the same manner. 'Any car which fails to maintain starting order during the ENTIRE formation lap . . .'

Well, as I have explained, and as the video of the event clearly shows, Michael only broke formation during certain sections of the formation laps and there were large sections of the laps when he remained in the prescribed starting order, in so doing staying inside the structure of the rule (a pedantic argument without doubt, but no more pedantic than the implementation of the rule itself).

Furthermore the rule states that Michael should have started the race from behind the last line of the grid. Following the delayed start due to Coulthard's stalled engine, there was plenty of time to inform Michael and ourselves of this requirement, and the same procedure could have been employed to get Michael's car to the rear of the field as was used for the Williams, yet no action whatsoever was taken to inform us of any breach of the regulations.

Let's forget about the delayed start for a moment and imagine that it never happened. Following the second formation lap there was no delay and I don't know how the officials were to be expected to discover a possible infringement of the rule, collect any evidence of an infringement, make a decision based on that evidence, and if necessary, move Michael's car to the rear of the grid, as the rule decrees they must do, before the Race Director got the event underway.

I simply don't believe there would be enough time, and I believe this adds credence to my previous explanation for the rule's origins. For example, if the rule's purpose was to prevent a car accelerating away and temporarily overtaking another, and, say, the infringement occurred at the bottom of Hanger Straight, then the Race Director would have very little time to be informed of the infringement before the cars returned to the grid.

I don't believe it would be possible for him to rely solely on television monitors to decide if the formation lap had passed without incident, as these can only show a few of the cars at one time. The television may be showing the lead cars while an infringement is occurring at the back, and vice versa.

I'm not accusing anybody of breaking any rules but who knows what the rear of the field was up to when the cameras were following Damon and Michael? As I see it, the only feasible way to inform the Race Director would be for any marshal who saw a possible infringement to 'red flag' the formation lap and allow his companions to carry that signal around the circuit and back to the Race Director. Then an official would have to go off and find the marshal in question and interview him on what he saw occur.

I don't believe that the marshals are there to, or would want to, take the decision to red flag and delay the start of a Grand Prix on the grounds of a possible breach of the rules, and if they did so the ensuing inquiry could delay the restart for a considerable time.

After the second formation lap the cars returned to the grid and formed-up in their correct positions. The official at the rear waved his green flag to signify the last cars were in position with their engines running, and on seeing that everything was in order the Race Director activated the lights and the Grand Prix began.

To my mind that should have been the end of the matter. No harm had been caused to any competitor and no advantage had been lost or gained by any competitor.

The Grand Prix was now underway and after discussing Michael's actions during the formation laps, the race officials decided that there had been a transgression of the rules and that they would have to penalize Michael for his actions. However, since they had missed the opportunity to send Michael to the rear of the grid on the first occasion, and on the second occasion there simply wasn't time to demote him (for reasons I have discussed), they decided to impose a time penalty on him.

Despite its lack of clarity, this was the intention of 'Stewards' Decision N°2', handed to Joan over half an hour into the race. As Benetton were now in possession of the Stewards' Decision it was up to us to act upon it. After several minutes of discussion and checking through our copy of the regulations we came to the conclusion that as no specific section of the regulations had been referred to – and that consequently there were no guidelines for us to follow – then the five seconds in question would simply be added to Michael's race time at the end of the race.

This method of imposing the penalty would require no action from us, and as we hadn't been asked to comply in any way this seemed logical enough. In the regulations there is a section which states that if a driver or team is awarded a time penalty then the team must be notified within fifteen minutes from the time of the transgression.

Joan signed the Stewards' Decision when it was delivered at 2.31 p.m. Because this document never referred to a time penalty, and since it was handed to us outside the 15 minute notification period, the time penalty section of the rule book was dismissed. I suppose it could be said in the officials' defence that the rule book doesn't actually state that if the notification is delivered later than 15 minutes the matter shall be forgotten. It simply states that the team must be notified within 15 minutes, full stop. Certainly the implication is there but it doesn't actually say so. If it doesn't mean that, however, what does it mean? If it means that the time penalty *can* still be imposed after fifteen minutes then why bother to state a time limit in the first place? Very curious. Very ambiguous!

As I mentioned earlier, with the issue of the 'Stewards' Decision N°3' we believed that the situation had been dealt with and that the matter was closed. However, a few days after the race we were notified by the FIA that following close examination of the race report by the FIA Observer present at the British Grand Prix, Benetton Formula Ltd and Michael Schumacher would be expected to appear before the World Motor Sport Council at a specially convened meeting in Paris on July 26th.

Flavio, Joan, Michael and our lawyers all attended the meeting in Paris, where they explained to Max Mosley and the World Council members the misunderstanding over the formation lap, the misunderstanding over the Stewards' Decision and the agreement with the Race Director to comply with the time penalty as soon as they knew about it. But none of this seemed to interest the World Council. What concerned them was Michael's disregard for the black flag. All the circumstances and confusion that led to the showing of it were irrelevant in their eyes. Michael had not responded to the black flag, and they wanted to know why.

We were not informed that Michael was to be shown the black flag and as I mentioned earlier it was only by chance that Joan happened to notice it when he had gone to find the Race Director. It is important to remember that the officials do not notify the team of their decision to show the black flag to a driver (that communication is strictly between the FIA and the driver concerned).

We were unaware of the flag, and consequently Michael received no radio message concerning the flag. Michael told the World Council that he couldn't act on the black flag for the simple reason that he didn't see it.

The last time I can remember anybody being shown the black flag was during the 1989 Portuguese Grand Prix at Estoril. Nigel Mansell had reversed his Ferrari in the pit lane, and in so doing had broken the appropriate rule. His penalty was to be shown the black flag and be disqualified from the race. For lap after lap he was shown the black flag and lap after lap he appeared to take no notice of it. He later collided with Ayrton's McLaren and both of them spun out of the race. Nigel later said that he couldn't act on the black flag because he didn't see it!

On both occasions, Nigel and Michael were racing at full speed and dicing for positions with other cars. Both had lost time, Nigel in his poor pit stop, Michael because of his believed add-on penalty, and both were concentrating on making up that time. I doubt very much that either of them would have noticed a lone flag – no matter what colour – held in a position they wouldn't normally look at, and which due to their speed would only be visible for a fraction of a second each lap.

I have never driven a Formula One car, I wouldn't deem myself able to do so, certainly not at racing speeds, only inches away from the car in front. I have, though, seen onboard camera footage of many drivers in action, as they constantly fight with the car and force it to go where they want it to go: left, right, hard on the brakes, throttle, right, left, avoid a spinning car, brake, throttle and so on.

I have no doubt whatsoever in believing that both Nigel and Michael failed to see the black flag. My argument is that the message that the black flag communicates is too important to be announced in such a quiet voice. The marshals posted around the perimeter of the circuit should each be issued with a black flag and a set of car numbers so that the message could be displayed to the relevant driver during his entire time on the circuit.

The system could be operated in exactly the same way as the red flags are displayed, the message passed on from station to station. The team should also be informed of the decision to black-flag the driver, and he could then be informed over the radio, a direct audible link from the team to the car.

But, at the end of the day, the World Council did not accept Nigel's defence in 1989, and it wouldn't accept Michael's identical defence five years later.

In '89, Ferrari were subsequently fined $50,000 and Nigel was banned from participating in the next race. When the World Council announced their verdict on Benetton we became aware of the incredibly steep inflation rate of Formula One.

Benetton was fined $500,000, Michael was disqualified from the Silverstone results and banned from taking part in the following two Grands Prix. There were also penalties handed out to the race officials. The Clerk of the Course at Silverstone had his licence suspended for a year, and Roland Bruynseraede was banned for life as Race Director (although his services were retained by the FIA in the reduced capacities of Official Starter and Safety Delegate).

These were stiff penalties, without doubt, particularly in light of the fact that the World Council's decision to punish the race officials seemed a clear indication that mistakes had occurred on all sides. There were more fines too. At the end of the San Marino Grand Prix, the FIA took away the various electronic control boxes, for the engine and gearbox management systems, of the first three cars to finish the race. These were Michael's B194, Nicola Larini's Ferrari and Mika Hakkinen's McLaren. This was to be the first of a series of random inspections by the FIA to check that none of the constructors had been using any of the banned 'driver aids', following the change to the regulations at the end of '93.

After an initial inspection of the boxes, the FIA asked Benetton, McLaren and Ferrari to supply the 'source codes' for their respective control boxes. The source codes allow the information stored inside the control boxes to be deciphered and analyzed, and all three teams agreed to supply the FIA with their codes. Ferrari's systems are produced by Fiat (for many years their parent company) and so their source codes were made available with the minimum of problems.

However, it was impossible for McLaren and Benetton to supply the codes immediately, as both teams have commercial partners that they needed to seek permission from. There are millions of dollars worth of technical development invested in the engine management systems, technology which feeds directly back into the very lucrative road car industry.

Despite everyone wanting to co-operate with the FIA, I'm sure all three teams were anxious to reveal that technology to as few 'outsiders' as possible. Remember, that when talking about Fiat, Ford, and Peugeot, we are talking about three of the biggest car manufactures in the world. The FIA had set a date for delivery.

Both teams reached agreement with their partners, and supplied their codes, but, unfortunately, not before the required time. A fine of $100,000 was handed out to both McLaren and Benetton for the delay in supplying the codes.

When the results of the hearing were announced, they sent shock waves around the sporting world, and the decision to ban Michael from the forthcoming race nearly brought civil unrest to at least one European country. The next event in the World Championship was the German Grand Prix at Hockenheim, Michael's home race!

The very idea that the tens-of-thousands of German fans were going to be denied the chance of seeing their potential World Champion compete in their homeland simply didn't seem possible. The decision of the World Council was made public immediately after the hearing on Tuesday afternoon, but this was only two clear days before the first practice session would be flagged underway.

By the time the news broke, the campsites in and around the forests close to the Hockenheim circuit had already begun to fill up. People had taken their holidays to coincide with the Grand Prix weekend, and thousands of fans had arrived early to vie with each other for the best and closest campsites to the circuit.

The German people are renowned for their love of the outdoor life, outdoor cooking and, particularly, their passion for beer. Most of the small towns and villages in the area had organized week-long festivals in large marquees that had been erected in any suitable nearby space. Inside these tents are long trestle tables where people sit in rows with friends and strangers alike.

They sit, they chat, they make new friends, they eat, they drink, they sing, they drink some more, and sing even louder. This had all generated a tremendous party atmosphere, and everybody was in high spirits, not just through the beer, but with the excitement and anticipation of the forthcoming race.

Germany has always had a long and distinguished association with motor sport, and their expertise in mechanical engineering is legendary, but the one thing they have never been able to achieve is their own Formula One World Champion. Now the realization of that dream was looking increasingly likely and, as the season progressed, Michael's points tally had been increasing with every race.

The news that the World Council had banned Michael from taking part in Hockenheim had been a devastating blow to the German people, and I imagine that the FIA office in Paris had been bombarded with phone calls pleading for them to reconsider their verdict and allow Michael to race. But their pleas were in vain – no amount of irate and distressed communication would sway the decision of the World Council.

Some of the fans had decided on a more direct and potentially very dangerous action by building huge piles of logs and branches around the perimeter of the track. They threatened to set them alight and destroy the circuit, forcing the Grand Prix to be cancelled altogether.

Banners were made from old sheets and sprayed with the message 'NO SCHUMACHER NO RACE'. The police and fire department demolished the bonfires, only to find them rebuilt the following day. They removed them in the morning, and they reappeared in the afternoon. Something had to be done before the situation got out of control.

There was only one way that Michael would be allowed to race. That was for Benetton to appeal against the decision of the World Council, and have the Silverstone incident reheard at a later date. This would allow Michael to race under appeal and, temporarily, his two race ban would be suspended.

However, despite this course of action proving very popular with Michael's fans it could prove very costly for us to pursue. Like Irvine's appeal following the Brazilian Grand Prix it might result in an even stiffer penalty being imposed upon us, and after the appeal Michael could be banned for three or even more races!

There was also another consideration to bear in mind: the circuit wouldn't suit our chassis half as much as our opposition's. The Hockenheim ring consists of a brief and winding stadium section, joined together by two very long straights, and although each stretch is partially broken up by a chicane the circuit is still extremely fast. It is an all-out power circuit, and as a rule of thumb it is normally the team with the most horsepower that crosses the line first. Over the past few years the first place honours at Hockenheim have been shared between the mighty and dominant McLaren-Hondas and the Williams-Renaults.

Honda withdrew its direct involvement in Formula One at the end of '92, but Renault, of course, is still very much involved, although in recent months even they have had to show due respect to the incredible power being produced by the latest Ferrari engines.

If there was any circuit where the 412 T1 should come into its own it would be here, where the Ferrari's blistering straight line performance should easily compensate for any deficit in its handling. We knew we would have to concede speed and lap times at Hockenheim, and that despite Michael's massive support it would be optimistic of us to expect to win. Purely from a performance point of view if Michael had to sit out for two races then Hockenheim would be an ideal venue to avoid.

The debate on whether Benetton should appeal continued without break for the next two days. On Thursday morning the alarm began its irritating beeping routine at 4.00 a.m., Judd commenced her irritating nudging routine five minutes later and the cottage began to smell of freshly ground coffee beans five minutes after that.

A coffee, a shower, a second coffee. Start the investigation to find the car keys. End the investigation to find the car keys, after remembering I have put them on top of my briefcase (so I wouldn't lose them), and just enough time for a final coffee before leaving home to catch the coach at 5.00 a.m.

'Good luck for the race, see you on Sunday night,' I called up the stairs.

'Turn the light off . . . and don't slam the door.'

'May the best team win!'

'Turn the light off!' Judd reminded me from underneath the quilt. I closed the door behind me and set off into the darkness. I don't know if it's possible for the colour of bedroom curtains to display emotion, but I'm sure I saw mine change from an annoyed translucent floral print to an angry jet-black as I drove out the lane and up the hill towards the factory.

There were several reporters waiting for us at Heathrow, all wanting to know more or less the same thing: 'Will Benetton appeal?', 'Will Schumacher race in Germany, or not?' and 'Does this mean Damon will win the Championship?'

We still had no idea whether Benetton or Michael had appealed, and we wouldn't find out until we arrived at the circuit, so apart from 'No idea. No idea,' and 'I certainly hope not,' we did not have an awful lot of information for them.

As we exited the customs hall at Stuttgart International we were faced with ten times the number of reporters that had been waiting for us in England. The majority of questions were fired at us in German, and as, unfortunately, I only speak English and a smattering of French, I had no idea what the reporters were asking.

I took a guess and when a microphone was pushed towards me I told them 'No idea', 'No idea', 'I certainly hope not'. This seemed to appease them, and eventually they walked off, nodding, scribbling into books, and comparing notes.

We sat and waited outside the terminal while Dave, Paul and Max (our minibus drivers) sorted out the rental contracts and went off to collect the transport. The weather in Germany was red hot, and as the minibuses didn't have air-conditioning we were pleased that the drive to the circuit took us along the autobahn, so we could benefit from the breeze blowing through the open windows.

After an hour or so we turned off the motorway and approached the circuit gates, slowing to a complete standstill and queuing up as security guards checked vehicle passes. Crowds of people lined the sides of the road, watching to see who was arriving. They stared through the windows of the minibuses and cars ahead of us, occasionally waving at the occupants and asking for auto-graphs if they recognized a driver's face, or turning away uninterested if they didn't. As we drew nearer to the gate an enormous man, dressed only in shorts and carrying a German flag, and sporting the sort of well-developed stomach only the most dedicated beer enthusiast can, walked towards us. He wiped the window clean and peered inside. When he noticed the Benetton Formula crest on our blazers his mouth fell open in surprise.

He pressed his face to the glass to get a better look, his suspicions were con-firmed when he noticed the 'Flying Colors' logo on our luggage stowed in the back. He tapped on the window. 'Benetton?' he asked. We didn't have time to answer before his question had changed to an exclamation: 'Benetton!' he called 'Benetton!!' His cry had an immediate effect on the people around him, and within seconds we were surrounded by cheering people, waving Schumacher flags, banging on the minibuses and chanting, 'SCHU-ME! SCHU-ME! SCHU-ME! SCHU-ME!' They obviously assumed that as the team had arrived Michael would be racing. We all thought it safer not to point out to the rapidly multiplying throng that it still wasn't certain that we would appeal, and there was a fair chance that J.J. might be driving Michael's car instead.

We waved back and continued on to the sanctuary of the paddock as quick-ly as possible. As we drove through the gates I wondered what sort of welcome lay in store for the Williams chaps when the big man and his impressive waistline wiped the dust from their windows and squinted inside to see who else had arrived.

The announcement the world had been waiting for was made later that afternoon. Benetton Formula and Michael Schumacher had decided to appeal against the decisions of the World Council. Consequently Michael Schumacher would be driving car number five in the 1994 German Grand Prix.

Both Flavio and Michael explained that the agreement to appeal had been made after long hours of debate, and that the final decision had rested with Michael. Benetton would support him in whatever he decided. Michael is a concentrated and deep-thinking person. He knew that if he decided to race, the pressure on him to succeed would be immense.

He knew that Ferrari would be a very powerful force here and that it would be his driving ability and not the performance of the B194 that would be the deciding factor in Sunday's race. He had thought long and hard before making his mind up. It wasn't fair, he told the press, to penalize the thousands of fans that had come to Hockenheim, and the millions of people who couldn't afford to come, but would nevertheless be glued to the radio and TV at home. He asked for the fans at the circuit to give him as much support as possible. 'I'll need it!' he said. The police and fire department must have breathed a huge sigh of relief at the news, and they began to dismantle the wood piles for the last time. They might now be able to have Sunday off, put their feet up and watch the Grand Prix at home, maybe even have a beer or two.

We were working on the cars in the pit lane garages when the news of the appeal was announced, and despite not actually being present at the press conference we knew Michael had decided to appeal by the sudden and dramatic increase in noise from the campsites, and the continuous shrieks from thousands of air horns.

Now, just to assist the people who may want to use this book for reference purposes, the chassis issue for Hockenheim remained the same as for Silverstone: 01, the emergency spare chassis; 04, for Jos; 05, for Michael and 06, the spare car.

Be careful! I've already seen several errors printed in various magazines and papers when references to our chassis numbers and driver allocation have been made. The next stage of the new safety measures had come into effect for this race. In an attempt to further reduce downforce it had been decided to compel the teams to lift the ride-height of their cars by the addition of a ten millimetre spacer that would be bolted to the flat underside of the floor. This would result in a 'stepped bottomed' car, allowing air free access to the underside.

The basic principle is that the lower we can run the car to the ground the less air can pass beneath, resulting in a 'low-pressure' area being produced below the car, and in relative terms this increases the pressure produced by the wings and bodywork above. The net result of this is that the car is pushed to the ground with greater force than would otherwise prove possible, enabling the drivers to corner at greater speeds.

The spacer would greatly increase air volume beneath the car, and so even out the pressures, slow the car's cornering ability, and hence provide a reduction in speed.

The spacer itself takes the form of a 30 centimetre wide piece of laminated, marine ply-wood, known as 'Jabroc'. It's just over ten millimetres thick, and when bolted to the car it runs the entire length of the floor. The Jabroc spacer is quite literally a plank of wood, and instantly became known as 'the plank'.

To me it seems an odd thing to be bolted to a Grand Prix car and looks completely out of place on our current state-of-the-art Formula One machinery. Anyway we'll talk more about the plank later. In Belgium this bizarre new arrival was to become the most controversial piece of plywood in the history of motor sport.

We were correct in our predictions of Ferrari's performance during qualifying, and by the end of Saturday's sessions they had secured first and second positions on the grid, Berger on pole with a time of 1m43.582s, Alesi 0.4 sec behind him. Damon had managed the third quickest time and Michael was fourth, just over 0.2 sec adrift of the FW16.

Michael's fans hadn't disappointed him in their support during Friday and Saturday. Every time he took to the circuit the grandstands became a swarm of German and Benetton flags, and as Michael made his way around the track his progress was followed by signal flares fired one after another from the stands.

It was an incredible display of support and encouragement for their potential Champion. Michael hadn't disappointed them either, he had driven the B194 to the absolute limit of his ability, throwing the car into the corners with great courage. He knew that Ferrari and Williams would out-drag him on the straights, but he made every possible effort to make up that time through the stadium section.

It is sometimes difficult for us to distinguish between the two Benettons when they are on the circuit. Both of the drivers' helmet designs are fairly similar and despite Michael's car having identification flashes, when they drive around the final corner, the sun reflecting off the bodywork, and the heat-haze shimmering on the track, it is easy to mistake one for the other.

It is important not to become confused in case Jon shows Jos the wrong pitboard or I show mine to Michael. However, as Jon and I leant over the pit wall it soon became very obvious as to which Benetton was which. We were forewarned of Michael's imminent arrival as soon as he appeared in the stadium section of the circuit.

The German fans went wild, flags waved, air-horns sounded, and fireworks and flares were set off. This continued as Michael came into sight on the start/finish straight and carried on until he disappeared into the forest section and was out of sight. On the other hand, when Jos drove through the stadium, rounded the final corner and drove down the straight it was possible to hear a pin drop! The grandstands remained silent. Not one flare was ignited nor a single flag waved (not even the unbiased Benetton flags).

I could almost sense Jos looking from side to side, wondering what he had done wrong. But the simple fact was that he just wasn't Michael and if it wasn't Michael driving past, the fans had no interest. Well, he hadn't done anything particularly wrong apart from spinning off in 04 during the first practice, and doing exactly the same thing in 05 during the afternoon. Jos had to borrow Michael's car during Friday's qualifying, as the damage to 04 had been too extensive for us to rectify before qualifying.

He had been handed 05 only after Michael had set his qualifying time, but, unfortunately, Jos had spun off during his first flying lap, and so finished Friday with a recorded lap time of over forty minutes duration. Overnight he was provisionally placed 28th and last, and since only the top 26 cars actually get to start the race we all hoped for better things on Saturday.

I think the effect of the reduced downforce had caught Jos off guard a little, but his morning spin was caused by oil dropped on the circuit following a Ferrari engine blow up. Thankfully things had gone better on Saturday and we finished up nineteenth on the grid. I think the main reason for this fairly low grid position was that Jos had been told to take it steady, and make certain that we qualified the car.

I wouldn't have thought it possible for Michael's support to have increased, but when the warm-up session was flagged under way the next morning there seemed to be even more flags waving and more flares in the sky than during the previous two days put together.

Over 150,000 fanatical fans had descended on Hockenheim, and every one of them cheered Michael on his way around the circuit. The support paid dividends, and by the end of the session Michael had put in the quickest lap of the morning. As I have said before, the warm-up isn't really a test of speed, but it does give a good idea of the confidence of the driver and the agility of the chassis in race trim.

It was apparent that Michael and his car were operating in perfect unison. Gerhard's Ferrari was less than a tenth of a second behind Michael's time, and Damon was only a fraction slower. It promised to be a very exciting race. Jos, like Michael, had reported that his car felt good, and although his lap times were nowhere as quick as his team mate's he was feeling more confident about the car's handling with every completed lap.

After the session we pulled the cars back inside and started the final checks before the Grand Prix itself would began at 2.00 p.m. An hour earlier we pulled our overalls and boots on, and at 1.30 the cars were dispatched to the grid. All was well and the only complaint was about how hot it was!

When the cars were released into their formation lap Joan reminded both Jos and Michael to remain behind the car in front, and I would imagine that every team manager in the pit lane did exactly the same with their drivers. As expected, all 26 cars paraded around the circuit together, nobody daring to budge an inch out of formation.

The lights turned green and the race was under way, but within seconds of the start several of the mid-field runners became tangled together as they fought for position on the run down to the first corner. Both the Minardis, both Jordans, Blundell's Tyrrell, Hakkinen's McLaren – in fact, a total of ten cars – were out of the race before the Grand Prix was even 20 seconds old!

Thankfully, none of the drivers were hurt, and they were all able to walk back to the pits unaided. Damon's car had also sustained damage. He managed to keep going but was forced to take to the pits for repairs.

Unfortunately, Coulthard had suffered a similar fate and both pitted at the same time – one with suspension damage, one for a new nose – resulting in a traffic jam in the Williams pits. Judging by the mechanics' body-language I doubted this was the sort of start to the race they had had in mind.

Alesi's Ferrari had apparently encountered electrical problems as he chased after his team mate down the first long straight, so he pulled off the circuit and became the 11th retirement of the opening lap. Initially it looked as though the race would be red-flagged, but the marshals managed to clear the debris from the racing line before the cars reappeared to begin their second lap. Both B194s managed to avoid trouble, the race continued and we gathered around the monitors to watch the opening laps, pleased to be in the shade of the garage and out of the sun's heat.

With Alesi out of the race, Damon in the pits and all the confusion and carnage behind them, the fight for the lead became a battle between Michael and Gerhard, and much to the delight of the crowd, and ourselves, the Benetton was closing on the rear of the Ferrari. For lap after lap the two cars screamed around the circuit only inches apart. Gerhard managed to pull away slightly on the straights, but Michael was all over the Ferrari through the stadium section.

On lap twelve Ross decided to put a temporary halt to the duel. Our cars would soon need refuelling, and after conferring with the engineers Pat radioed to Michael to come in for his first pit stop.

Ross turned towards us and pressed his transmit button, 'OK chaps, this is a Schumacher stop. I repeat this is a Schumacher stop. Let's be ready for him.'

We got into position, I heard the air guns being tried and gave the rear jack an almost involuntary final check. Michael's new tyres were removed from their blankets and carried outside. Simon heaved the fuel hose of the 'Schumacher rig' over his shoulder.

Then Pat's voice was on the radio: 'Forty seconds', then a little later, 'Ten seconds,' and finally, 'He's in the pit lane'. Michael charged towards us and braked to a standstill in perfect position, the main-plane of the front wing just nudging onto the front jack. Simon connected the fuel hose to the filler valve, and Ken and I lifted the car. There was a flurry of activity as the wheels were removed, and instantly the fresh tyres replaced them. I had a quick glance towards the front just in case they had encountered any problems, at the same time I heard the rear wheel nuts being driven home, the speed and note of the air-guns slowing to indicate the nuts were tight.

After the fuel had been delivered, Simon pulled at the hose to release it from the car, it didn't free itself at first and he had to have a couple of attempts before it finally uncoupled. A quick glance left and right to confirm that the wheels had been changed, and simultaneously Ken and I released the car off the jacks.

It dropped to the ground and back into Michael's control. He had increased the engine revs and selected first gear while the car was still in the air, the sound of the Ford ZR V8 rose to a deafening howl, and as soon as Ken jumped back, and Mick removed the BRAKES ON sign he was off, the new tyres squealing down the pit lane. Without wasting a fraction of a second Michael was back in the race, charging around the circuit in pursuit of Gerhard's Ferrari.

Two laps later Ross was on the radio again. 'OK chaps, this is a Verstappen stop. This is a Verstappen stop. He'll be in at the end of the next lap.' Jos's tyres were unwrapped and carried outside. Another check of the jacks and air-guns, the 'Verstappen rig' hose was lifted up and we were ready.

'Ten seconds,' Christian told us. Jos peeled off the circuit. 'He's in the pit lane now.' Jos shot into the pit, I ran in behind and threw the jack into position. As soon as Simon had the fuel-hose on, Ken and I lifted the car. I heard the machine-gun-like clatter of the air-guns as the wheel nuts were removed. I glanced to the front of the car to check on their progress, but my attention was caught by something else: Simon was struggling with the hose, it didn't look as though it was connected properly, the angle of the nozzle seemed too steep for it to slide onto the filler valve. Simon tugged at the hose to try and reposition it, but the nozzle and valve had become jammed. He took his right hand off the nozzle and tried to move it further down the hose to obtain better leverage.

As he did so, however, fuel sprayed out between the nozzle and filler valve. We had been told that this couldn't happen, that it was impossible for fuel to flow unless the nozzle was fully engaged, and that the valve would close before the nozzle was disconnected. Well, the impossible had just occurred, and fuel from the rig was spraying all over the car, over Jos and ourselves.

The next few seconds seemed to last for an age, and events appeared to unfold in slow-motion. On seeing the fuel spraying into the air my initial reaction was disbelief: I thought it must be water that someone was splashing on us by mistake, that one of the marshals had set off an extinguisher in error.

A fraction later I focused on where the spray was coming from and I realized what was happening. My next thought was relief that it hadn't instantly erupted, my mind recalling a childhood memory of when I had thrown a few drops of paint brush cleaner on to our coalfire. Being only five or six years old the instantaneous flash and roar of flame had scared me, and the image has remained with me ever since.

Most people, of course, were looking at the wheels they were changing, and hadn't seen the fuel spraying from the nozzle. The fuel washed over the bodywork and onto our overalls. As people realized what had happened they began to jump back from the car.

We still had the car on the jacks and I didn't want to let it down as I had no idea whether the wheel nuts were tight or not. I don't blame anyone for standing clear of the car, it was an instinctive reaction, and without doubt the correct thing to do. The only reason I stayed with the rear jack was because I held it at full arm's stretch and aided by the length of the handle I had managed to get about six feet away from the rear wing.

The fuel had now stopped spraying, and some people had arrived at the same conclusion as myself, and when after a moment or two the fuel hadn't caught fire they moved back in towards the car in an attempt to finish changing the wheels. They were obviously concerned that if Ken and I let the car down then Jos would possibly try and drive off. It was at this precise moment, about two seconds after the fuel spray, that it finally ignited.

My vision of the car was suddenly replaced by a bright light as a sea of white flame erupted out of the fuel. It washed over and engulfed the car in an enormous fireball. At the same time there was a loud rushing noise similar to the air movement in an underground station just before the train arrives.

A fraction later I felt the heat of the burning fuel through my gloves, I remember thinking that it didn't seem as intense as I had expected, it was hot but not painfully so. The white light changed to bright yellow, then orange. Shapes began to form, and I could once again focus on the scene in front of me.

My gloves and overalls had caught fire, but there was no shock or panic at this stage, I suppose it was too soon for that, I just thought the whole situation seemed very odd. The flames burning on my outstretched arms reminded me of Dali's 'Burning Giraffes'!

I was told later that in times of danger and when the body needs to fight for survival it is normal for the mind to try and distract itself from panic. The body's reactions in a situation of self preservation dramatically increase, and the mind compensates for this by making time appear to slow down.

I remember thinking, 'OK, you're alive. You're on fire but at least you're alive. You ought to think about putting yourself out. Try rolling on the floor, that should do it.'

I can't remember letting go of the rear jack, it could be that the force of the fire knocked me over, but I don't think so. My next memory is of rolling over and over on the ground. Every time I was facing skyward I saw flames coming from my overalls and thought that I'd better keep rolling.

My progress was stopped, and I felt people jumping on me and hitting the flames out. I had been heading towards the McLaren pit, and had been met halfway by their mechanics as they had started to run towards us to help.

'It's OK, Steve, you're out!' I heard someone say.

'Get my gloves off quick! My hands are burning!'

The heat was now intense – my hands felt as though they had been plunged into boiling water. 'Get these bloody gloves off!' I yelled again. The McLaren mechanics grabbed my arms and began pulling and tugging at the gloves. I was being dragged along the ground in their urgency to help, but that was of no consequence, as all I wanted was to be rid of that intense heat, and at last they came off. I opened my eyes and saw the gloves smouldering on the ground in front of me.

'It's OK, Steve, you're fine,' a voice reassured me. I was breathing in short, sharp gasps – the realization of what had just happened was beginning to sink in and the slow motion effect of instinct and survival had worn off.

I looked at my hands, expecting to see them burnt and blistered, but apart from looking rather red, and the hair being singed off the back of them, they were fine. I lay on the floor for a few seconds letting my breathing slowly come back to normal.

'OK Steve?' someone asked. I took a couple of deep breaths, sat up and pulled my balaclava off. 'Yes, I think so', I replied. I looked in disbelief at my scorched sleeves and smoking gloves.

The Sparco clothing had done an incredible job. Certainly without the protection they had provided, many of us would have been critically injured or killed. I had escaped relatively unscathed. Some of us, however, hadn't been so lucky.

I got to my feet and walked towards the car. The fire had been put out and a cloud of white extinguisher powder was beginning to settle on the ground. Most of the paintwork had blistered in the heat and what wasn't blistered was either blackened or covered in white powder.

This was all of no importance, of course, the main thing was that the cockpit was empty. I couldn't see Jos anywhere, but the mere fact he was out of the car was a good sign. Inside the garage the scene was reminiscent of the aftermath of battle. Tools and equipment were strewn everywhere; several people were lying on the ground, while others were still trying to pull their smouldering overalls off.

A voice at the back of the garage was shouting to the marshals, 'Medics! Quick!' I saw Dave being carried off down the pit lane on a stretcher, and a few minutes later I heard the first of several helicopters chopping their way through the air as they evacuated the injured to the Hockenheim hospital.

Dave, Simon, Wayne, Jakey, Ken and Paul Seaby had all been taken for treatment. Jakey and Ken hadn't been burnt (although both of them had their overalls set alight by the burning fuel), but their eyes were streaming, and both had developed a serious cough after inhaling the white extinguisher powder that the marshals had released onto the car. Out of the others it was Simon who had suffered the worst. Because he is the closest to the fuel-hose, he wears a full-face helmet, but unfortunately the fuel had managed to run down the inside of his visor and had caught fire after it was inside the helmet. Consequently he had received some fairly serious burns to his face.

Mick came over and asked how I was. I inquired about Jos. He too had received some burns to the face as, like Simon, the fuel had run down inside his helmet and then ignited. He had panicked slightly, and forgotten to remove the steering wheel before trying to climb out.

It had been Greg's quick response to the fire that had helped him. As soon as the fire had started, Greg had discharged our big 20 kilogramme halon extinguisher, which he kept playing over the flames, in and around the cockpit area until the fire was out.

It must have been absolutely terrifying for Jos to have been strapped inside the middle of it all, but after the flames had gone he managed to climb out unaided, and had walked off to the motor home to escape from the media.

While all this was happening Michael was still in the race, of course, and it wouldn't be long before he would need to come in for his second pit stop. However, it would have proved impossible for us to have worked on the car. We had lost six men, and most of us that were left had received some sort of injury, either from the fire itself, or from tripping over pit equipment in desperation to get away from it.

In the end it was the hand of fate that finally solved the predicament for us. Michael's engine suddenly emitted a burst of smoke, it started to misfire and with the engine coughing and spluttering he slowly drove around the circuit, back into the pit lane and retired from the race.

Michael sat in the car for a few seconds, bitterly disappointed that his race should end this way. He eventually climbed out and walked to the back of the garage, surprised at the state of Jos's car, and visibly shocked as he became aware of what had occurred.

Joan, Pat and Christian in France.

Michael and Benetton Technical Director Ross Brawn.

Frank Dernie (left) talking with Tom Walkinshaw and Jos.

Chassis 04 on the grid in France, having been built into Jos's race car following the brief life of 07.

All the teams put their bodywork in front of the garages.

Bernie Ecclestone chats with Flavio.

Michael decides to try the car in the rain at Spa. I decide to have another coffee.

Jos leads Gerhard around Spa.

Michael looking so happy and relieved to have won the Belgian Grand Prix –
a few hours later the victory was snatched away.

Michael Schumacher.

The crowd at Hockenheim.

German flags signal a sea of support.

The ill-fated pitstop at Hockenheim. The fuel has sprayed all over us, Jos and chassis 04.

And then the fuel ignited.

Gerhard went on to win the race, adding a long awaited victory and another ten points to Ferrari's tally, giving them a total of 52. Both the FW16s failed to score. Coulthard had been forced to retire with an electrical fault, and Hill, despite making it to the end had finished a lap down in eighth. That left Williams unchanged with a total of 43.

Bearing in mind the six points that had been taken off us following the Silverstone race, Benetton had a total of 67. We were still leading the Constructors' Championship, but with a greatly reduced margin of only 15 points.

So the German Grand Prix and the month of July came to a close.

Chipping Norton was still and quiet as I drove home in the early hours, and apart from the two permanently smiling chaps and their hand-painted Kebab van, the whole town was asleep. It wouldn't be long before I was asleep too.

The warmth of the bed soon had the desired effect, and my eyes grew very heavy. One by one I slowly recalled the events of the day, and as my mind released the thoughts and began to relax I gently started to drift off.

My final thought was of the burnt car, the significance of it had only just connected with me. Chassis 04 had struck again!

# AUGUST

The first of August was a day of rest. The trucks wouldn't be back in the country until Monday night, which gave the rest of the team the day off. I spent my time writing 'July', watching the video of the Hockenheim race and replaying the ill-fated pit stop, frame by frame, in an attempt to analyse what had happened, and how different people had reacted.

The first time I saw it on TV I was surprised at how dramatic the fire had been. I had no idea at the time how high the flames had risen. The Paddock Club, the first class corporate hospitality area, is directly above the pit lane garages at Hockenheim. The spectators had been very lucky not to have been seriously injured.

In the morning I strolled up the hill to the newsagent. The amount of press coverage the fire had received was incredible. Not just the back pages either, but splashed across the front of every local and national newspaper was the story of the 'HOCKENHEIM HORROR' the 'PIT LANE TERROR' and even 'THE IGNITED COLOURS OF BENETTON'. The fire had generated more media interest than if a 747 had crashed, killing everyone on board.

The telephone was forced to work overtime as friends called to see if I had survived in one piece. I was astonished at how many people remembered me from when I had lived in Loughborough, and it was good to hear from them. Initially the conversation centred around Grand Prix racing, and they wanted to hear all about the fire, of course, but after a few minutes I managed to change the topic to the subject of mutual acquaintances and what they had been up to. It made a pleasant change to catch up on all the local news.

It's sometimes difficult to explain to our friends that Formula One takes up so much of our lives that it becomes near impossible to make plans to meet up for dinner, go out to the cinema, or even get together for a quick beer. It's frustrating to have to say 'Sorry, but I'm afraid I won't be able to make it!' over and over again, even when the proposed date may be three or four months off.

People, and I don't blame them, simply can't accept how much time this profession consumes. After all, to the majority of the world we only appear to actually work for six seconds every two weeks. Well, that assumption is probably quite exaggerated, but several people have asked me if the teams fly out to the races on the Sunday morning.

Other familiar remarks include 'Surely you can't make ends meet by working just two days a month! You must have another job to support you in between races?' and 'What do you do during the Winter? If you have all that time off between November and March how come we never see you?' and 'I didn't know Benetton made cars, don't you have to buy them from somewhere?'

Although without doubt, these questions are bizarre, it's quite fun to see how some people view our profession. Paul Seaby called me in the evening. He and most of the others had been released from hospital and they had flown back to England during the course of the morning. Simon, however, had been kept in for further treatment, and it would be a few more days before he would be able to rejoin us.

At 8.30 the following morning we were back at the factory to begin the rebuild, and prepare the cars for round ten of the World Championship, the Hungarian Grand Prix, held just outside the magnificent and historic city of Budapest.

Because of the length of the road journey to Hungary, and the need to ensure that they would arrive in time, our trucks would have to leave for Dover no later than Saturday afternoon. Silverstone had been booked for the shakedown on Saturday morning, and so this left four days in which to complete the 'turnaround'. Not very long, but providing things went to plan, we would be ready without the need to work extra long hours.

However, there was a lot to do and we would all be kept busy. Max, Ken, and Jon had a new car to build. The composite department had finished the next new chassis, and with the arrival of 08 the decision had been made to halt production of the B194. Grand Prix car collectors take note, if you ever see a 'B194-09' coming up for auction, beware, it isn't one of ours!

Chassis 05 took over the role of Emergency Spare, and chassis 01 was returned to the Test Team (with many thanks for the loan of it, and even more thanks that we hadn't needed to use it). Chassis 06 remained the spare car. Meanwhile, 04 had been given a comprehensive check-over following Hockenheim.

The fire had resulted in only minor damage to the actual chassis. It had been the car's bodywork and paintwork that had submitted and finally succumbed to the heat of the burning fuel. And so, denied the opportunity to at last be rid of the wretched thing, we had no choice but to strip the car, remove the gearbox and suspension, and send everything into Sub-Assembly to be 'crack-checked'.

The fire had alarmed everyone involved with the sport, and had frightened most of the drivers and mechanics alike, from all of the Formula One teams. The main worry was that if it had happened once, then it could happen again. We had only lost about three litres of fuel before Simon had pulled the nozzle back from the car, and the valve had sealed again. The potential disaster that could result with 150-litres of fuel spraying into the air doesn't bear thinking about. Everybody in the pit lane was keen to get to the bottom of the problem. On Tuesday, the rig manufacture Intertechnique, together with Benetton, and an independent body specializing in accident causes, the Accident and Failure Technical Analysis Company (AFTA) slowly dismantled the rig and began to investigate the reason for what had happened.

Each component of the car's refuelling valve and the rig's nozzle was methodically studied, measured and microscopically scrutinized. AFTA asked to see Intertechnique's assembly drawings, so they could cross-check the size and tolerance of the various components against the dimensions that the drawings called for. However, Intertechnique wouldn't agree to this, claiming 'confidentiality of design' and after everything had been carefully examined Intertechnique decided to take the valve assemblies back with them to France, where they would compile their report and send a copy of it to the FIA.

The most puzzling thing, and without doubt the aspect that worried us most, was how the fuel had managed to flow through the nozzle before it had been fully engaged onto the car. As I said before, we had been told that this was impossible, but that reassurance was now somewhat redundant. The report by AFTA pointed out that it is possible for the nozzle to be misaligned when attempting to locate it onto the car, and that there is no real 'lock-on' device built into the nozzle assembly, it is only the action of the man pushing the nozzle onto the car's valve that keeps the couplings mated.

The fuel valve in the nozzle should only open once the nozzle and car valve are coupled together, and the fuel valve should close again as soon as they become uncoupled. I believe the accident was caused by the fuel valve in the nozzle opening by fluke chance when the nozzle and car valve had become misaligned and jammed together.

Then, as Simon moved his arm down the hose, he took his weight off the nozzle, thus allowing the valve to reseal (as it is designed to do), and that is the reason why only a relatively small amount of fuel was lost.

On Wednesday morning Joan called the race team together for a meeting to discuss the fire. He asked what our thoughts were on the matter and how we felt about refuelling the cars in Hungary. 'There is a possibility that the FIA will ban it (refuelling), but we don't know that, and we can't count on it happening', Joan told us. 'There also is a possibility that the FIA will ask Intertechnique to redesign and replace the fuel couplings on all the rigs, but again we can't rely on there being a new system by the next race.'

'We therefore have to face the possibility that nothing will change, and that if we compete in the next race we will have to refuel using the same system as before. Each of you must decide for yourselves whether you are prepared to refuel with the old equipment. I cannot guarantee that what happened in Hockenheim won't happen again in Budapest.

'I'm sure all of us will try one thousand per cent to ensure that, if we have to refuel, then it will be done as safely as it is possible to make it. But I cannot guarantee it won't happen again. We have given Sparco the burnt overalls back to analyze. They are interested in how they stood up to a genuine accident situation, as opposed to a laboratory test. New overalls will be with us within a few days, but the decision of whether you will refuel or not is one you must make on your own. There is no shame in deciding you don't want to, but we must know before we leave for Hungary. If they allow refuelling to continue, then to be competitive we have to refuel, because, for sure, the others will.

'There's no point in racing in Hungary if we don't refuel. We will be miles off the pace. We may as well stay at home. The fight for the Championship will be over. Talk it over with your wives or girlfriends. Each of you must make your decision. Take your time. Let me know what you've decided in a day or so.' He left us alone to ponder the situation.

Up until that meeting I had, possibly naively, thought that refuelling would be banned from Hungary onwards. I hadn't even contemplated the idea that we would have to continue with it. I had assumed that the remainder of this season's Grands Prix distances would simply be reduced by sufficient laps to allow the cars to start the race with a full tank, enabling them to run to the end without the need for refuelling.

The mood in the race bay was sombre. I had been one of the lucky ones, I had come out of the fire with only superficial injuries (two sore hands and a small scorch around my right eye which had only made its presence known after my hands had stopped nagging me). Some of the other mechanics had received far more serious burns and I doubted if anybody would relish the prospect of having to carry out any future refuelling stops.

As work progressed on the cars there was little conversation. People were in deep thought, debating with themselves whether or not they felt willing to go to Hungary with the possibility of another fire.

On Wednesday the 10th, the FIA issued a press statement concerning the investigation into the fire, in which they concluded that the cause of the blaze was that a filter had been removed from the rig, and that a 'foreign body' had passed down the fuel-hose, resulting in a valve failing to close properly.

Benetton Formula was also summoned to appear before the World Motor Sport Council to answer a charge that the rig had been 'modified' due to the removal of the filter. This press statement came as terrible shock. As if it wasn't bad enough that we had been involved in such an accident, there was now speculation that we had caused the fire deliberately!

The filter in question was a later addition to the original specification of the rigs. It was fitted because some teams had been complaining about finding machining swarf left in the rigs during their production (as I mentioned in March). However, we strip, clean and service our rigs after every Grand Prix and our fuel is filtered through a much finer-grade filter than the Intertechnique item. We have never found evidence of swarf or debris of any description inside the rigs, following their initial clean-out at the beginning of the year.

It is not possible that the cause of the fire was through swarf holding the valve open, as there was never any swarf in there. Besides which, if the fuel valve had been held open by swarf, the fuel would have carried on spraying until the rig was empty as the valve would have been unable to seal. It just didn't add up.

Yes, the filter had been removed, but only because it was a redundant item. Benetton had never made any secret of the fact that it had been removed. Remember that the rig had been investigated on the Tuesday after the race. There was plenty of time for the filter to have been refitted if the team had felt any need or inclination to do so. As far as I'm aware, Benetton had sought permission to allow the filter to be removed, and that permission had been granted.

Unfortunately, the go-ahead had been given during the course of a conversation, and consequently the team had no documentation to clarify the situation. I don't believe for one second that Benetton was responsible for that fire. However, the thing that bothered me was that if people read that Benetton had brought the fire upon themselves, then it was most unlikely that the governing body would ban refuelling, or even look into re-designing the equipment.

We flew out to Budapest on Thursday morning. I don't think any of us were looking forward to Sunday afternoon, especially if we had to work with the same equipment, but despite the dangers of a possible recurrence, every member of the race team had agreed to refuel if needed.

I had thought about the fire on several occasions and when Judd asked me if I was worried about the prospect of refuelling in Hungary, I said to her, 'Yes, it does worry me. It even scares me a little. But if we have to do it, then so be it'. It's very much a personal decision, and a difficult thing to explain. As I'm sure you're more than aware by now, the struggle for the Drivers' and Constructors' World Championships becomes a way of life. And if trying to win the World Championships requires me to refuel, then – despite the fact that I would rather see the back of it – I have to deem refuelling as an acceptable risk. Maybe other people had different reasons for continuing, I don't know.

Steve Bird is a pleasant, friendly sort of chap, helpful and always smiling. He is one of our Test Team gearbox mechanics. At least he used to be. He had volunteered to take over the role as 'refueller' from Simon. Simon's face was still in a very delicate condition and his injuries made it impossible for him to wear any protective clothing. He had been advised to stay at home and rest. The last thing Simon needed now was to pick up a skin infection from any of the oil fuel, and smoke, to be found at a Grand Prix.

He and Joan had gone through the pit stop routine with Steve, and together they had practised the drill until our new recruit was happy and felt comfortable with the procedure.

I was very impressed that Steve had volunteered for this quite obviously hazardous job. I had joined him for a coffee at the airport, as we waited for our flight to begin boarding. When I inquired what had made him ask Joan if he could come along, he paused for a few seconds and mulled the question over.

Then he said 'Well, one of us was going to have to do it. Besides which, I have several hobbies, and all of them are far more dangerous than refuelling ever is.' He didn't venture to tell me what his leisure activities might include, but if they made refuelling a Grand Prix car appear safe by comparison I didn't think I had really the courage to inquire about what he did for relaxation.

I first visited Budapest in 1990. When I originally saw the city I had an odd feeling of *déjà vu*. As we drove through the streets, past the ancient buildings, some of which are riddled with the bullet scars of past conflicts, I sensed that I knew the place, and that I had been here before. Scraps and fragments of weathered posters hung like rags on old boards, their messages long since washed away and forgotten. The people watched us drive along, both curious and suspicious of who we were and what we were doing.

It was the strong, almost methane like, smell of cabbage soup drifting through the minibus window that eventually triggered the memory. Airstrip One. All it needed was a gritty wind and a glass of Victory gin, and Budapest would have been the living interpretation of Orwell's '1984'. Even the wording on the apparently home-made banners, hanging opposite the pits seemed a little contrived. They said things like: 'We love Formula One teams', and 'Gerhard Berger is my favourite driver, but good luck to all!'

Now, however, following the changes to the political structure of Eastern Europe, things seemed to have changed a little. You can now buy polystyrene encased burgers, the streets are more dangerous, drinks cost twice as much, and most of the trams appear to have been replaced with BMW and Mercedes sports saloons. Whether or not these changes turn out for the better only time will tell. But, regardless of any politics, the splendour of Budapest's opulent past is still apparent, and parts of the old city are still very beautiful.

Following the FIA press release about the fire, I was a little apprehensive as to how the other teams would view the situation. Would they believe that we had caused the fuel spillage, and if they did, would they consequently treat us with scorn and contempt? Or simply ignore us altogether?

The media seemed to be in two minds on the subject. Certain sections of the press had started to run stories suggesting that maybe Benetton had become a little too successful, and that our rate of scoring needed to be kept in check. The papers which survive on sensationalism had printed stories condemning the team as cheats, saying that our speed in the pit stops throughout the year wasn't simply a result of having a good system, good equipment, and hours of practice. But that our agility was a direct result of tampering with the rig. Pure nonsense. And they knew it was. But in their defence, I suppose their objective is to sell newspapers and the story of 'MAN READS BOOK WHILE WIFE WATCHES TV' is not really going to do it for them.

On our arrival at the circuit my fears of condemnation were proved to be unfounded. Everyone I talked to, up and down the pit lane, showed only concern for us. They asked who had been injured, how Simon was getting on, and if Jos would be driving. Jo Ramirez and Dave Ryan (from McLaren) inquired how I was, and said how much they appreciated the fact that I had sent a brief letter to Ron Dennis, in which I thanked his mechanics for their quick work in putting my overalls out during the fire. 'Good gracious!' I said. 'Don't thank me. Let me thank you! It was an absolute pleasure.'

People wanted to know what we thought had caused the fuel spillage, and what we had found when the rig had been dismantled. McLaren had issued their 'refuellers' with special air-fed helmets, manufactured for use by fire brigades. They are designed to enable the wearer to literally walk through fire.

The members of the McLaren crew who, during a pit stop, would stand with their backs to the pit lane had been issued with helmets to protect themselves, in case they involuntarily jumped back into the path of an oncoming car.

The chaps who would normally work between the garage and the car had elected not to wear helmets, to enable them to have a slightly better field of vision. The Jordan mechanics had all been issued with Arai crash helmets, painted in their team colours. In fact nearly everybody in the pit lane had been issued with as much new and innovative safety equipment as the market could supply.

The majority of team managers had got together and were exchanging information as to where the various new equipment could be bought. We were all impressed with the protection that the air-fed helmets could offer. Steve and Martin, one of our truckies, who helps support the fuel-hose during the pit stop, would be issued with them for the next race.

The new equipment, the exchange of ideas and the concern for every team's safety, coupled with the fact that the Intertechnique engineers had arrived with a box full of components, and had proceeded to replace parts in everybody's fuel-valve assemblies, all helped to convince me that no one in the Formula One fraternity believed that the fire was connected with the fuel filter.

I believe that the majority of teams were in favour of banning refuelling there and then, but to do so requires unanimous agreement, and unfortunately that wasn't reached. So on Sunday afternoon we would have to continue with it. This wasn't popular news, but as I said before, if we have to, then so be it.

Over the two days of qualifying we saw many of the cars spinning off the circuit. The Hungarian is one of the most tight and twisting tracks we visit. It is, in complete contrast to Hockenheim, nearly devoid of straights, but with an abundance of demanding corners. Top speed is reduced, and the cars need as much downforce as possible. We would have liked to have used the high downforce rear wings (which I wrote about in Aida).

However, the regulation changes regarding downforce reduction, had put these outside the rules. Some teams were suffering more than others. The Ferraris had been in their element in Germany, where the long straights had allowed them to take full advantage of their abundance of horsepower. But Budapest is all about handling, and Berger and Alesi had both been complaining about the stability of the cars all weekend. Ferrari had been constantly revising their chassis. In fact they had made so many modifications that from Magny Cours onwards they had renamed it the 412-T1/B. They were still having problems, and from what I could see, their chassis had started to suffer from oversteer as opposed to the understeer which had troubled them at the start of the season.

I think the loss of available downforce, allied to the track's slippery surface had caught many drivers off-guard. During Saturday afternoon Jos had spun off during his first timed lap. He had managed to drive back to the pits, but the shunt had damaged the gearbox, and we were unable to get him back out again. Jos had done well on Friday, qualifying the car in sixth position.

Unfortunately, everyone else had improved their times the following day, which effectively meant that he slipped down the grid to start the race from twelfth place. Even Michael had spun during Saturday, an event which over the last couple of years had become very rare. However, he had secured pole position well before his spin, and with a time of 1:18.258 he was over half a second quicker than Damon's FW16, and just short of two seconds clear of David Coulthard, who had done an excellent job of driving the other Williams to third place on the grid.

After breakfast on Sunday morning I was sitting on one of the tool cabinets at the back of the garage, drinking coffee and quietly pondering life. We always arrive at the circuit well before the cars have to run, just in case of any emergency, so (providing things are in order) early morning is the most relaxed time of the day. Jos came into the garage and sat down next to me. 'You're very quiet!' he said, 'Are you worried about the pit stops?'

'A little I suppose, but not too much. Are you?' I asked.

'A little, but it'll be alright!' he said. Then added, 'Well, if it's not the pit stops, why are you so quiet then?'

I paused for a second or two and then told him, 'The thing is Jos, I've been writing a diary, well, more a book I suppose, about the team and what we get up to.'

'Really! Am I in it?' he asked.

'Of course you're in it! We're all in it. You, Michael, Ross, Huub. Everyone.'

'Huub! What did you write about Huub?'

'Remember the restaurant, when all the lights went out?'

'In Estoril?'

'In Estoril, yes. Well I wrote about him then.'

'I didn't see you writing anything in the restaurant.'

'I didn't actually write anything in the bloody restaurant!'

'Who are you writing it for?'

'Well, I don't know really. Originally it was going to be just for me. A sort of hobby. But, to cut a long story short, a publisher has been in touch with me. They want to print it and put it in bookshops, so everyone can read about us!'

'Did you write about chassis seven at Magny Cours?'

'Yes, I did. And when you spun off during the race!'

'Oh . . .'

'The thing is Jos, we haven't scored a single point so far. I don't want to have to write that we went all year without scoring a single bloody point!'

'And Brazil? Did you write about Brazil?'

'Yes.'

'That wasn't my fault.'

'No. Everyone knows it was an accident.'

'Writing a book is going to be good, isn't it!?'

'Do me a favour this afternoon Jos, will you?'

'Of course. I'll score a point for us today. Wait and see!'

The warm up proceeded without problems. At 1.00 p.m. we changed into our new overalls. Sixty minutes later, 26 Formula One cars screamed off towards the first corner, and the 1994 Hungarian Grand Prix began. Michael sped away, with Damon close behind. Jos also made a good start up to ninth by the end of the first lap.

We sat in silence watching the monitors, waiting for the radio message from Ross, informing us as to which driver he was going to call in first, and advising us to stand by. I walked around the garage for a while. Although I didn't feel particularly nervous, I nevertheless found myself pacing up and down. In the end I walked outside, leant on the rear jack and tried to take my mind off the impending pit stop by watching the activity in the pit lane. After a few minutes of standing in the sunshine I felt relaxed and at ease. Then a radio keyed-up. It was Pat Symonds. 'In for tyres at the end of this lap Michael. Please acknowledge.'

'OK,' replied Michael.

'Alright chaps, this will be a Schumacher stop. Let's be ready for him,' said Ross. Michael's tyres were brought out and unwrapped from their blankets. '40 seconds,' Pat informed us. The air-guns whirred. Steve lifted the fuel hose onto his shoulder. 'Relax chaps, take your time, nice and easy,' Joan told us. '10 seconds' Then, 'He's in the pit lane.'

As soon as the car came into view the procedure became automatic: there was no time for second thoughts. Steve pushed the nozzle onto the car, Ken and I lifted the jacks and the others set about changing the tyres. I glanced at the front, checked the back, and as soon as Steve disconnected the nozzle we released the car back down. Mick checked to see that the pit lane was clear, lifted his board, and Michael pulled away.

Joan was straight on the radio, 'Well done boys, great job! Bloody great job!' We all breathed a huge sigh of relief. 7.5 seconds. Not bad, not bad at all. I felt much happier after that, we all did. We carried out a total of five successful and quick pit stops during the race. In my opinion, the speed of those pit stops was the best possible answer we could give to our critics.

Damon temporarily led the race until he too pitted for fuel. As the Williams entered the pit lane, Michael regained the lead, and he disappeared into the distance. The circuit is notoriously difficult to pass on, but Michael's ability to deal with backmarkers and his skill in weaving through traffic is now, I believe, second to none. It wasn't long before he had managed to get close to 40 seconds ahead of the field, at which point Pat radioed to Michael, asking him to back off slightly and give the car a chance to relax a little.

This domination of the race was, of course, very impressive, but what was even more impressive to me was that by lap 52 Jos had managed to get up to sixth. Not only that, but he was gaining on Alesi's Ferrari, in fifth place. Jos had been pounding round the circuit in a very determined drive. This could be it, fingers crossed and we could actually score some points.

I looked over at Bobby, he gave me a very nervous and concerned look back. Dave walked over. 'If he dares go into a gravel-trap now . . .' Jakey sat on the ground, deep in thought. He seemed to be trying to make mental contact with Jos, willing him on. Take it steady. Take it steady. Wayne was glued to the monitor, watching the times flash up lap by lap. Lap 53, 54, 55 keep going Jos. Then, on lap 59, car number 27 disappeared off the screen. Alesi had retired with gearbox trouble. Jos was fifth. 'He'd better not go off!' Dave warned. Jos kept on pushing, there were only four cars ahead of him now. Damon's FW16 was in second place, he and Michael had lapped the entire field by this stage.

David Coulthard was third in the other Williams.

Martin Brundle was in fourth place in the McLaren. At this stage we would have been more than happy with the three points for fifth place. Then on the next lap we found ourselves elevated to fourth. Coulthard had been under too much pressure from the McLaren, and car number 2 had spun off. I didn't want to think how the Ferrari and Williams mechanics must have felt, we might be sharing the same emotion soon enough. 'Keep going Jos!' Lap 61, 62, 63. Jos was still circulating, pushing hard, chasing after Brundle's McLaren.

My heart jumped as Michael's radio cut in, fearful that something had happened to his car, and that we could lose the lead. But it wasn't anything to worry about, I think Michael had become a little bored, since he had been told to take it easy. Because he didn't need to concentrate on his own position so much, he had been thinking about Jos's race, possibly to keep his mind alert and avoid any errors through lack of concentration. 'Pat, can you tell me where Jos is?'

'Er, yes Michael, he's currently in fourth place, way behind you.'

'OK.' Then a few seconds later, 'And who's third, Brundle?'

'Yes Michael, the order is Hill, Brundle, Verstappen, Blundell, Panis.'

'OK. How far behind Brundle is Jos at the moment?'

'About nine seconds.' Lap 73 advanced into lap 74. Including this lap there were just four more to go. Michael was back on the radio. 'If I keep at this speed, Martin may have to unlap himself to get away from Jos. If he does, tell Jos to unlap himself too. This will give him an extra lap to try and catch Martin, and if anything happens to the McLaren on the last lap . . .'

'OK, Michael, we'll tell him. But please concentrate on your own race first!'

'OK, Pat.'

Brundle was all too aware of Jos behind him, and he had little choice but to overtake Michael and attempt to put some distance between Jos and himself. Jos had been informed of what Michael had suggested. He duly unlapped himself from the race leader, and set off in pursuit of the McLaren.

Lap 75, Lap 76 and Michael crossed the start/finish line to begin the final lap of the race. Jos was still chasing after Brundle. We walked over to the pit wall, and waited for Michael to complete the last lap and take the chequered flag. The Benetton rounded the final corner, and Michael crossed the line to win his seventh Grand Prix of the year. Then Damon crossed the line to add another six points to his and the Williams totals.

We waited for Martin and Jos to come round, but only one of them came into view. The McLaren had stopped during the final lap. Jos crossed the line in third position. We were ecstatic. At last! Thank God! At last! Four points! Four beautiful points! And a podium position as well! We shook hands, we slapped each on the back, we shook hands again. It was a wonderful moment. A truly wonderful moment. Joan cut in on the radio, 'Well done chaps! Fantastic! Fantastic job!'

We walked down to the podium to watch Michael and Jos accepting their awards. Michael looked as happy as always, and Jos was overjoyed with the result. Waving at us, waving at the crowd, waving at the cameras, waving at everybody and everything. He had good cause to be happy too. In that split second it took to cross the finish line Jos became the most successful Dutch Formula One driver in history. His family, and indeed his country, must have felt very proud.

Later, as we were packing the equipment away, Jos came in to say thank you, his hair still soaked in Champagne. 'I'm sorry Steve!' he apologized.

'What for?' I asked.

'Well, this morning I only promised you one point. I didn't think we'd get on the podium. I hope that doesn't mess your book up!'

'No, that's alright Jos. I'll just write that you finished sixth.'

'Don't you dare!' he laughed.

So chassis 04 had finally come good, and the four points we had scored meant that each crew and each driver had scored points towards the Constructors' Championship.

The situation after the Hungarian Grand Prix looked like this: Benetton, 81; Ferrari, 52; Williams, 49; McLaren, 17. And in the Drivers' Championship: Schumacher, 76; Hill, 45; Berger, 27; Alesi, 19; Verstappen, 4 (14th); Lehto, 1 (22nd).

During the flight back to England I thought about the events of the race. Michael had been perfectly correct about the possibility of the McLaren failing, and if I hadn't heard him say it myself, I would have found it hard to believe. It must have been bitterly disappointing for Martin to have stopped on that final lap (apparently an electrical fault, the car just cut out).

As I have already told you, Martin drove our car throughout '92, and we had suffered our fair share of bad luck together. I genuinely wanted Martin to do well this season. For the entire duration of the flight I tried as hard as possible to feel regret for what had happened to him at Budapest, but it just wouldn't come!

Besides, Martin had already scored, and had already been on the podium. Second in Monaco, and three points in Budapest (having been classified fourth). I feel sure he'd forgive me a few moments of self-congratulation.

There have been many books written on the subject of motor racing, and Formula One in particular. The majority of them refer to the *Circuit de Spa Francorchamps* as being magnificent. Yet from a mechanic's point of view, the facilities at Spa are far from magnificent. The garages are small and dark, and the pit lane is narrow. When we arrive in the morning the marshals don't want to let anyone in, and at night they close all the gates and don't want to let anyone out. However, as far as the race track itself goes, I would have to agree with the authors. Spa is a splendid setting for a Grand Prix and the circuit is steeped in Formula One history.

The track cascades up hill and down dale, climbing long straights, round sweeping bends, and through almost impossibly tight hairpins. Spa contains one of the most famous sections of race track in the world, Eau Rouge. When you look at a plan view of the circuit layout, you could easily overlook Eau Rouge. It appears almost non-existent, like an insignificant squiggle. Maybe even a mistake caused by the artist sneezing while drawing. This would be, of course, a very bad assumption to make.

In reality Eau Rouge is an incredible corner. The track slowly creeps around the tight La Source hairpin and suddenly plunges at full speed downhill, past the 'old pits' and straight towards a slight left, at the bottom of the hill. The circuit bottoms out and immediately changes direction back to the right, careering upwards and on towards a sweeping left. Eau Rouge is all about elevation and speed. The drivers have to commit themselves 100 per cent to get it correct. Too much speed going in and it's too late to do much about it on the way out. It was at Eau Rouge where Alessandro Zanardi had his big accident in the Lotus last year.

There is one thing you can be absolutely certain of at Spa, and that is the unpredictability of the weather. The circuit is set amongst the rolling hills and dense firs of the Ardennes forest. In the morning it can be pouring with rain, with a thick mist cutting the visibility down to a mere few yards. The skies can be black with cloud, giving the impression that it has been raining for weeks, and that it has every intention of continuing to do so.

However, within an hour of arriving at the circuit, the clouds have vanished, the sun is shining, and any remaining water is gently steaming off the circuit. Within two hours the track is bone dry, and Spa will try and convince you that it hasn't seen rain in ages. If you are fool enough to be taken in by this charade then Spa will trick you again as the clouds return, the mist rolls down the hills and it immediately starts to pour.

This year was to be no exception to the rule. From Thursday to Sunday the weather simply couldn't decide what it wanted to do. It was raining. It stopped. It was sunny. It was cloudy. It was raining. There was, however, one big difference to previous years. The famous Eau Rouge corner had been altered. It had been decided that the corner was too quick for its adjoining run-off area. Following the FIA's commitment to improve circuit safety, there had been plans to build extensive gravel-traps around Eau Rouge, but the work would have taken too long to have the circuit ready in time for this year's race.

A solution had to be found and a compromise was reached. A chicane was built at the bottom of the hill. This would require the cars to change down through the gearbox, trundle through the chicane, and accelerate away. No spectacle, by any means, but much slower. Fingers crossed and all being well, 1994 would be the first, last and only time we would have to race here without the corner as it should be.

We had arrived at Spa in good shape. The turnaround had been fairly painless, and we had plenty of time to carry out the rebuild. In complete contrast to Hungary (and with the obvious exception of Silverstone), Spa is the shortest journey our transporters have to make. They didn't have to leave for Dover until Tuesday night, which gave us ample time to prepare for the race weekend. There hadn't been any damage to either chassis during the previous race, and the allocation remained the same as for the Hungarian Grand Prix, so if you are hunting for chassis numbers, you'll have to flip back a few pages.

Friday morning started dry, but within a few minutes of the first practice session beginning, the skies darkened and it began to rain. Spa is a long circuit, and being just short of seven kilometres, it is, in fact, the longest track we visit. It's quite possible that the far side of the circuit, around Les Combes and Rivage, might be bright and sunny, while down in the pits at La Source the rain will be teeming down.

As soon as we noticed the first drops start to fall, the engineers radioed to Michael and Jos, informing them of the rain as there could be disastrous consequences for a very powerful and extremely fast racing car to be pounding along on slicks, exiting a sweeping bend, when suddenly the driver finds himself in the middle of a downpour. Then the skies really opened up. Pat and Chris called the drivers back in and within a few seconds the pit lane was full of cars slowly returning to their garages, as the engineers from most of the other teams made the same decision. We removed the slicks, dried the cars off and waited to see if it would stop raining. It didn't.

After about ten minutes Ross asked us to change the wings to the high downforce levels. There was a strong possibility that the afternoon qualifying session would be conducted in the rain. We needed to set the cars for wet conditions, and give Michael and Jos a chance to evaluate them. Even if it stopped raining in time for qualifying, the information we would learn and the data we would acquire would prove extremely useful, as Sunday afternoon could well see a wet race. Michael drove for just nine laps during the morning, Jos completed ten. That was all we needed really, we didn't want to risk damaging the cars before qualifying began at 1.00 p.m. We pulled the cars back inside, checked the oil consumption, pumped the fuel tanks out, and waited.

When the circuit opened for qualifying the rain had turned to drizzle, which made it difficult to know what to do for the best. The drizzle might just be a slight lull in the weather, with heavy rain returning at any moment. Or the rain could be moving away, over the hills, resulting in the circuit drying out, and obviously producing better track conditions later in the session. Most teams chose to go out, get a time on the board, and then wait and see.

Over the hour-long session the track gradually started to dry, and the last few minutes of the session became very busy. In the final five minutes, a definite dry line could be seen around the majority of the circuit. It was now a gamble of whether to risk going out on slicks, or stay with wet tyres.

If the cars could maintain grip then slicks would obviously produce a quicker time, but drive slightly off-line and into water, and the car would be in the gravel. It was the teams that had elected to run right at the very end of the session that benefited most, as the dry-line finally joined together to cover a complete lap. Jos managed a time of 2m 22.218s, putting him sixth on the grid. Michael had gone out on slicks, and with a time of 2m 21.494s we all thought he'd taken provisional pole. However, in the final seconds of the session, Rubens Barrichello flung his Jordan over the line in a time of 2m 21.163s, to beat Michael by 0.331 sec.

By Saturday the rain had returned with a vengeance, and a rich, deep mist hung over the track. The weather was far more severe than Friday, and it soon became apparent that the best course of action was to leave the cars sitting in the pits. When the circuit closed for the day at 2.00 p.m., the Jordan garage went wild. At just 22 years old, Rubens Barrichello had become the youngest man in Formula One's history to take a pole position. It was also the first pole for Jordan Grand Prix as well, and they were all clearly – and audibly – overjoyed with the situation.

On Sunday afternoon the weather, in true Spa tradition, had changed again. The sky was blue, the sun was bright. It was a perfect summer's day in late August. The race itself went very well for us. Barrichello made a good start, and the Jordan led the field round La Source, down the hill, and through the Eau Rouge chicane. But on the climb up the other side, Michael pulled out, passed the Jordan, and from then on the race was his.

Rubens had made no attempt to resist the manoeuvre. He was well aware that he had found himself in a privileged and responsible position by taking pole, and that in reality the Jordan was no match for the Benetton or the Williams chassis. We carried out four pit stops during the course of the race, two for each driver. All of them were quick, and although we were still very cautious, my confidence was much better here than it had been in Budapest. Instead of sitting in silent contemplation in between pit stops we had started chatting again, and the atmosphere was a little less tense.

About halfway through the race Ross pressed the transmit button on his radio. 'Can we have some Schumacher tyres in the pit lane please, quickly!' he said, 'Michael has spun, he's still going, but let's be ready. He may have flat-spotted the tyres, or even damaged the car.'

A second later Michael switched his radio on. 'Sorry about that!' he apologized, 'I think the tyres are OK. I'll take it steady until the next pit stop. Sorry!' I walked over to the monitor just in time to watch a replay of the spin. Michael had just negotiated the right/left section at Fanges, and as he began to position the car on the short straight, at the approach to Stavelot, the rear of the car broke away, and the momentum of exiting the left-hand bend caused the car to spin through 360-degrees. The car spun down the kerbing, just missing the gravel trap, thankfully ending up back on the track. If he had gone into the trap it would have been very difficult for him to have regained the circuit and driven back out.

Jos was driving another good strong race. His third place in Hungary had boosted his confidence no end. On his return to Holland he had been treated as a celebrity. The mere fact that he was driving in Formula One had made him a popular chap, but to step off the plane with four points to his credit had turned him into a national hero. His family run a small bar/cafe in Montfort, and whenever the races are televised, the locals flock inside to watch TV. The bar had apparently been full during the Hungarian race, and when Jos had stood on the podium, waving at them in celebration, the resulting party had lasted all night and well into the next day.

The two FW16s had also been going well, and for the majority of the time David Coulthard had been ahead of Damon. But in the closing stages of the race he had developed transmission trouble, and with the car stuck in gear he dropped through the field from second to fifth. A great disappointment, as it had looked very promising for him to take his first podium finish.

Michael took the chequered flag well ahead of the others. Damon finished second and Jos was fourth, just behind Mika Hakkinen, who claimed the last place on the podium for himself and McLaren. As Michael, Damon, and Mika sprayed *Moët et Chandon* over each other, we shook hands with the Williams and McLaren mechanics, congratulating each other on another successful

Grand Prix. Williams were pleased with the result, as Damon's six points moved them ahead of Ferrari in the Constructors' Championship. Williams was now second, and with the 13 points we had just scored they trailed Benetton by 37. Ferrari had failed to finish the race and dropped to third.

Do you remember me telling you about the Jabroc spacer cum skidblock (known as the 'plank') that was introduced to the cars at Hockenheim? And can you recall me saying that in Belgium one of these planks turned out to be the most controversial piece of ply-board in the history of motor sport? Well, this was the reason why. After every Grand Prix, the cars that finish the race are driven to a scrutineering area, from here, depending on their finishing position, the drivers either walk back to the pits or climb the stairs to the podium. It is in *parc-fermé* that the final legality checks of the weekend are carried out. The cars are weighed, the wings are measured. Once or twice a year the engine capacity is checked (just to make sure none of the teams have substituted a 4-litre engine), and occasionally fuel samples are taken.

Since Hockenheim the scrutineers also check the thickness of the plank. As I mentioned before, the plank was introduced to force the teams to raise the ride-heights of their cars to a minimum of 10 millimetres. If, after the race, the plank is less than nine millimetres thick (the teams are allowed a one millimetre margin) the car is deemed to have been running too low, and is therefore illegal. When Michael's plank was measured, there was a certain area where the thickness was down to 7.4 millimetres. I feel that it's important to point out that this excess wear wasn't consistent over the entire length of the plank, nor was the wear tapered (from the front of the car to the rear, or vice versa), it was in one patch about 20 centimetres back from the leading edge. Charlie Whiting informed Ross about the wear, so Ross reminded Charlie about the incident where Michael had spun the car down the kerb during the race and that the wear to the plank must have been a direct result of that accident.

It couldn't be caused through normal running on the track because the wear would be uniform, or at least follow a mathematically regular pattern.

In the amendment to the regulations regarding skid blocks there is a section which allows for accidental damage to be taken into consideration. The rule states that in the event of accidental damage reducing the thickness of the skid-block below nine millimetres, the skid-block should be removed from the car and weighed. If the weight of the skid-block after the race is within ninety per-cent of its original weight, then the skid-block should be deemed to be legal (each plank is serial numbered and weighed after production, and the figures are registered with the FIA). Charlie asked Ross to remove the plank from the car so he could weigh it, and cross reference the figures. The plank was weighed and found to be within the 10 per cent tolerance allowed in the regulations.

This ruling concerning accidental damage is something I find a little ambiguous. When Michael's plank was weighed, it was within the allowed weight tolerance, which was all well and good, but theoretically, if any car had an accident which removed 20 per cent off the plank's weight, or indeed, had a section of its plank ripped clean off, the car would be illegal because it had suffered too much accidental damage. Or if two cars had a slight altercation with each other, and both spun off the circuit but managed to keep going, eventually finishing the race in first and second position, I find it difficult to accept that the rules can pass one car as legal, but disqualify the other because it had suffered a greater degree of accidental damage.

Anyway, Charlie took the figures of the plank wear and the plank weight into the Stewards' Office. Later that evening, five hours after the end of the race, the Stewards of the Meeting issued 'Stewards' Decision Number 3' which announced that the skid block of car number 5 was below the acceptable dimensions, and that the Stewards did not consider the wear to be the result of Michael's accident.

Apparently the Clerk of the Course had visited the scene of the spin and had certified that 'The concerned kerb is flat and that no piece of wood could be found either on top of or at the side of the relevant kerb'. Consequently the car and the points achieved by its driver were to be disqualified from the results of the 1994 Belgian Grand Prix.

I find the statement by the Clerk of the Course concerning the scene of the accident a mite mystifying.

I have always thought that the very reason of a kerb's existence was to dissuade the drivers from going too wide, preventing the cars from excessive straightlining of the corners, and in so doing keep the drivers 'honest' to the circuit layout.

If the kerb was flat it would simply be an extension of the useable track. Surely to be classed as being a kerb it must be raised, and the video of the spin clearly shows that to be the case. The statement says '. . . on top of or at the side of the relevant kerb.' Well if the kerb has got a top and sides how can it not be higher than the track?

The top of the kerb certainly wasn't flat either, it was serrated in order to produce a 'rumble strip', again in an attempt to dissuade the drivers from using it. And then there is '. . . no piece of wood could be found.' There wouldn't be any 'pieces' of wood to find. The spin would have simply worn the Jabroc away. I suppose it may have produced microscopic particles of wood-dust, but most of these would have been instantly burnt, turning to smoke by the friction and heat produced by the speed of the spin.

As I understand the interpretation of the regulation this statement (however mystifying) should have proved irrelevant and quite superfluous to the outcome of the meeting between Charlie Whiting and the Stewards of the Meeting. Benetton and the race officials all agreed that Michael's skid-block was undersize; both parties agreed that the skid-block had suffered accidental damage; and both parties agreed that the skid-block had clearly passed the required test as specified in the FIA regulations. Surely that should have been the end of the matter?

We had to leave for the airport before the stewards' decision had been released. The rumours of what had happened started to circulate in the Brussels departure terminal, but we were in the baggage hall at Heathrow before the stories were finally confirmed. People had telephoned home to say they were back in England, and their families told them what had just been on the 9.30 p.m. news.

I was watching the endless stream of bags slowly tour the luggage belt, feeling both tired and unwashed, and dreading the pending coach journey home when Bat came over to tell me. 'No, not again,' I sighed, 'I can't believe it. If it's not one thing it's another! What do they expect the plank to look like? The whole world just saw us spin over that kerb.'

However, at the end of the day, feeling thoroughly fed up, picked on, and miserable wasn't going to change anything. Michael had been disqualified and that was that. We would, of course, appeal the decision, but for the time being we had no alternative but to accept the situation.

The revised results meant that everybody moved up a position. Damon claimed an additional four points for first place, Jos gained an extra point for third, and David Coulthard an extra point for fourth. And, if nothing else, the new results certainly brought the Championship much closer together, which could only be good news for the media. The gap between Williams and ourselves had just been reduced to twenty-three points.

While in the Drivers' Championship, instead of the gap between Michael and Damon being thirty-five points, it had suddenly reduced to twenty-one. An instant reduction of fourteen points! On Tuesday the 30th, only two days after the FIA had disqualified the car in Belgium, Michael went to Paris for the appeal hearing of the two-race ban following the British Grand Prix. The hearing concluded with the FIA International Court of Appeal saying that they could find no new evidence to justify changing the original decision of the World Motor Sport Council.

Michael's second place would remain removed from the Silverstone results, and the two race suspension would have to be imposed, so Michael would not be allowed to participate in the forthcoming Italian Grand Prix at Monza and the following Portuguese Grand Prix at Estoril.

# SEPTEMBER

Flavio had asked J.J. if he would stand in for Michael and drive the car at the Monza and Estoril races. There had been five Grands Prix since J.J. had stopped racing, he needed little persuading to put his overalls back on and get behind the wheel again.

Ross had decided to leave 08 at the factory and thus avoid the risk of anything happening to our newest chassis, which could then be stored for Michael's return. 08 had only been used for Hungary and Belgium, and its limited mileage made it the most desirable chassis. A lower mileage monocoque should be more resistive to 'flex' (barring accident damage or similar), resulting in a lack of misleading feedback which can create problems for the drivers and engineers as they try to compensate for any chassis movement.

The decision to put 08 into storage meant that Max, Ken, and Jon would require another chassis to prepare for J.J. They were reunited with 05, a perfectly sound chassis that had been the emergency spare for the last two races and, prior to the arrival of 08, Michael's race car.

We then needed a replacement chassis to fill the position of the emergency spare. Because of the loss of 02 and 07 earlier in the season we only had two possible alternatives, 01 or 03. The test team was currently using 01, which meant the choice was more or less, already decided, so 03 was forced out of retirement.

Paul, Paul and Lee stayed with 06 for the spare car, and we remained with the old clonker – chassis 04 – for Jos. I had actually grown quite fond of it by now and hoped 04 would stay with us until the end of the year. It had been through several accidents, even surviving the inferno in the Hockenheim pit lane relatively unscathed, and despite all its misfortunes – and consequent repairs – still handled perfectly well. I felt it would be a bad omen to try and get rid of it now.

Prior to the trucks leaving for Italy we had paid another visit to 'Britain's Premier Drag Racing Venue'. J.J.'s enthusiasm at the prospect of driving again didn't seem to extend to a shakedown at Santa-Pod. I can't say that I blame him either. Up, down, check for leaks. Up, down, up, down; 'It's fine', pump the fuel out. 'Next.' Up, down, check for leaks. Up, down, up, down. You can just imagine.

I sat in bed the next morning, drinking coffee, and making the most of the opportunity of a lie in. I was listening to the 'Today' programme on the radio, and enjoying the presenter's ability to make politicians squirm in their seats and become all tongue-tied and panicky trying to defend themselves.

Just when it seemed that the MP was about to confess to everything and admit that the other party had been right all along, the interview was brought to a swift conclusion to make way for a news update. The name of a Formula One team on the news always makes the ears prick up, so when I heard the presenter say 'McLaren and Benetton' it immediately grabbed my attention.

The report said that McLaren International had been summoned before the Motor Sport World Council to answer claims that following a routine inspection of their electronic control modules by the FIA, they had apparently used a fully automatic up-change facility on the transmission of Mika Hakkinen's car at the San Marino Grand Prix.

They were to go to Paris the next day, Wednesday the 7th, together with Benetton Formula, who were there on two different matters. Firstly, to appeal against the disqualification of Michael Schumacher and his Benetton Ford from the results of the Belgian Grand Prix. And secondly, to answer charges relating to the pit lane fire that occurred during the German Grand Prix.

The investigation into McLaren's control modules had been carried out after they had managed to supply the source codes I told you about in 'July'. We had also been investigated, as had Ferrari (although Ferrari's investigation had been carried out a little sooner, because of their ease of access to the codes). The FIA had found that all three teams' control modules had contained various forms of 'driver aids' that had been banned at the end of last season and I would imagine that every other Formula One team in the pit lane had these same driver aids in their control modules.

Because of the complexity of the electronics in the engine and transmission systems it is no simple matter to remove these functions, as many of them inter-connect with differing control systems. For example, the complete removal of 'traction control' could affect the basic fuel injection and ignition timing of the engine management system.

By far the quickest, easiest, and safest way of complying with the current regulations was simply to disarm them. This was the course of action that Benetton had decided on, and was obviously what Ferrari and McLaren had done as well.

With McLaren being called before the FIA it meant that all three teams had attracted media attention over their electronics. At the Pacific Grand Prix, Charlie Whiting had discovered that in one of the practice sessions Ferrari had used a system which apparently altered the point at which the rev limiter cut in, and hence reduced the engine power.

He had told Ferrari not to use this system again until its precise functions could be ascertained. Some of the press had assumed this meant Ferrari had been using a form of traction control. I really couldn't see them doing so for a minute (I didn't even bother telling you about it at the time). Why would they? There was so much to lose by being thrown out of the Championship that it simply wouldn't make sense to use it.

When Benetton had been inspected, the FIA had found that we had a 'launch control' facility in one of our control modules. The FIA had looked at the data, investigated the electronics and issued a press release clearing the team of any breach of the regulations: '. . . the best evidence is that Benetton Formula Ltd was not using launch control (an automatic start system) at the 1994 San Marino Grand Prix,' said the statement.

Again, some papers reported that if Benetton had the facility for launch control then they must have used it. I don't believe so for a second. If that was the case J.J. wouldn't have stalled on the grid at Imola. 'Er, yes,' they said, 'well maybe it was only activated on one car.'

These arguments just didn't add up. As a Constructor we would obviously want both cars to do well, so surely it would have been more logical to have given our new and inexperienced drivers the electronic assistance. And now it was McLaren's turn to go under the spotlight. I couldn't see McLaren breaking the regulations any more than Ferrari or ourselves and I felt sure the situation would be resolved with a satisfactory conclusion.

I spent Wednesday writing, listening to the radio, and waiting to hear the outcome of the meeting in Paris. The news finally broke late in the afternoon. Benetton were cleared of any charge of causing the pit lane fire by the removal of the filter. The FIA press release had said that during the hearing it had emerged that there was a possibility that another competitor (Larousse) had been given permission by Intertechnique to remove their identical filter as early as May.

A letter had been produced to this effect, and there was a drawing from Intertechnique showing how to remove the filter from the rig. McLaren had told the World Council that their up-change facility had only been installed because they thought that it was legal from their interpretation of the regulation. There had been no intention to deceive the FIA and run an illegal driver aid.

The World Council pondered the matter and agreed to accept McLaren's explanation. The system was not to be used again, but there was no penalty imposed on the team. They also advised McLaren that during the investigation into their software, the FIA investigators had discovered a 'glitch' in the McLaren electronics which had been sending a faulty signal from their gearbox control module to their engine management system, resulting in a loss of engine performance. A problem that McLaren could now set about curing (I thought this was very decent of the FIA).

The third matter of the day wasn't resolved with such an amicable conclusion as the two previous issues, at least not for Benetton at any rate. Despite the fact that we had shown the World Council photographic evidence that the kerb where Michael had spun was in fact sharply serrated and over four inches high, and that a read out of Michael's telemetry showed the rear suspension to be in full 'droop' during the accident (the rear wheels hanging in the air, as the car slid and spun down the kerbing) and that the same telemetry showed the front suspension to be in excess of full 'bump' (the front suspension bending under the full load of the car as it falls back onto the tarmac), the appeal against the Spa disqualification was rejected.

The press release had said that the World Council could find no reason to interfere with the Stewards' Decision, but they were quick to point out that in no way did the FIA think the ride height of car number 5 had been set deliberately low to infringe the regulations.

Well, at the end of the day, we have to have a governing body to oversee the sport, and we have to accept the decisions of the World Council. At the conclusion of the meeting, Max Mosley had stated that it was the World Council's unanimous view that the filter had been removed in complete good faith. Personally, that comment meant more to me than the reinstatement of the 10 points for the victory in Belgium. Millions of people had seen Michael win in Spa. The World Council had cleared Benetton of any deliberate infringement at Spa, we could score the points again.

Chipping Norton was still fast asleep when I departed for Monza on Thursday morning. The alarm had been set for 4.00 a.m. and I had left the cottage thirty minutes later. It was cold, dark, and I was looking forward to a few days of Italian sunshine, but when we landed at Milan a few hours later it was pelting with rain.

Like Spa, Monza is one of the most famous circuits in the world, it is set amongst the parkland of the old royal palace, and the track is surrounded by ancient trees. The layout of the original circuit included two huge banked sections, which really resulted in two separate circuits, the 'road' course, which we know today, and the banked oval, being joined together by the main pit straight.

The cars would travel around the road circuit and then enter the oval from the right hand side of the pit straight, lap the banked oval and then exit back onto the road circuit on the left hand side of the pit-straight. In its original form the circuit was incredibly fast, and over the years, unfortunately, Monza has tragically claimed the life of many courageous drivers – Alberto Ascari, Wolfgang von Trips, Jochen Rindt and Ronnie Peterson, to name but a few, and there have also been a number of spectators and marshals killed or injured. All terribly sad. Nowadays, of course, safety precautions are much better, and the old banked circuit hasn't been incorporated in a race since the 1960s. The pit straight has been left at its original width, and remains the widest section of race track I have ever seen. But despite the loss of the oval and the introduction of chicanes to slow the cars down, Monza is still very quick.

There is one other facet to Monza that is simply impossible to overlook. As you drive through the park gates and head towards the paddock you are greeted by a sea of scarlet flags, scarlet hats, and scarlet T-shirts. Like Imola, Monza is within striking distance of Maranello, and is without doubt, the original home of the *tifosi*.

Some people will argue that Monza is the only true mecca of Ferrari devotion, and I certainly wouldn't argue the point, but I must say that I have always seen more constantly intense and noisy vigilance at Imola.

In some ways, the long straights of Hockenheim are similar to Monza, and as Ferrari had done so well there, it was to be expected that they would be trying harder than ever to emulate their earlier success. The pressure is always on Ferrari when we race in Italy. If they do well the media loves them and the entire team are hailed as national heroes. They have clearly demonstrated to the watching millions that Ferrari and Italy are still the greatest names in motor racing.

By Friday morning the rain had decided to leave us in peace. The sun was shining, and Monza was very pleasant. However, that was about the only good news of the day as far as Benetton was concerned. We were having all sorts of problems getting chassis 05 set up for J.J. He was complaining of understeer, and whatever we tried to do to cure the problem seemed to produce little change to his lap-times. If you recall, we had a similar problem in Canada when J.J. had been driving 04.

It was a frustrating situation for all of us. Obviously J.J. was trying as hard as possible, and he was keen that this weekend should go well for him, but he just wasn't happy with the car and when he finished Friday's qualifying session in 16th place he looked most unhappy.

Jos had never driven at Monza before, and he too had some initial problems with the set-up. Like J.J., he started the day with too much understeer, but after adjusting the wing settings we managed to improve the handling and were able to qualify the car in 14th place. Although this provisional grid position was far from perfect, Jos seemed much happier at the end of the day and was confident that we could go a lot quicker in Saturday's second qualifying session. During Friday Jos had driven over a kerb and through one of the gravel traps. He had managed to drive back out again and returned to the pits so we could remove the stones from the brakes and radiator ducts, and inspect the chassis for any possible damage.

While Tim was checking the car he noticed a small crack in the underside of the monocoque, undoubtedly a result of the chassis striking the kerb as it glanced over the top of it. Mick had a look, and then Ross came over to see what should be done. 'Well, we've seen a lot worse,' said Ross, inspecting the crack, 'but any damage is obviously bad news. Can you repair it Tim, or is it a job for the Composite Department?'

'No, I think we can fix it here. I'll fetch Reg and we'll do it tonight,' Tim assured him.

'OK. You and Reg repair this one for Saturday, and I'll get the spare car chaps to start preparing 03 (the emergency spare) for Sunday morning. We'll use 04 tomorrow, just in case Jos has another 'off', and you can keep an eye on the repair every time he comes into the garage. That means we can prevent any potential damage to 03 on Saturday, and allows us to use it for his race car if everything seems OK during the warm-up. Then we'll send 04 to the Composite Department when we get back to England, and they can confirm whether we can continue with it until the end of the season. I can't see a problem though, the damage is fairly minor. I'm sure your repair will cure that.'

So, while Dave, Bobby, and I proceeded with the normal post-running checks, and prepared 04 for Saturday's free practice, Tim and Reg started to repair the chassis. Meanwhile Paul, Paul, and Lee unloaded 03 from the transporter and began the process of turning the Emergency Spare chassis into a complete car. Oz supplied the three of them with new wishbones and uprights for the front suspension, and Cosworth issued Jos's race engine, so much of the work could be carried out at a steady pace over Friday, Saturday, and Saturday night.

Williams and Ferrari had been having far more success than Benetton. Jean Alesi had taken provisional pole (much to the obvious delight of the Tifosi) with a time of 1m 24.620s. The two FW16s were sitting second and third on the grid, with Damon just ahead of David Coulthard by 0.135 sec. Gerhard's Ferrari was fourth, a mere 0.046 sec behind Coulthard.

Saturday was a day of mixed fortune. Both Jos and J.J. had made improvements in the morning, and during his first two attempts in the qualifying session Jos had managed to move up the grid from fourteenth to tenth. He had got used to the Monza circuit now, the car was working well, and he was very confident that he could improve his grid position again. But when he came back into the pits after that second run we noticed a hole in the bodywork (side pod) around the left-hand radiator duct.

It appeared to be stone damage at first, but when we looked inside the duct the reason for the damage became obvious. The on-board camera, mounted on the rear wing of Pierluigi Martini's Minardi, had fallen off, bounced along the circuit and smashed into our car. Jos would have been driving at close to 200mph when the car and camera collided.

The speed and force of the impact had staved the camera into the duct, breaking a hole in the side pod on its way through. It had then crashed through the bottom of the duct, and had finally lodged itself in the carbon floor. If the camera had bounced on a slightly different trajectory it could easily have hit Jos instead of just the car. Once again he had been very lucky.

We worked as fast as possible to change the damaged floor, radiator duct and side pod, in order to give Jos another run on the circuit, but even with the help of the spare car crew we weren't able to complete the work in time. The most annoying thing was that we only missed our deadline to get the car back out by less than two minutes. And so we had to settle for 10th place on the grid. J.J. managed to improve on his Friday's qualifying time by over 1.2 sec. However, others had improved even more, which resulted in J.J. slipping further down the grid, and, unfortunately he would have to start the Italian Grand Prix from twentieth position.

Ferrari had done a splendid job and managed to claim the whole front row of the grid for themselves. Jean Alesi had finally secured his first ever pole position. As he and Gerhard stood on the pit wall, waving at the cheering fans in the grandstands, he was quite obviously delighted and looked very proud to have achieved that career milestone while driving a Ferrari at Monza.

The Williams drivers finished in third and fifth position (Damon had lapped just over 0.3 sec quicker than his team mate). Hill and Coulthard had been split by Johnny Herbert's Lotus, which had been fitted with a new specification Mugen-Honda engine. And Johnny, Lotus, and Mugen-Honda had surprised everyone (and themselves I think) with their renewed competitive performance.

Tim and Reg had made an excellent job of repairing 04. As a precaution we had inspected the chassis every time Jos had returned to the pits, but there was no evidence at all that the damaged area was likely to be problematic. However, it was only sensible to change to chassis 03 for the Grand Prix, and thoroughly check 04 back at the factory before committing it to another race distance.

Because of the amount of work that had been carried out on 03 since Ross had decided on Friday's plan of action, there was probably less for Dave, Bobby, and me to do than would otherwise prove necessary for a standard Saturday night race preparation, and the three cars were finished at a very reasonable 10.00 p.m.

In Sunday morning's warm up Jos reported that 03 didn't feel anywhere near as good as 04 had done the day before. The cars had been set up exactly the same, and the springs and dampers had been swapped over from 04 the night before. In theory both cars should have reacted exactly the same.

'No, this car definitely feels much softer,' said Jos. So Christian sent Jos back out in the spare car to get a comparison. 'There must be something wrong with that one,' commented Jos on his return, 'The spare car is much more like 04 was during qualifying.' We changed the tyres on 03 and Jos tried again. 'No, it's not the tyres, it feels exactly the same.'

Once the warm-up was over we checked the set-up on the flat patch, but everything was correct. The general consensus of opinion was that the chassis itself was at fault, and (as I described a few pages ago) the high mileage of 03, combined with the extensive repair work that had been carried out to the bottom of the chassis (after Michael's Silverstone shunt while testing there in June) had possibly resulted in 03 simply becoming too old and tired to be of any real use to us any longer.

Ross wanted 03 sent to Silverstone after we returned to England so we could carry out a proper investigation when we had more time. But for now, of course, if 03 had some sort of problem, then it couldn't be raced. Jos would drive the spare car in the afternoon.

In the event, however, it really wouldn't have made much difference which chassis Jos used, his race was over after only a couple of laps. At the start of the race there had been several minor collisions as the field fought for position at the first chicane. The end result of which was a blocked track, leaving the race officials no alternative but to stop the Grand Prix.

Unfortunately, during the opening lap of the restarted race Jos's Benetton became tangled with Alessandro Zanardi's Lotus, leaving both cars with cut rear tyres. Jos limped the B194 around the circuit and back to the pit lane, but by now the damage was far more than just a ripped tyre. The remains of the flailing tyre had been battering the car, eventually the bodywork had broken away, exposing the engine oil-cooler and that too had been badly damaged. We were left with no alternative but to retire the car from the race.

J.J. had only marginally better luck himself. He did manage to finish, but following a ten-second time penalty (for speeding in the pit lane) he was unable to get any higher than ninth place. The time penalty was a result of a defective wheel-speed sensor which controls the car's 'pit lane speed-limiter'.

J.J. had been coming in for his pit stop, pressed the switch to activate the limiter – and nothing happened. By the time J.J. realized what had happened (or not happened, in this instance) it was too late, he jumped on the brakes, but had already driven through the speed-trap. And so, as a result of Jos's early retirement from the race and J.J. finishing in ninth position we began packing away without scoring a single point.

The race was one of mixed fortune for Ferrari and Williams. Jean Alesi had been in excellent form during the first section of the race. A gap had been developing between himself and Gerhard, and it looked as though the stage was set for him to win his first Grand Prix, and for Ferrari to finish first and second, the prospect of which had sent the *tifosi* into raptures.

Unfortunately, following Jean's first pit stop the gear selector failed, leaving the transmission in neutral as he tried to pull away from the pits. Nigel Stepney and the mechanics quickly dragged the Ferrari back, and with the howl of the V12 screaming in frustration they frantically tried to cure the fault, but it was no use, the problem lay inside the gearbox itself. It was a lost cause.

It was so disappointing for them, and you could sense their complete despair at the situation. No, it can't be! Not at Monza! Not today! Not when we were winning the race! Alesi jumped out of the car and stormed off, and the Ferrari was pulled very solemnly back inside the garage.

However, even with car number 27 out of the race, Ferrari were still winning, as the lead had been taken by Gerhard Berger. There was still a fair chance of a Ferrari victory at Monza, and the *tifosi* were giving Gerhard their complete support. But only a few laps later – and as a result of a slow pit stop – Gerhard slipped to third position, and handed the lead to Damon Hill.

In fact with David Coulthard being directly behind his team-mate the two FW16s were now running first and second and, quite understandably, neither the Ferrari personnel, nor their throng of supporters looked too pleased about it.

The pit lane garages are allocated to the different teams depending on their standings in the Constructors' World Championship from the previous season. So, as reigning Champions, Williams enjoyed the prestige of having the garage closest to the pit lane entrance. McLaren were in the second garage, Benetton had the third, and so on. The Ferrari pit was located between ours and Ligier's. Unfortunately for Ferrari, Oliver Panis shot into the Ligier pits at exactly the same moment as Gerhard was trying to leave. The two of them very nearly hit, and Nigel Stepney was close to being trapped between the two cars as they manoeuvred into and out of position.

This unfortunate coincidence delayed Gerhard from leaving the pits for several precious seconds, and it was during this time that the Williams cars moved ahead. In the grandstand opposite, the crowd were visibly and audibly most perturbed, cat whistling, shouting, and signalling to the people in the Ligier pit.

Although I only speak a few words of Italian, the actions of the *tifosi* made it perfectly clear that they strongly disapproved of the timing of the Ligier pit stop. When car number 28 finally rejoined the circuit in third position I was sure I heard a distinct rumble of thunder from the direction of Maranello.

With Hill and Coulthard storming around at the front of the field it appeared a near certainty that we would see Williams finishing the Grand Prix with a maximum sixteen points, but during the closing seconds of the last lap David Coulthard's FW16 began to lose speed and drop back from Damon. As they charged for the line, his car eventually slowed to a complete stop.

After all the hours of work that everyone at Williams, driver and team alike, had put into getting that FW16 to within sight of the finish-line it had simply run out of fuel. Damon took the chequered flag to win the race, and Gerhard shot past Coulthard to snatch the six points for second. Mika Hakkinen claimed the last place on the podium and four points for him and McLaren.

When the results of the race were printed they showed that Coulthard had been classified as finishing in sixth position, and he had been awarded the final point of the Grand Prix. It probably seemed little compensation after such an impressive drive, but at least he and his mechanics had something to show for all their efforts.

The Williams combined score of eleven points reduced the gap between themselves and Benetton to twelve points, making the current scores: Benetton, 85; Williams, 73; Ferrari, 58; McLaren, 29. In the Drivers' Championship, Damon had closed the gap between Michael and himself to just eleven points: Michael, 76; Damon, 65.

As soon as the flag drops at Monza the crowds rush towards the pit lane. Many of them bring wire cutters to open up huge holes in the safety fences as they charge over the track. Their main quest, of course, is to get as close as possible to their beloved scarlet cars, and obtain anything they can find as a souvenir. But in a country so passionate about Formula One it isn't only Ferrari that has to worry about post-race security. Over the years teams have lost thousands of pounds worth of equipment: TV monitors; air-guns; pit stop jacks; wheel-nuts; wheels and radios. Even entire pit stop gantries have all disappeared.

The very second the winner crosses the line it is vital to get everything inside the garage as quickly as possible, and get the doors firmly closed. The fans at Monza cram themselves against the garages, banging on the doors and shouting in sheer exuberance at being within touching distance of the otherwise incredibly elusive world of Grand Prix racing.

In the rush to get everything and everyone safely inside before the hoards descend, team personnel occasionally get left behind and become trapped on the outside. If that happens to anyone the best thing they can do is slide their FOCA Identification pass underneath the nearest garage door to where they are, irrespective of which team they belong to, and hope the mechanics will see it and lift the door just enough to get them inside. While they attempt to scramble through the gap the mechanics inside will try and keep the thousands of excited fans on the outside.

We managed to escape fairly lightly this year. We only lost one piece of equipment. Mick's 'BRAKES ON' board must now be an unusual conversation piece in a house somewhere in Italy. In the rush to get everything in the garage the board had been left behind. It had survived the intense heat of the Hockenheim fire with only minor burns, but it had stood no chance whatsoever against a swarm of desperate souvenir hunters.

As soon as the trucks were back at the factory, we stripped chassis 04 and sent it into the Composite Department to be thoroughly inspected. Then Dave, Bobby, and I were on our way to Silverstone with chassis 03. The test team were already there, and the idea was to let Jos drive 03 and the test car. If he still thought there was a handling problem with 03 then we would try and identify whether the chassis itself was at fault.

It was raining at Silverstone. Nothing too unusual about that, of course, but we needed the circuit to dry before we could carry out any useful 'back-to-back' tests. In the wet the track is constantly changing, and as the drivers gently feather the throttle and brakes it becomes very difficult to get a proper comparison between cars. We stayed there for two days, waiting for it to stop raining, but the Silverstone weather was having none of it.

At the end of the second day we had no choice but to give up and return to the factory. We simply couldn't afford to waste any more time there. 04 had been given another clean bill of health, and we only had two days in which to rebuild it into Jos's race car before the trucks would have to leave for Portugal.

Because we hadn't been able to confirm whether 03 was still serviceable, there seemed no point in taking it with us. Chassis 08 would be used as the spare car. 06 replaced 03 as the Emergency Spare chassis, and J.J. would stay with 05.

Damon was obviously keen to take full advantage of Michael's absence from the Portuguese Grand Prix, and, with all due credit, Williams, Renault, and their two drivers completely dominated the race at Estoril. They started the race from second and third on the grid, and were the first two cars to cross the line at the end, Coulthard directly behind his team mate.

Gerhard had succeeded in securing pole position for Ferrari, but his race was finished after only seven laps when he pulled off with transmission problems. From that point on, the honours always belonged to Williams.

We seemed to have set-up problems all weekend. Possibly not as much as at Monza, but it was still very frustrating. Jos had qualified in tenth place, which I suppose has been about his average for the races he has driven in, but with J.J. unable to get any higher than fourteenth, the lap times made it appear that Benetton were simply off the pace.

It was obvious to the whole world that without the efforts of our number one driver we were nowhere near as competitive. As engineers and mechanics there is only so much we can do to increase our performance level. The rest must be achieved on the circuit.

Jos crossed the line in fifth place, and scored two points for himself and the team. J.J. failed to finish, spinning off into the gravel with only ten laps of the race remaining. McLaren scored five points at Estoril – Hakkinen third, Brundle sixth – but despite this very respectable result they had now dropped out of contention to win the Constructors' Championship.

There were only three teams still in a position to be able to clinch the title: Williams (who had just overtaken our lead), Benetton, and Ferrari. The scores:

Williams, 89 points; Benetton, 87 points; Ferrari, 58 points.

Damon's win had reduced Michael's lead in the Drivers' Championship to a mere one point: Michael, 76 points; Damon, 75 points.

# OCTOBER

It was the way the rain lashed directly in the face that seemed to annoy most people. The fact that it felt about minus 10 degrees and that our clothes did nothing to prevent the howling wind blasting through to chill the very life out of us wasn't really our main complaint. We could accept that, it was normal. But why did the rain have to travel parallel to the ground, instead of merely falling from sky to earth and follow the more traditional laws of physics?

We all knew the weather at Silverstone would be back to normal by October and that the wind, the cold, and the rain were to be expected. But today Silverstone simply wasn't playing to the rules of the game. However, despite the weather's unfair advantage, none of us objected to being there, most days we did, but not today.

It was Monday the 3rd and Silverstone was playing host to the second Annual Grand Prix Mechanics' Charitable Trust Day. The Trust was originally founded by Jackie Stewart several years ago, to provide for the families of Formula One mechanics in the event of injury or illness.

We all appreciate that the Trust is there, and although I hope I will never have to make use of the funds, it's reassuring to know that people have our wellbeing at heart. Jackie had asked for a handful of volunteers from the British based teams to come to Silverstone and assist with the running of the event.

So there we were, wet, cold and more than happy to be of service. The event had been a sell-out, with the two hundred tickets being sold well in advance. The lucky few were going to be given the chance to lap Silverstone as passengers of the world's greatest drivers.

Several major manufacturers had donated cars for the day and drivers from the British Touring Car Championship, rallying and, of course, Formula One had volunteered to drive them. Last year the drivers didn't really know what they were letting themselves in for, and the event had started on quite a formal footing.

For the first few laps the drivers took it relatively steady. They drove around the circuit trying to explain to the guests their particular driving techniques and the various lines through the corners. Then, as racing drivers inevitably do, they started to get curious as to how quickly the cars could actually go.

Their lap times started to drop. Just a couple of them at first, I don't want to mention any names, but it was Derek Warwick and Johnny Herbert actually, then others soon began to investigate their machines' potential. On their return to the pit lane smoke was pouring from the brakes, and after an hour of touring round, constantly restocking with eager passengers, the cars were ready for a rest.

Fortunately, most of the manufacturers had supplied a back up team to carry out any necessary maintenance. The red-faced and profusely sweating mechanics worked flat out, changing tyres and replacing brake pads. I overheard one young apprentice complaining that he thought the day had sounded 'a bit of a doddle. A day out of the garage, a free trip to Silverstone, meet some famous drivers. Just some fancy press day. Nothing to it!' Wrong.

It made a refreshing change to stand back and watch someone else desperately working as fast as possible. We loved every minute of it. Especially after the apprentice had come out with the hilarious 'What are you lot doing here? I thought you only worked seven seconds a fortnight!' He had come out with that superb piece of satiric comedy at 9.30 p.m. in the morning. He didn't look quite so chirpy by 4.00 p.m.

That first year set the standard, and this year was conducted in much the same manner. The cars were thrashed to within an inch of their lives, then handed over to their suppliers to be turned around and thrashed again. The weather did nothing to detract from the fun of the day, and in fact, the drivers reported how enjoyable it was trying to keep the cars on the tarmac, something not all of them managed.

Our names were drawn out of a hat to see which driver we would be with, and Bob and I found ourselves paired with Ukyo Katayama. In the morning the guests had 'timed slots' with each driver, to ensure everyone had a fair chance of driving with the top names. After lunch, during the afternoon session, the guests were free to join the queue for whichever driver they wanted.

Our job was easy enough. Check the guests' names against our sheet, sort them out with a helmet, and make sure they were securely installed in the car. 'Please make sure you keep the seat belt fastened,' we told them, 'Not just in case of an accident, but without it you'll be thrown all over the place.'

'And possibly be really sick too!' added Bob. When they climbed back out after their first trip, some looked like young children again, big bright eyes and enormous smiles, unable to talk quickly enough to describe their experiences. I found one chap that needed some help to get back out of the car.

'Can you give me a hand?' he said in a quiet voice.

'Of course, are you O.K.?' I asked. We sat him down while he caught his breath.

'Do you think I could have a glass of water?' We quickly fetched him a drink.

'Are you alright?' I asked again.

'Do you feel sick?' asked Bob. The man didn't look pale or anything, just a little dazed.

'That was . . .' he paused for another gulp of water, 'That was . . .' again he stopped short, searching for the right word.

Eventually he gave up and decided to create his own, '. . . unbloody believe-able!' With that he stood up, thanked us for the water, and walked off to join the queue for a trip with Mika Hakkinen.

In the afternoon the weather calmed down a little, the rain stopped, and the wind began to dry the circuit. This allowed the guests to experience the cars under different conditions, and from what I could see everyone seemed to thoroughly enjoy themselves, drivers and guests alike. It was a good day and I hope we carry on having them for many more years to come.

There was one major alteration to the schedule for round 14 of the '94 World Championship, and that was the venue. We should have been visiting the brand new *'Circuit Autodromo Municipal de la Ciudad de Buenos Aires'* in Argentina (I hope you pronounced that correctly and didn't just skip over it). But, unfortunately, the circuit was so new that it hadn't been finished in time.

There had been stories circulating for months that the race would be can-celled, and several circuit owners had approached both FOCA and the FIA to try and stage the replacement Grand Prix. In the end – and just to disprove what I told you in February – the race was awarded to Jerez in Spain, and the event was renamed the European Grand Prix. I would have quite liked to have visited Argentina.

I have never been there, and different places are always interesting to inves-tigate for the first time. However, while chatting on a plane, a stewardess once told me that the trek to Buenos Aires is a 15-hour flight, the longest non-stop flight in current service. On the strength of that alone, I was perfectly happy to go back to Spain for the third time in eight months.

There had been other interesting developments too. Nigel Mansell had signed with Williams to drive car number 2 for the remaining three Grands Prix of the year. The Indycar season had finished, Nigel had completed his contract with Newman-Haas and he was extremely keen to return to Formula One.

David Coulthard must have been very disappointed to have to step down, especially after his superb drives at Monza and Estoril. But although Mansell's return meant that Coulthard's season would finish prematurely, he had already done more than enough to impress the Team Managers up and down the pit lane, and I feel sure Coulthard will be racing in Formula One in '95. Not nec-essarily in a Williams, perhaps, but definitely in one of the major teams.

There were also driver changes at Lotus and Ligier. Lotus had been struggling financially all year, and in the end they were forced to put Johnny Herbert's contract on the market to raise money. A deal had been agreed with Ligier, and the teams had exchanged drivers. Johnny caught a flight down to Magny-

Qualifying in Hungary. Jos and Christian talk via the radio. Dave Redding is standing directly behind Christian, while Bobby and Jakey are leaning on the rear wing.

Pat Symonds (far right) and the Cosworth engineers study the constant stream of data being accumulated from the cars' telemetry systems.

Hungary. Jos and chassis 04 on route to score their first ever points.

At last! Michael and Jos finally get to share the podium.

Damon, Michael, and Jos wave to the world. The party in Jos's home town carried on right through the night.

Everyone had worked extremely hard to be able to savour this moment. When it finally came, it was definitely worth all the effort.

Joan and Jos on the grid at Monza.

On the grid at Estoril. This was to be JJ's last race for us. Notice how Jon is using the bonnet as a shield to stop anyone photographing the Benetton suspension.

Michael shakes hands with Damon in Jerez. This was Michael's first race
back with us, following his two race suspension.

Another victory celebration
for Michael and Benetton.

Tom Walkinshaw chats with Johnny Herbert (in Ligier overalls).

Tom Walkinshaw chats with Johnny Herbert (in Benetton overalls).

Michael at Adelaide, the final Grand Prix of the year.

Michael walks back to the garage after the collision with Damon. He has just become the 1994 FIA Formula One World Champion.

British team, Italian owners, German World Champion.
The United Colors of Benetton pose for the cameras at the end of a very long year.

Cours, and Eric Bernard would find himself driving a Lotus 109C in Jerez.

Now that Michael's two-race ban was over, chassis 08 was returned to Max, Ken, and Jon, to be used as Michael's race car while chassis 05 was given to Paul, Paul, and Lee to be rebuilt as the spare car. Dave, Bobby, and I serviced and prepared 04 for Jos. The emergency spare chassis remained 06.

On Saturday the 8th, the transporters departed for Plymouth harbour to catch the Sunday lunchtime sailing to Santander and begin their final European trip of the season. When they returned from Spain the tools, spares, and equipment would be removed, and everything would be loaded into pack-horses in readiness for the final two races of the year in Japan and Australia.

We would fly out to Jerez on Thursday morning, which meant we could have a few days' rest, away from anything to do with Grand Prix racing.

The bathroom was really beginning to take shape now. My neighbour, Jon, had been coming in whenever he had a spare hour or so, and one by one, jobs were being crossed off the list. The window frame had been completely stripped, and sanded, and varnished. New hinges had been fitted to the door frame, and the door had even been fitted to the hinges, and when I returned home on that Saturday afternoon, the bathroom walls gleamed at me with their bright new paint.

'What about the floor?' Jon asked, 'Have you decided? Tiles? Carpet? Carpet tiles? Or shall we rip the hardboard up and sand the floorboards?' I hadn't thought about what to put on the floor. I'd got so used to seeing the hardboard, I didn't even notice it any more.

'Ah, yes, the floor, right, I don't really know. Oh, how about that sea-grass stuff? That always looks quite fun.' I'd seen it in those converted school houses in the free Sunday magazines, where the lounge has twice the floor area of my entire house, and there are always two or three Beagles sleeping in front of a log fire. If it was good enough for the more affluent and discerning Beagles of the community, I thought it must be good enough for my bathroom.

'Well, I wish you the best of luck trying to find it.'

'Why do you say that, Jon?'

'It's sometimes difficult to get hold of,' he warned. 'You had better ask how long it's going to take the shop to order it. People might promise they can get it, they might even be able to produce a sample. But a roll of the actual stuff itself . . .'

'But it only looks like old string and seaweed! It's not like the materials are hard to come by, surely. Alright, well, leave it with me. I'll look into it to-morrow.' After visiting a carpet shop the next day I fully appreciated Jon's warning.

'Sea-grass? Yes, we can get sea-grass,' promised the girl. Then her brow began to furrow and she looked at me with inquisitive eyes. 'When did you want it?'

'Well, as soon as possible. How long is it likely to take?'

'If they have it in stock, you can have it tomorrow.' She smiled. That sound-ed more like it. 'But if they haven't, and our suppliers have to order it them-selves, it could be six months.'

Six months? I couldn't believe it. How could it possibly take six months to get hold of a few lengths of dead seaweed? Formula One can stage three-quarters of a World Championship in six months!

'Look,' she said, 'leave me your number. I'll have a go. I'll give you a call and let you know what I find out. It comes from China.' I think 'China' was supposed to explain it all. 'China? It sounds more like it comes from the Moon.'

'It's not from the Moon. If that was the case, we'd have to call it lunar-grass!' Her joke caused her to shake and giggle with laughter. I wrote my number on her notepad and left her to wipe the tears from her face. I drove back home with the distinct impression that the quality of British comedy was in steep decline.

Three things had remained the same in Jerez. The weather was still nice. Sunny, warm, but not too hot to work in. The Don Tico had managed to retain its terrible soapy smell. And there didn't appear to be any local interest in the Grand Prix whatsoever. I half expected to see a banner with 'NO INTEREST AND NO STRONG VIEWS' hanging in the grandstand, but obviously the locals couldn't summon up the motivation to make one.

The media was having a field day. Michael had returned, and in the post Estoril test he had been straight back on the pace. In his enforced absence Michael had spent his time fitness training, and he looked in excellent physical and mental health. The two-race ban had only served to increase his motivation, and he was obviously pleased to be back. He was relaxed, he was smiling, and he was very confident of success. The photographers crowded round him whenever he stepped out of the motor home or the garage, and with Nigel Mansell back in the pit lane as well, if Michael wasn't available, there was another big media target to head for.

The first qualifying session turned into a bit of a disaster for us. Heinz-Harald Frentzen had gone out for his first run as soon as the circuit opened at 1.00 p.m. followed a few minutes later by Ukyo Katayama's Tyrrell. Frentzen had just managed to set a time when Katayama's engine blew up, spraying oil all over the track. For some reason, best known to himself, Katayama didn't immediately pull off, but continued to slowly tour the circuit, laying oil all over the racing line. When eventually the Tyrrell ran out of momentum, leaving Katayama no choice but to park, the damage had already been done, and the circuit had turned into an ice rink.

The teams tried to avoid going out for as long as possible, to try and give the oil a chance to disperse, but eventually the pressure of the clock forced people on to the tarmac. Unfortunately, Jos only managed to complete two laps before he spun, and we finished the day in 28th position. Michael had managed to get his car to third place on the grid, despite complaining that the chassis didn't feel right. He couldn't quite describe what he thought the problem was, but he could definitely sense that something was wrong. Damon took the provisional pole, and the time from Frentzen's Sauber was good enough for second position.

That evening, during the engine changes, the reason for Michael's handling fault came to light. The left-hand lower engine mounting stud had sheared off in the chassis, allowing a slight degree of flex between the front and rear of the car. Because of the stud's position it had been impossible to notice this problem during the routine inspections we carry out throughout the sessions and the broken stud was only visible once the floor had been removed in preparation for the engine change.

Jos came in to the garage for a chat while we were working on the car. He looked particularly fed up and was very apologetic about what had happened during qualifying. It wasn't really his fault, it was just unfortunate that the circuit was in such a poor state when we went out. We had to try and qualify at some time. 'I hope it doesn't rain tomorrow, Jos!' said Bob.

Fortunately it didn't rain and the next day Jos qualified the car in twelfth place. And after replacing the broken stud in 08 Michael declared the handling of his car to be much better, finishing Saturday afternoon on pole position. Damon was right behind him, and Nigel Mansell had driven the other FW16 to third position, one place ahead of Frentzen's Sauber. The circuit was in much better condition on Saturday, and apart from Alesi, who spun and stalled early in the session, everybody seemed able to go about 1.5 sec a lap quicker than Friday.

Michael drove a superb race on Sunday, and went on to take the chequered flag nearly 25 sec ahead of Damon. This gave Michael a four-point advantage on the day, and extended his lead in the Drivers' Championship to five points, making the scores 86 points to Michael, 81 to Damon. Both Nigel and Jos failed to finish, each spinning off into gravel-traps during the course of the race. Although this was disappointing for us (and, of course, for the crew of car number 2 in the Williams camp), the results of the European Grand Prix meant that we regained the lead in the Constructors' Championship by two points. Benetton, 97 points; Williams, 95 points.

We had the next three days off as we waited for the trucks to get back. I spent the time writing about what had happened to us during August and waiting for the girl from the carpet shop to ring. On Monday I wrote about the investigation into the fuel rigs (the girl from the carpet shop didn't ring). On Tuesday I began telling you about the events at Hungary (the girl from the carpet shop still didn't ring). On Wednesday I completed my account of the race at Budapest and started writing about Spa, and when the 5.00 p.m. news came on the radio, I gave up waiting for the girl to ring, and I got in touch with her.

'I said I would call you when I had some news. I don't have any news, so I haven't called you,' she explained. There was just a touch of irritation in her voice. I think the stress, induced by the high pressure world of domestic floor coverings, was beginning to tell. We were back into work at 8.30 a.m. Thursday morning. While we started to strip the cars down, the truckies began loading the packhorses and Oz started to sort the abundance of paperwork necessary to satisfy the British, Japanese and Australian Customs Authorities.

All the teams have to give a detailed list of everything they intend to export abroad, the precise weight of each packhorse must be declared and the boxes then sealed. There are also declarations that must be signed to say that everything we import to Japan is only there on a temporary basis, that it will then be exported to Australia, that everything we import to Australia will only remain for the duration of the Grand Prix and it will then be exported back to Britain.

Of course, as soon as the freight lands back in England the Customs Officers require certification that everything they see before them is everything that they saw leaving for Japan a couple of weeks earlier. One mislaid form, or one missing label and we might not have any equipment waiting for us at Suzuka or Adelaide. Car 6 was to have a new driver for the final two races. Johnny Herbert had impressed many people when driving the Ligier in the last Grand Prix, and an agreement had been arranged between both teams to allow Johnny to test a Benetton B194 at Barcelona on the Thursday and Friday following the Jerez race.

Johnny had jumped at the chance of being able to demonstrate his ability in a Championship leading car, and had managed to get within 0.4 secs of Michael's best time, which he had set on Friday morning. Later that afternoon, while we were preparing the cars, Mark Owen, our test team chief mechanic, sent a report of the test back to the factory, containing only good news for a change.

As soon as we saw the lap times we suspected that Johnny would be asked to drive for us in Japan, and a few days later the situation was finalized. Johnny's contract was still with Ligier, but they had loaned him to us for the remainder of the season.

Jos was disappointed not to be driving, but he had been very understanding of the situation and was willing to stand down if it would benefit the team. We were going into these last two races fighting for the Championship and Johnny had a lot of experience of both the Suzuka and the Adelaide circuits. Jos, of course, had none. He would still join us in Japan and Australia, putting his race shirt back on, wearing a radio headset, and picking up as much useful information from Michael and Johnny as possible. At least that's what he said. I think he was coming along for the party that would undoubtedly follow the last race, as much as for anything else.

The final shakedown of the year was conducted at Silverstone. It wasn't raining, just bitterly cold. We had to work in a marquee tent, as the old pits were being demolished to make way for brand new facilities to be built.

'I bet you boys are going to miss these old pit lane garages, and all the nostalgia that's associated with them', said one of the marshals. I looked at Dave and thought about the endless number of freezing days and nights we had spent there. Dave looked at me, obviously thinking the same. We both looked at the marshal, 'No.'

We left for Japan on Sunday the 30th, flying with the same airline as when we went out to the Pacific Grand Prix, All Nippon Airways. It was going to be another hideously long trip, and I wasn't looking forward to it in the slightest. All cramped up for twelve or fourteen hours, then another flight, then a two hour coach journey, time differences to adjust to. Jeff's coaches got us to Heathrow's Terminal Three in plenty of time and after we had negotiated the rigmarole of checking in, we went for a coffee and a bite to eat.

To pass the final half hour I went for a stroll around Duty Free. Everything was more or less the same as before, but at least I was doing something, instead of just watching the clock slowly tick round. Whisky bottles, brandy bottles, teddy bears wearing T-shirts, Rolex watches, Mont Blanc pens, girls offering useless gifts if you buy certain cigarettes, furry covers for golf clubs which seem to cost more than the club itself. All the normal things. In the corner of the departure terminal was a small sign: Berry Bros and Rudd Ltd. it announced. I went over to see what the Berry brothers had for sale. I had only been there for a few minutes when Ken and Bat walked over: 'Steve! Come on, we've got to go. The 'last call' light has been flashing for twenty minutes.'

We shot off for the departure gate. I had to double check the number on my boarding pass when I found my seat. No, it was correct. I had been upgraded to Club! That made the flight to Japan far more appealing. I made myself comfortable, sipped a glass of orange juice, and wondered if All Nippon Airways could emulate their British Airways counterparts by issuing the Club passengers with something to reduce the risk of skin dehydration from the drying effect of the cabin air.

# NOVEMBER

Until the body clock finally resets itself to local time, the thing about waking up in a country with a nine hour time difference, is that you're awake instantly. One second you are deep, deep asleep, with no concept of ever being alive and the next second BANG. Wide awake. You feel fresh and alert, as though you've just plunged yourself into an ice cold pool. For most people this is an odd sensation and something that takes a little getting used to. Certainly that's the case with me. It normally takes me about ten minutes to slowly come round, as, one by one, the senses gradually and begrudgingly start assessing the situation, and begin to cautiously assemble any available information, Have I got enough time to go back to sleep? No. Am I late? No. Can I smell coffee? No. Right, well get up and go and find some.

It was just 6.00 a.m. when I sprang into life, which wasn't too bad at all. It's a poor start to the day if you're wide awake at two, or three o'clock in the morning. There's no chance of getting back to sleep and by 4.00 p.m. you'll be struggling to keep your eyes open. If that happens, you must avoid taking a late afternoon nap 'Just for ten minutes'. Believe me, it doesn't work. You'll sleep until midnight, and the next day will be twice as bad. It's most important to get it right that first night. When I opened the bedroom curtains I realised exactly why Japan is known as the land of the rising sun. The sunrise was simply magnificent.

Our hotel was one of the tallest buildings in Yokkaichi, and my room overlooked the town, down to the docks and onto the waterfront. The sun was just creeping over the horizon. It was enormous, rich dark red in colour, with bright flashes of fire burning within it. Moments later it had risen to about a quarter its full size and its colours changed from dark red, to scarlet, and to orange. A few seconds more and it had left the sea behind, slowly lifting itself into the sky. It started to lose its definite shape, as the heat caused the sky to shimmer and haze around it. The colours changed again. From orange, to bright yellow, eventually into brilliant white, finally becoming too intense to look at. It was certainly a spectacular start to the day.

The area around Suzuka is far more industrialized than Aida, and the exchange of trade between East and West has resulted in the hotels being familiar to seeing and dealing with foreigners, so they can handle the whines and moans of European visitors with less confusion. Therefore, the 'I can't eat noodles for breakfast! I want bacon and eggs and toast and marmalade!' brigade can normally be appeased. I don't say that out of pretentious snobbery, I'll be the first to admit that I'd prefer cornflakes and a strong coffee, as opposed to a traditional Japanese breakfast, but some people just refuse to adapt to their surroundings.

The breakfast room at the Yokkaichi Miyako has a buffet laid out, so you can help yourself to whatever there is. It may not have been traditional English in the purest sense of the words, but it seemed to go down better than the cold fried eggs and potato salad we had in Aida.

We left for the circuit at 9.30 a.m. All we were going to do was unload the tools and equipment, get the cars unpacked, and prepare the garage with the banners and so on. We had three days before the first practice session, so providing nothing terrible had happened to the cars while in transit, we would have plenty of time to prepare for Friday. Suzuka is about a 30-minute drive from Yokkaichi. The roads are always busy, with hundreds of bicycles, scooters, cars and trucks, all riding or driving along in mutual respect for each other.

No one seems to speed. No one jumps red lights. No one adjusts the washer jets on their minibus to spray people standing at the side of the road (well, none of the Japanese that is). I've said this before, but Formula One mechanics are a sore bunch, and for some people, adjusting the washer-jets to point outwards became priority job number one. I felt sorry for the poor pedestrians. They had no idea where the spray could have come from, and while they were looking around, trying to figure out what had happened, they would be sprayed again. Terribly immature, I know, but the shouts of 'Quick! Squirt him! Squirt him!' and the resulting cheers from scoring a direct hit, still makes me smile.

I often think that in some ways travelling with a Grand Prix team is merely the grown-up version of Cub Scouts on a camping holiday. Formula One is incredibly popular here and every year the Grand Prix is completely sold out. Consequently, so many people apply for tickets that all sixteen rounds of the World Championship could take place at Suzuka, with a different audience at each race.

On the Tuesday, Wednesday, and Thursday before the race weekend, the local schools bring the young children into the circuit to watch the teams preparing for the race. Dressed in their matching sailor-style uniforms, they walk down the stairs in pairs to sit in the main grandstand opposite the pits, watching us working away. If anybody wearing team-clothing walks past the grandstand when they are there, the children give a polite and appreciative round of applause. By 4.00 p.m. we had finished unloading everything, and the banners had been erected. The cars had survived the trip from England intact, and we were looking in good shape. Mick called it a day. 'Alright everyone, that's enough. Let's go. Same time tomorrow.'

I think most of us were glad to finish when we did. There were an awful lot of tired, jet-lagged eyes in the garage. The ice-cold plunge, wide-awake feeling I had experienced at 6.00 a.m. had long since worn off. As soon as we departed for the hotel I started to drift off to sleep, and the next I knew, we were back at Yokkaichi. Shower. Change. Out. To do anything else would result in a sleepless night.

For Europeans, socialising in Yokkaichi isn't easy. It can be done, of course, but it isn't easy. As you walk about the streets there are hundreds of signs advertising various bars and clubs. Curiously, about half of them are written in English. The bars have names like 'Ace of Spades', 'Bar California' and even 'English Pub'. Most of them are in high-rise blocks, two or three of them on each floor and one building can contain anything up to 20 such establishments.

However, open one of the thick wooden doors and you normally find a tiny room with just enough seats for five or six people, and a small bar in the corner which appears to have nothing but whisky bottles behind it. The owners prefer to select carefully their amiable clientele, and on seeing four or five Westerners looking through the door, their reaction is to cross their arms into an 'X' to signify they don't want you to go inside which is fair enough, it's their bar after all. These places are small drinking clubs, frequented by business men after work. Most of them drink nothing but whisky, and the bottles behind the bar belong to the customers. They are paid for in advance, labelled, and saved for their next visit.

Over the years we have opened hundreds of these doors, but it's very hard work getting served. Occasionally, one of the owners has waved us inside, but the idea of paying 200 pounds for a bottle of scotch quickly makes one look for cheaper alternatives. There are lots of far cheaper, and much more interesting places to visit, but the problem is finding them. There are three main difficulties in tracking them down. The biggest problem is the language. None of us speak Japanese.

As a group we can get by in most of the major European tongues, and if we start to struggle there's a fair chance the waiter can speak English. But Japanese, to me at least, is unfathomable. So asking someone if they can recommend a good restaurant isn't really feasible. The second problem is a variation of the first. Japanese calligraphy is a complete mystery. I mean, even if you can't speak any French or Italian, we do, at least, share the same alphabet, and it's possible to have a go at translating some of their written words. For example: 'vin rouge', 'vino rosso', 'birra', 'biere', 'ristorante', and, of course, 'pizza' are all more than obvious, and translating just a couple of them will ensure you won't go hungry. But, to the uninitiated, the artistic brush strokes of the Japanese, offer no clues at all.

The final problem is the lack of visual clues. As soon as you get off the main roads in Yokkaichi the streets become very narrow. The buildings are close together, their windows are small and usually steamed up. In Europe a restaurant or bar is fairly easy to identify. In Japan not so. The doors are always shut, and at first sight everywhere looks either closed or private. One helpful clue is the sight of a red lantern hanging outside. This seems to be associated with eating establishments, as opposed to any other form of trade. But, at the end of the day, the only thing to do is open a few doors and look inside. Despite the old and unprofitable appearance to these back street buildings, most of the doors open automatically. Some doors slide open to reveal bars, packed with people, and clouds of cigarette smoke billow outside through the open door. Others reveal small stir-fry restaurants. Again, clouds of smoke pour outside, not from cigarettes but from the hot-plates and woks, as the chefs go about their profession. It was into one of these smoke and steam-filled places that we went for dinner. The inside looked more like a kitchen than a restaurant. Three small tables, and chairs to accommodate 12 people (if all the tables had been occupied, it would have been impossible to have moved in there). From what we could make out it appeared to be run by a husband and wife team. The two of them seemed pleased to see us. We waved and nodded at each other in welcome, and Madam showed us to a table. She brought out hot towels and chopsticks. It was pointless looking at the menu, so Bob was dispatched to try and communicate with the chef and decide what we were going to eat. Bat walked to the fridge, pointing at the bottles of cold beer through the glass door. Madam indicated that he should serve himself, smiling in what I took to be a 'make yourselves feel at home' kind of way. He returned with beer for five. Bob returned with an unconvinced look about him. 'What did you order for us?' asked Ken.

'Chicken, I think. It's difficult to know really. Every time I pointed at his different ingredients, the chef just made a chicken impression. At least I took it to be a chicken impression. Anyway, maybe chicken. And rice. Well, rice or noodles. I pointed at both, and he just nodded'.

'I'm sure it'll be fine Bob,' said Jon. 'Here, have a drink.'

'Cheers!' toasted Ken. We chinked glasses and awaited dinner. Two beers later, a large plate of chicken wings cooked in hot chilli sauce, and five bowls of boiled rice arrived at the table. 'Good old Bob'. Some of these places aren't always as clean as they might be but this one was fine, and the food, although fairly basic, was good too. One evening last year during a similar stroll about town, we came across a bar infested with rats. The place had looked clean enough from the outside and, to be fair, even the interior appeared sanitary. The inside of the bar was as large as my lounge, which to give you a better idea is about the average size of a living room.

The counter was in the middle of the room, with the bar stools around the outside. The floor, where the customers would sit around the bar, had been raised a little, giving the effect that the counter itself had been set lower down. At one end of the counter a doorway led into a tiny kitchen, effectively leaving three sides of the counter to sit around. We had managed to order a drink from the waitress, and were quietly chatting away, when Bob suddenly became interested in something behind the counter. 'I'm sure I just saw something run into the kitchen!' he said.

'Where?' asked Ken. A couple of us looked to where Bob pointed, but there wasn't anything to see. After a few seconds we started chatting again. Bob, however, was convinced he had seen something, and wouldn't take his eyes from behind the bar. 'There it goes!' Bob cried out.

'A rat! I saw it as well,' Ken agreed. We all looked. It wasn't long before another one showed itself. The girl behind the counter appeared to take no notice. Occasionally one of the rats would run straight over her feet. This made her look, but she displayed no more interest than if a pet cat had been rubbing against her leg. She looked down, she saw them, she ignored them. The rats waddled from the bar into the kitchen, had a bit of a nose about and waddled back again. They didn't seem to be in any particular hurry to go anywhere, and obviously didn't consider it necessary to hide themselves either. They must have been living in relative luxury underneath the false floor. The owner of the bar saw us watching his rats going about their business.

He put a quietening finger to his lips, 'Shh!' he whispered, and then a few words of English, just decipherable through a heavy Japanese accent, 'Mickey Mouse. Secret.'

'Mickey Mouse! Secret? That's no secret! It's an enormous rat infestation!' The rats had sent shivers down my spine, I couldn't wait to get out of the place. Fortunately the beer we had drunk had been out of a bottle, which made me feel a bit better. The idea of drinking anything from his beer pumps, that may have been open to the atmosphere, with the casks possibly stored underneath the floor was revolting.

That was last year. We had often talked about the Rat Bar since that night, and how nonchalant the staff had been in their reaction to the rats. Occasionally, during the course of the year, the suggestion had been made that on our next trip to Yokkaichi we should try and find it again, to see whether it was still open for business, or if the health and safety people had closed it down. As individuals I don't think any of us wanted to go anywhere near the place again, but as a group, motivated by sheer morbid curiosity, we decided to go and search the place out.

We had a few false starts, turning right instead of left and going down dead-ends, but eventually we found it. 'This is it!' exclaimed Bat, 'The Rat Bar! And the lights are on!' I hate rats, which I have always thought to be a fairly sound opinion to have of them, and I don't mind admitting that it was with more than a little trepidation that I walked back inside, and, for me at least, it was with great relief that we discovered the bar was under new ownership. Thankfully, the rats didn't appear to have been included in the inventory of fixtures and fittings when the terms of sale had been agreed. However, the lack of infestation resulted in the bar losing its almost macabre attraction. We soon left, and as it was now nearly midnight we decided it was time to get some sleep.

The grid positions for Sunday's Grand Prix had been decided on Friday afternoon. We didn't know this at the time, of course, but 20 minutes before Saturday's qualifying began, rain started to fall. Heavy rain, too, and it lasted for the rest of the day. Following the results of the last race, Ferrari had dropped out of contention for the Constructors' Championship. It was now a straight race between Williams and Benetton. By the end of Friday's first practice the top four times reflected the fact that both teams were trying as hard as possible to secure this particular trophy.

Michael was quickest, then the two FW16s (with Mansell leading Hill). Johnny had also driven well, and had managed to achieve the fourth fastest time of the session. J.J.'s name was also on the time-sheet. He had been approached by Sauber to drive car number 29 during these last two Grands Prix. He was still under contract to Benetton, but Flavio had agreed to release him for a return to his old team and thus help them out. Karl Wendlinger should have been driving, and with no disrespect to J.J. I was sorry he wasn't able to. Like J.J. earlier in the year, Wendlinger had made a tremendous recovery.

Since regaining consciousness in June, he had gone from strength to strength. Karl had worked extremely hard to regain his fitness and stamina in time to drive the Sauber in Japan, and he had very nearly made it. He had tested the car in France and in Spain, but his neck had started to hurt (again similar to J.J.) and he had decided that to drive too early could possibly do him more harm than good. Yet I thought it was very fitting that Sauber had asked J.J. to step in for him. Karl and J.J. had been team mates at Sauber during '93. Both had been seriously injured during the year, and both had been incredibly determined to drive again. I'm sure one would approve of the other helping out.

During the Friday afternoon qualifying session it was a Sauber that broke up the Benetton/Williams domination of the grid. J.J.'s team mate Heinz-Harald Frentzen, finished the day in third position. Michael would start the race from pole. Damon was next, just under half a second off the leader. Nigel Mansell had dropped to fourth, and Johnny was fifth.

Because of the deluge on Saturday afternoon it was simply impossible for anybody to improve on their grid position. The two Pacifics didn't even bother moving out of the garage. Their drivers, Gachot and Belmondo, had been 27th and 28th on Friday and as only 26 cars are allowed to start the race, it would have been pointless for them to have run.

We sent both Michael and Johnny out into the rain, to get a feel for the cars in the wet, and to see what the drainage of the circuit was like. It was important to know where any puddles of water would form, in case it started to rain during the race. It could end in disaster if a car exited a corner, to find standing water or a stream running over the line to which the driver had committed himself.

The Saturday night race preparation seemed to take a long while. Because of the data we had acquired during the wet session the engineers had a lot of set-up calculations to do before they could release the job lists to us (at least that's the reason they gave for keeping us waiting). The weather forecast for Sunday gave a high possibility of rain, but we couldn't just set the cars for wet conditions on the strength of that alone. We would have to have dry settings as well. So, while Ross, the engineers and the drivers pondered over what they wanted to do, we began the standard preparation work.

New engines were fitted in all three cars. The gearboxes were inspected and new gear ratios installed. The brake discs and pads were removed, measured, and the figures given to Pat and Chris so they could calculate the anticipated wear during the race and thus specify the type and thickness of the replacement material. Drinks bottles were fitted. The suspension was checked. Wishbones inspected for any cracks around the welds, bolts checked for tightness, upright bearings for any play. In fact, every single component on the car received its due attention.

We were leading both World Championships. If we finished first and second tomorrow, we would win them both. The atmosphere in the garage reflected that situation. I'm not saying we worked in complete silence, each of us concentrating with such intensity that you could hear a pin drop, but there was a definite difference, a mood of expectation. I'm sure most of the team had contemplated what it must feel like to be World Champions. I remember chatting to Tim about it at Magny-Cours, but that conversation was over four months ago. Then it had been purely wishful thinking, I couldn't really focus on it as being a definite possibility. But now, here we were on the evening before it could actually become reality.

The Constructors' Championship was established in 1958. Many famous teams had claimed the trophy over the years: Vanwall, Cooper, Ferrari, BRM, Lotus, Brabham, Matra, Tyrrell, McLaren and Williams have all been winners during the Championship's 36 year history. Tomorrow could see our name added to the list and all of us were doing as much as possible to ensure the cars stayed reliable.

Michael – and Damon, I'm sure – had been under a tremendous amount of pressure in Japan. He couldn't step out of the garage without being hounded by film crews. Everyone wanted an interview with the Championship leader before these final two races. Saturday might be their last chance to interview him as a contender for the Championship. By Sunday he could be World Champion, and everybody wanted his thoughts on that prospect before tomorrow's race. Michael had remained calm and unruffled. He had given the interviews, signed the autographs, shaken hands with hundreds of fans and remained polite and patient through it all.

It was 1.30 on Sunday morning before we had finished work, and it had just gone two o'clock by the time we had driven back to Yokkaichi, showered and got to bed. The alarm woke me up three hours later. We had to leave for the circuit at 5.30 a.m., which left me half an hour to lie there for a few minutes, shower again, find a clean race shirt, and get back into the minibus. By this stage of the week I had adjusted to the time difference in Japan, and I certainly didn't awake with a BANG. When I opened the curtains it was still dark outside, but the sound of the rain hitting the window told me not to expect another spectacular sunrise.

The roads around Suzuka were crawling with traffic, slowly making its way towards the circuit. Hundreds of people were queuing at the gates, all wrapped in brightly coloured anoraks or sheltering under umbrellas. It may have been raining, but the weather had done nothing to dampen the spirits and enthusiasm of the Japanese fans. It had been raining when we left the paddock a few hours earlier. It was still raining when we returned. It rained during pit stop practice. It rained during breakfast. It rained during the warm-up. It was a wet race.

As the cars sat on the grid prior to the formation lap, the weather changed from bad to worse. During this final half-hour, it's fairly normal for the drivers to climb out, have a last stretch, and maybe even a few words with one of the film crews. But today the drivers had no intention of getting out. They sat under umbrellas, keeping dry, and the film crews would just have to interview someone else. While these interviews are going on, the mechanics are constantly fussing, checking that everything is in order, or trying to look as calm and serene as possible, when the car suddenly decides to throw a tantrum.

Every Formula One team in the pit lane can recall stories of last minute problems on the grid. Oil leaks, water leaks, fuel leaks, bodywork fasteners breaking, air bottles for the engine's pneumatic valve system losing pressure or starter-motors deciding not to work. The list is endless. At least one team or another has had problems during every Grand Prix this year.

Thankfully both of our cars were fine, and as the rain poured down I spent most of the thirty minutes crouched at the side of the car, sheltering under Johnny's umbrella. I expected the start to be delayed, but it wasn't, and at 1.00 p.m. (the race always starts one hour earlier at Suzuka) the cars were flagged away for their formation lap. They began a slow amble around the circuit, but even at this pace the tyres threw clouds of water into the air. At racing speeds the visibility would drop close to zero.

The lights changed from red to green and the Grand Prix began. The cars disappeared into a thick fog of spray. Mansell made a poor start and, by the first corner Johnny was up to fourth place. By the second lap he was up to third, as Frentzen went off the circuit. Within minutes of the start Michael and Damon were already in a race of their own, over 10 sec clear of the rest. The weather deteriorated again and hail stones were mixed with the rainstorm. The conditions became impossible. The officials made the decision to dispatch the Safety Car, and slow the cars down until the weather sorted itself out.

At the same instant as the yellow flags started to wave around the circuit, Johnny led the rest of the pack onto the main straight. The track was flooded with water, and the hail only helped to make conditions worse. There was simply no traction at all and Johnny aquaplaned off the circuit, merely trying to drive in a straight line. He was fine, but the car was out of the race, and the prospect of winning the Constructors' Championship in Japan was over. I felt really miserable. Damn it! We had been looking good up until then.

A second later, Ukyo Katayama's Tyrrell slammed into the pit wall. He too had done nothing wrong, but had just lost control on the straight. Katayama hadn't been as lucky as Johnny, and was limping badly. He was helped back to the Tyrrell garage by two of the marshals. Pat was straight on the radio.

'Michael, the Safety Car has gone out. Be careful when you come onto the main straight. Johnny has gone off, so has Katayama, there may be debris lying . . .' SLAM. Pat broke off in mid-sentence as a Simtek also collided with the pit wall.

'Michael, there are cars going off all over the place! Be very careful!'

'OK Pat. The conditions are terrible out here. Are they going to stop the race?' asked Michael.

'Not at the moment, we believe the Safety Car will stay out for the time being. We'll let you know as soon as we know more.'

'Where's the Safety Car now? I can't see it.'

'From what we can see on the monitors, it's further around the circuit to where you are. Just keep cruising around, he'll find you.'

'OK. How's Johnny?'

'Fine. He lost it on the straight, but he's not injured.'

'O.K.'

The Benetton slowly toured round the circuit, and eventually found the Safety Car. The entire field then closed up behind Michael, and followed him around the track in formation. After a few laps, the rain started to ease slightly. The decision was made to recall the Safety Car, and resume the Grand Prix. However, within a lap of trying to race again, both Minardis and one of the Ligiers had collided and Berger's Ferrari had stopped. A few laps later Morbidelli's Arrows had also spun off. His car had hit the barrier very hard, and he had been lucky to escape injury. Then Martin Brundle's car aquaplaned off the circuit, just where the marshals were trying to move the wrecked Arrows. The McLaren knocked one of the marshals over and the race was immediately red-flagged to a halt.

The impact had broken the marshal's leg and he was taken straight off to hospital for treatment. Martin's car had collided with the guard rail, ripping the suspension off the right rear and the left front corners. Although badly shaken, he climbed out the McLaren unaided and was obviously concerned about the marshal's injury.

The Grand Prix was eventually re-started about 30 minutes later. The hail had stopped and the rain had reduced to a more acceptable level. The results of the race were to be decided on the aggregate times from both 'legs'. This system always appears to me to be terribly complicated, as the time differences and positions of the cars as shown on the monitors, do not necessarily tie up with what is occurring out on the track. It becomes easier not to watch the pictures from the circuit cameras, and just concentrate on the time sheets instead.

Michael pitted five laps after the restart. The pit stop went well, but, unfortunately, by the time he rejoined the circuit Damon had taken the lead – both on the circuit and on aggregate times! Damon pitted seven laps later. He had managed to build enough of a lead over Michael that he retained first place by 7.5 sec, although on the circuit the two cars were actually close to 14.5 sec apart, as Michael had started this second leg of the race with a 6.8 sec advantage over Damon.

The Benetton simply tore around the circuit in pursuit. He didn't have to pass Damon to regain the lead, he just had to get within 6.8 sec of him as this would reduce Damon's aggregate lead to zero. Lap after lap the Benetton closed on the Williams advantage. This had genuinely become a race against time, and it made an interesting change to see a Grand Prix decided this way. Damon's lead started to drop. The FW16 crossed the timing line. We waited. The B194 crossed the timing line. The lead was down to 6.2 seconds. They shot off on their next lap. Damon crossed the line. Michael crossed the line 5.8 sec. Then 5.7 seconds 5.3, 5.2, 4.4, 3.4, 1.3, 0.4. The next time Michael drove past the line he had regained the lead by 1.1 seconds. 'Michael, you must keep pushing,' Pat informed him, 'We must build up some time for your second pit stop. We don't think Hill will pit again. You must keep pushing!'

'OK. I'll try!' replied Michael.

The Williams shot down the main straight, seconds later the Benetton did the same. Michael's lead started to rise, 2.0 sec, 3.3 sec, 3.7 sec, 'Stand by chaps', said Ross. Pat radioed to Michael. 'OK Michael. In at the end of this lap. In at the end of this lap. Please acknowledge.'

'OK. Coming in.'

The tyres were taken out of their blankets, and carried outside. '40 seconds,' said Pat. '20 seconds.' I could hear the air guns whirring behind me, as they were given a final check. 'He's in the pit lane!' The B194 sprinted down into position. Fuel-hose on. Car up. Tyres changed. Fuel-hose off. Car down. Seven seconds! Taking into account the time lost through coming into the pit lane, the seven second stop, and the time lost exiting the pit lane, when the Benetton crossed the timing line again we had given the lead to Williams by 14.6 sec.

There were only nine laps remaining and they were some of the most exciting laps I've ever seen. Once again Michael set off after Damon, and once again the time difference started to fall, 14.1 sec, 11.9, 10.0, and then 8.3 seconds. Both Michael and Damon were driving at the absolute limit. At times it looked as though Damon might have been driving the Williams too hard, as it twitched and slid around the corners, but he managed to keep it under control and kept on pushing. Michael was also driving very hard, and still the time between them kept dropping, 7.0, then 5.2 sec. Three laps left, 4.2 sec, then 2.4 seconds. On the last lap Damon was really throwing his car into the corners, the Williams seemed poised on a knife edge between gripping the circuit and spinning off. He crossed the line and took the chequered flag, but we had to wait for Michael to cross the line before we knew who had won. The Benetton shot down the main straight, and crossed the line 3.3 sec behind the Williams.

Those last ten laps had kept everyone enthralled, and the shouts of encouragement for both drivers from up and down the pit lane had made Suzuka seem as though it was hosting the Grand National rather than a Grand Prix. With the four point advantage for winning the race Damon was now only one point behind Michael in the Drivers' Championship. Mansell had finished in fourth place, giving Williams a tally of 13 points on the day, and a grand total of 108. Michael's six points gave us a total of 103. The lead in the Constructors' Championship had reverted to Williams, and they were obviously delighted to have kept both title battles open until the very last race of the year.

I can't admit to feeling half as delighted as the Williams camp. It would have been wonderful to have finished first and second here, and clinched both Championships before Adelaide. The accident was in no way Johnny's fault. We had simply been caught out by the weather. I just had a feeling that we would do better than we did. Our car has been particularly short of luck this year. Damn it! Damn it! Damn! It really had been very frustrating.

Then something happened, which although being perfectly apt, nevertheless seemed to add insult to injury. One of the circuit marshals came into the garage, and walked over to where Dave and myself were sitting (and feeling sorry for ourselves) on the tool cabinets. The marshal appeared to be in his early twenties, and was keen to try out his English on us. 'Excuse me Sir?' he said. I thought he was going to ask us for some Benetton stickers. 'What can we do for you?' Dave inquired.

'Excuse me Sir. The Benetton crash machine is ready to carry home. OK?'

'Thank you,' I replied, 'we'll go and fetch it.'

'Thank you, Sir. Goodbye!'

'Yes, goodbye.' What he had said was obviously a poor translation from Japanese to English, but his wording wasn't far wrong. The Benetton Crash Machine. That just about summed up our season.

The race might have finished, but we still had hours of work ahead of us. The first practice session for the Australian Grand Prix was only five days away. In that time we had to rebuild the cars, fly everything and ourselves down to Adelaide, clear the freight through customs, get the freight to the circuit, unload, prepare the garages, and finalize the cars to run on Friday morning.

It was important to do as much of the rebuild work as possible here in Japan. It was a very tight time schedule to begin with and if the freight was delayed in transit for any reason we might not make it for Friday's qualifying session. And if it rained on the Saturday, (as it did here in Japan), we wouldn't even be competing in the last race, never mind fighting for any Championships.

We worked on the cars until about 11.00 p.m. We still had work left to finish off, but the freight was beginning to leave and if we wanted the cars to be in Australia when we arrived there, we had to get them to the airport immediately. While we had been changing engines and uprights, the truckies had been busy loading the banners, wheel-rims, and any tools and equipment we weren't using – and some we were using. So by the time we had fitted the 'travel steering wheels', travel floors, and waterproof covers, everything else had been packed too. By this time we were all very tired, and feeling the effects of only having had three hours sleep the night before.

However, as we had to leave the hotel at 3.15 a.m. to catch the flight to Australia the next morning, there was no chance of a lie in. We got back to Yokkaichi at 11.30 p.m. There seemed to be two schools of thought on the subject of the early start. Some decided that the best way to tackle the potential problem of oversleeping was not to go to bed at all, and turn the occasion into an all-nighter. Others, myself included, decided to get a couple of hours sleep and take the risk.

I seemed to have my eyes closed for no longer than 10 seconds before the alarm went off. I had taken the precaution of packing before I went to bed, to give myself as long as possible to shower and get dressed. I walked down to the coach feeling fairly terrible, but when I saw the people who had decided to stay awake all night I was pleased I had been to bed. They looked dreadful, especially Jon, who looked particularly bad.

I can't tell you much about the flight to Australia. I slept the entire duration of the trip. All I know is that the 747's landing was bumpy enough to wake me up and when I opened my eyes we were in South Australia's state capital.

For the last four years we have always stayed at the Ramada Grand Hotel. Out of all the hotels we visit during our world tour, this is my personal favourite. It is very smartly presented, very comfortable, and the staff go to a great deal of trouble to ensure we have everything we need. I am always impressed with their service, and how genuinely friendly their staff are. The Grand is located just out of the city centre at Glenelg – Adelaide's seaside suburb – and the building's exterior is as impressive as the hotel's service. It stands right on the seafront, a big, bold looking building, with an 'Art Deco' style about it. Some of the rooms have glass doors which open onto a huge communal balcony, big enough to play cricket on, and all the rooms facing the sea come complete with splendid views of the ocean.

However, the rooms on the opposite side of the hotel, which look back towards the city, don't have balconies and command splendid views of the car park. Despite being just as comfortable as their sea-facing counterparts, they just aren't as much fun. And, unfortunately, on arrival at the Grand's reception on Monday evening, we discovered that it was into one of these 'city view' rooms that Reg and myself had been booked. After checking in and unpacking, the first job was to put our dirty race shirts into the hotel's laundry. The next job was to go for a beer in the hotel's bar. After that and some pasta for dinner, I retired to bed for a decent night's rest.

The majority of the Adelaide circuit is constructed by making use of the city streets. But the pit straight, the garage complex, and the return section of track leading into the final corner are housed in the middle of the Victoria Park Race Course. That first and last section of the circuit is a purpose-designed and permanent piece of tarmac, but everything else is temporary. The barriers, the grandstands, the garages, the hospitality suites, everything. It all goes up before we arrive, and it all comes down when we leave.

When fully assembled, the resulting facilities are excellent, and in my opinion the garages are quite simply the best we visit. They are spacious, well lit, watertight, and the roller doors glide with blissful ease in their frames – and, believe me, there aren't many circuits in the world that can claim that.

Thankfully, the freight was waiting for us at the circuit, and over the next three days we managed to have the garage prepared, and the three cars built and ready to run in time for the first practice session.

On Friday morning we left the Grand at 6.30 a.m. The practice session was due to begin half an hour earlier than normal, at 9.00 a.m. This was done to allow the session to finish at 10.45 a.m., instead of 11.15 a.m. It was Friday, 11th November – Armistice Day – and at precisely 11.00 a.m. the circuit fell silent.

As we stood in quiet remembrance I looked up and down the pit lane, observing the different people around me. Australian, British, Italian, Spanish, French, Dutch, Japanese, German, Finnish, Swiss, Brazilian, Irish, American, and many more. There seemed to be people from nearly every country on earth. As we stood there remembering those who had died and suffered in the terrible conflicts of the past, it felt rewarding to work within such a cosmopolitan sport and an industry which unites so many of the world's people.

Michael had an accident during the final two minutes of qualifying. It happened on what would have been his last flying lap of the afternoon. He hit the tyre barrier on the exit of the chicane at the end of the pit-straight. The impact ripped the front and rear wings off the car, as well as the front and rear suspension off the left hand side. I was very relieved to see Michael climb out the car uninjured. When he returned to the garage he looked fine, and what had obviously been a fairly major shunt appeared not to have shaken him at all.

'Are you sure you're OK. Michael?' Ross inquired.

'Yes, I'm fine. I just tried to relax during the shunt, and not tense any muscles. I'm OK.' and then after a slight pause, 'Sorry about the car!'

On its return to the garage a quick inspection of the car was all that was needed. The front wishbones had been ripped off with sufficient force to damage the suspension mountings. Chassis 08 was finished. Mick started to unload the emergency spare. Jon began to remove the bent suspension, steering rack, master cylinders, dashboard and so on while Ken and Max started on the engine, gearbox, and fuel system. Oz assembled a stock of new parts for the replacement chassis, handing them to the spare car crew to begin the assembly. After a couple of hours the two chassis were ready to be swapped over. Chassis 08 was lifted off the high stands and put to one side, while the emergency spare was lifted into position to replace it and become Michael's race car. The work steadily progressed during the course of the evening, and by 2.00 a.m. we had three cars finished and ready for Saturday's practice. Just to clarify which those cars were, car 5 was now chassis 06. Car 6 remained the same one we had been burdened with for most of the year, the cursed 04. The spare car was the same as in Japan, 05.

As at Suzuka, Saturday's qualifying was a washout. So the grid was set with Friday's times, which had seen Mansell on provisional pole with a time of 1m16.179s. Next was Michael on 1m16.197s. Damon was in third position with 1m16.830s. Johnny was a little further back, and with a time of 1m17.727s he was seventh on the grid. I'm sure he would have gone a lot quicker on Saturday if the rain had held off.

In testing he had been much closer to Michael's times than he was here, and I think he just needed more experience with the car. Not so he could play around with different set-ups, but more time getting used to how the car reacts, and how far it can be pushed before it lets go. Nearly all of the drivers we have had in the B194 during the year have commented on the car's unique handling characteristics, and how difficult it is to drive until they get used to it.

On that note, we began the very last Saturday night race preparation of 1994. I was pleased it was the last one too. It had been a long season, and it seemed an age since we were preparing the cars for the Brazilian Grand Prix. Tomorrow afternoon either Williams or ourselves would be World Champion Constructor, and either Michael or Damon would be World Champion Driver. No more ifs and buts, no more mathematical probabilities, no more anything. The season would have to stop, and we could go home.

We changed the engines. We changed the gear ratios. We measured the brakes, and gave the figures to Chris and Pat (I bet you know this routine better than we do by now). We had a coffee. The engineers pondered their data. We had another coffee. The set-up sheets arrived. We checked the looms for any sign of chafing, and any suspension welds for signs of cracking. We checked the suspension bearings, and the upright bearings. Once again we went through the car with a fine-tooth comb.

One by one, the different teams completed their work and slowly the pit lane began to empty. We finished at around midnight, and were back at the Ramada Grand 20 minutes later. It had been another long day, but despite feeling tired it was difficult to get to sleep. I lay awake thinking about the race and what might happen during tomorrow's long, 81 lap charge around the streets of Adelaide.

The thing that concerned me most was Williams's five point lead in the Constructors' Championship. If Michael and Damon finished first and second respectively, and the other two cars failed to score, Michael would win the Drivers' Championship, which would of course be a wonderful result, but we would lose the Constructors' Championship by one point. One single point after sixteen races. I've always been a big believer in fate and the philosophy of 'what will be, will be'. There was no point in worrying or fretting about the situation. Things would resolve themselves soon enough.

At about 1.15 p.m. the following day, we were getting changed into our fire-proof overalls. There was a quarter of an hour to go before the pit lane exit opened, allowing the cars to form up on the grid. The small personal fire extinguishers, which we would wear during the fuel stops, had been kept out at the back of the garage in one of the large freight containers, which the race organisers had provided the teams with storage space. While Bobby and Dave finished getting ready, I walked off to collect our three extinguishers.

Saturday's rain had moved away during the night, and although it was still fairly cloudy, when I glanced up at the sky, it appeared that it would stay dry for the race. In complete contrast to the pit lane and the hospitality suites, which were bustling with people, the area in between the containers was almost deserted, and apart from myself, the only other person there was Frank Williams, enjoying a few minutes of quiet contemplation before the start of the race. I wished him and his team good luck for the afternoon.

'Thank you, and good luck to you as well.'

'I would love to win here, Frank. It would mean an awful lot to me if we could win this Championship.'

'Well, whatever happens, we'll both enjoy today,' he said.

At precisely 2.00 p.m., the final and all-deciding round of the 1994 FIA Formula One World Championship began. Michael and Damon both made excellent starts. Nigel Mansell didn't, and by the end of the straight, Michael was leading the race, with Damon tight behind in second place. They were in a league of their own, and by the end of the first lap the rest of the field had dropped way behind.

Before long the third placed McLaren of Mika Hakkinen was trailing the first two cars by over 13 sec and still the leaders pulled away. The pace being set by the Benetton and Williams was incredible and there didn't appear to be any performance difference between the two chassis. Johnny had spun in the opening laps, which had dropped him to fifteenth place, but he had managed to keep the engine alive. This obviously wasn't the sort of luck we needed if we were going to score any points, but the car was still running and it was still very early days.

Then Blundell spun, elevating Johnny to 14th. There was still hope. But not for long. Johnny pitted on the very next lap, 'I'm stuck in fourth gear,' he told us, 'I've still got drive, but I can't change up or down.' Hydraulic oil dripped from the rear of the car. A pipe had fractured, and we had lost oil pressure to the gear selector mechanism. There was nothing we could do. Johnny's race was finished, and as far as car 6 was concerned, the '94 season was over. Two laps later Mansell passed Barrichello's Jordan to take fourth place and I began to sense the Constructors' Championship slipping away.

Meanwhile at the front of the Grand Prix, Michael and Damon were still pounding round at a terrific rate and it looked as though it might be the pit stops that could break the fight up a little. But not so. Michael and Damon came in at the same time, we both did very quick stops and both cars shot off down the pit lane in the same order as they had entered. We had given Michael about a half second lead over Damon, but this was soon used up, passing back-markers.

So they set off again, lap after lap, driving at the absolute limit. At some points on the circuit Michael would pull out a slight lead, and at other points the Williams would claw it back again. And then, on lap 36, the cars hit each other.

Michael had managed to get about two seconds ahead of Damon, and had just entered the 90-degree left, short straight, 90-degree right section, between Flinders Street and East Terrace. His car ran wide on the entry, he ran over the grass, and clipped the wall. He had driven back onto the straight, just as Damon came round the left-hander. Damon had seen Michael go wide, but I don't think he saw the contact with the wall.

Then Damon saw the gap between the Benetton and the right-hand corner and went for it, but as Michael turned in to drive around the corner himself, the gap disappeared, and the cars collided. The impact flicked the Benetton onto two wheels, it came back down, ending up in the tyre barrier on the opposite side of the track. Michael climbed out the car uninjured, but his race was obviously finished. At that precise moment, Williams Grand Prix Engineering became the FIA Formula One World Champion Constructor of 1994.

Damon had managed to keep going, but the collision had bent the top left-front wishbone. The FW16 slowly toured the circuit, and drove back into the pit lane. Patrick Head came over to the car and inspected the damage, but it was no use trying to repair it, and I would imagine that to replace the broken wishbone would have taken them 10 or 15 minutes. Damon's race was also finished. The Renault engine fell silent, and he climbed out the car. As he did so, Michael Schumacher became the FIA Formula One World Champion Driver of 1994.

We had done it. We shook hands, we slapped each other on the back, we waved at the crowd in the grandstand, and the crowd waved back. The German journalists went crazy. The Ferrari mechanics cheered and waved. It was a wonderful feeling, as much one of relief as anything else. We had kept our heads down while the flack was flying, and simply carried on doing the job. It was over. It was time to pack up, shower, change and celebrate.

Nigel Mansell went on to win the race and as he crossed the line it was time for Williams also to celebrate. We walked down to their garage to congratulate them, and at the same time they walked over to us to do the same.

'Congratulations Patrick!'

'And congratulations to you. One each. That seems fair enough!'

# DECEMBER

I began making tentative plans about writing my account of the life of a Grand Prix mechanic at the start of the 1992 season, but for several reasons I thought it best to wait a little longer. I felt I needed more experience of the unique environment of Formula One to be able to comment on life within it, and so I decided to delay a while and begin writing during the '93 season. However, at the start of the following year I discovered that there were two other books being planned about Benetton Formula and, regardless of the fact that these were to be written from an entirely different perspective from the one that I intended to pursue, I still thought it best to postpone the project for another year. If I didn't start writing in '93, then I would start writing during '94, after all, I was in no particular rush, and the extra time would give me greater opportunity to ponder how best to go about things. Throughout '93 I devoted any spare time to scribbling brief details about what life was like when we travelled away, and how people reacted to our different destinations. Learning to take notes proved an immense help, as much of what we do happens so quickly that events can become a blur. We fly in, we qualify, we race, we fly out. By the end of the '93 season I was keen to begin writing.

At the start of December, during a shopping trip to Banbury, I bought myself a small word processor from Dixons, and in between tiling the bathroom I spent my time reading the manual and trying to figure out how to use it. In the end it was very simple: I threw the manual in the bin, randomly pressed the various function keys, watched what happened, and on January 1st, I commenced work on page one.

When I began telling you about the cottage where I live and the launch of the B194, I had no idea that 1994 would unfold into such an incredible, turbulent and tragic year. I never imagined I would have to describe some of the awful incidents that befell us. J.J.'s testing accident at the start of the year, and Jos's accident in Brazil. It was only by the grace of God that both of these incidents didn't prove fatal. And then Imola. I very nearly gave up and stopped writing after Imola. I didn't know what to say, or how to say it. I'm a mechanic, not a professional journalist, and my feelings and emotions on that terrible weekend were somehow too private to commit to paper.

Only two weeks later at Monaco, Karl Wendlinger had that dreadful collision with the barrier, which was followed by Andrea Montermini's accident at the very next race. And, of course, there was the fire at Hockenheim. Probably even worse than being burnt in the heat of the fire itself was the reaction of certain sections of the press with regard to the cause of it. The media can be incredibly quick to condemn, but so very reluctant to apologise.

And what of refuelling itself? It seems very sad that so much has been done to improve driver safety, with the re-design of the circuits, and the reduction of the cars' performance, and yet, come the first race of 1995 the mechanics will be expected to lift those fuel-hoses over their shoulders and continue with a practice which has been witnessed by the whole world to be potentially lethal. If we are asked to do it again, then I'm sure we will do, but refuelling is simply not necessary and somehow it just doesn't seem fair. On the whole, we had been incredibly lucky at Hockenheim. Next year, or the year after, others – from whichever team – may not be so lucky.

I really wanted to win the Constructors' Championship this year. I suppose that must be the ambition of everyone in the sport, and if we had won, I would obviously have been delighted. However, in some respects I'm rather pleased we didn't win. Simtek and Williams have each been through a truly dreadful season, and yet despite their losses they both carried on pushing forward. As Simtek is such a new team it must have been a constant struggle simply to be able to continue racing. But they persevered, and in the end it was a struggle they won. Every member of the Simtek organisation deserves an award, just for their determination to continue with the season.

Williams was obviously under public scrutiny far more than Simtek, and this team also did a marvellous job of pulling itself together and continuing onward. The loss of Ayrton must have been horrendous for them, and the whole team demonstrated great courage in the months that followed. Race after race they constantly seemed to improve the FW16, they consistently scored points with it, and I believe all three cars claimed victories by the end of the year.

We hadn't been able to achieve the same level of combined results as Williams, and it was, without doubt, Michael's exceptional driving abilities that had scored the vast majority of Benetton's points. He finished the season on a total of 92. Jos managed to score 10. J.J. scored one and Johnny unfortunately scored nothing.

The Constructors' World Championship is a team award, and as a team, the Williams drivers had produced a string of point scoring results in the second half of the season. Damon finished with a total of 91 points, David Coulthard scored 14 and Nigel Mansell finished with 13 points. Considering what the team had to endure, I'm more than happy that Williams finally managed to clinch the title. There is always next year, and I always try to remain optimistic. Hopefully 1995 will be the year Benetton's name is added to the Constructors' Trophy, and maybe, just maybe, *our* car may win a race. Just one, just once.

The numbers on the cars will change next season. As the new Formula One World Champion, Michael's car will proudly display the number 1, both on the nose and the rear wing end plates. It is a Grand Prix tradition that this number is reserved for the current World Champion, and number 2 is the preserve of whoever his team-mate will be. Moreover, 1995 will be the first year a current Formula One World Champion has elected to defend his crown in the following season's competition since Ayrton claimed his final title at the end of 1991.

There would also be some changes to the car crews for next year. On his return from Adelaide, Dave Redding resigned his commission and departed for Woking to join McLaren International. Dave, Bobby, and I have worked together as a crew for years. I have enjoyed working with Dave. He is very good at his job, and he normally managed to remain fairly calm as he tried to work his way through the night-time job lists on his own, as Bobby and I wandered off for another coffee and a chat.

I wish him all the best at McLaren. I don't know who will take over from Dave, but it could possibly result in shuffling several people around until a proper and workable balance is restored. All I know is whoever takes the job is going to have their work cut out. We said goodbye to Cosworth in Adelaide as well. From next year the team will be known as Mild Seven Benetton Renault. Ever since I joined Benetton the cars have been powered by Ford engines, and during the past five years I got to know the Cosworth mechanics and engineers very well. We have all spent many hours together, chatting and having a few drinks at the various bars and restaurants we have found ourselves in over the years. Cosworth have signed a deal with Sauber for '95, so we'll still be able to keep in touch with them.

I never heard back from the girl in the carpet shop, but other than the flooring, the bathroom is finished. I might start on the bedroom next. Flavio, Joan, and Mick have been kind enough to extend my holidays over Christmas, which has been a great help to me, and since I returned from Australia I have been busy writing up the events of the last couple of months, and trying to meet Weidenfeld & Nicolson's deadline for publication. As you are currently reading the final chapter it's safe to assume I managed to complete the work in time.

The time now is exactly 11.15 p.m., Saturday, December 31st. This gives me just 45 minutes to finish writing these last few paragraphs. That might seem like plenty of time, but you don't know how many corrections I'm going to have to make. On the table in front of me, just to the side of the word processor, is a small glass mounted painting, by the French artist Pierre Soulages. I discovered the painting at the airport, prior to the journey to Suzuka. It was quietly waiting for me inside 'Berry Brothers & Rudd Ltd' – the little shop in the corner of Heathrow's Terminal Three.

Soulages's work normally consists of generously applied, thick, bold brush strokes and although he was born in 1919 his creations are still referred to as 'modern.' The painting I've got in front of me is mainly blue. Dark blue background, strokes of lighter blue on top. My painting isn't an original, I don't know how much his work commands, but I doubt I could even match the opening bid. It isn't even a print and the copy I've got hasn't been reproduced on high quality art paper and in fact Pierre's brush strokes have been confined to the very top of the paper. The artist's work has been reduced to such a degree to allow space for some lettering underneath. Just below an impressive golden crest, depicting two rams holding a shield, there is something written in ornate flowing script. The legend reads:

'1976. CHATEAU MOUTON-ROTHSCHILD'.

Two hours ago I slowly cut away the top of the foil capsule, gently eased the cork from the bottle, and carefully set the bottle down to rest and allow the fruits of Pauillac to take their first breath of air for 19 long years. Experts would probably have insisted that I should decant it to remove the sediment, but I haven't. I want to hear the wine as it slowly pours from the bottle to the glass. The bells have started ringing in the church at the end of the lane. It must be midnight.

Well, I hope you enjoyed your world tour with Benetton. Just before I fill my glass and drink a toast to 1995, let me thank you for joining me and may I wish you 'all the best' and a very happy New Year.

Cheers!

# INDEX

*The Benetton team is fully indexed; other names and topics are indexed selectively. Subheadings are in alphabetical order or, where appropriate, in chronological order of events. Illustrations are not indexed.*